# Levinas and Kierkegaard in Dialogue

INDIANA SERIES IN THE PHILOSOPHY OF RELIGION
MEROLD WESTPHAL, EDITOR

# Levinas and Kierkegaard in Dialogue

Merold Westphal

INDIANA UNIVERSITY PRESS
BLOOMINGTON AND INDIANAPOLIS

This book is a publication of

Indiana University Press
601 North Morton Street
Bloomington, IN 47404-3797 USA

http://iupress.indiana.edu

*Telephone orders*    800-842-6796
*Fax orders*    812-855-7931
*Orders by e-mail*    iuporder@indiana.edu

MANUFACTURED IN THE UNITED STATES OF AMERICA

**Library of Congress Cataloging-in-Publication Data**

Westphal, Merold.
Levinas and Kierkegaard in dialogue / Merold Westphal.
p. cm. — (Indiana series in the philosophy of religion)
Includes bibliographical references and index.
ISBN-13: 978-0-253-35082-4 (cloth : alk. paper)
ISBN-13: 978-0-253-21966-4 (pbk. : alk. paper)
1. Lévinas, Emmanuel. 2. Kierkegaard, Søren, 1813–1855.
I. Title.
B2430.L484W47    2008
194—dc22

2007039623

1  2  3  4  5    13  12  11  10  09  08

To **Dom Balestra**, in friendship

# Contents

# ACKNOWLEDGMENTS

Earlier versions of these chapters have appeared in the locations indicated below. Permission to publish these revised versions is gratefully acknowledged.

Introduction—five paragraphs, as indicated, are taken from "Levinas, Kierkegaard, and the Theological Task," *Modern Theology* 8, no. 3 (July 1992): 241–61.

Chapter 1—"Levinas and the Immediacy of the Face," *Faith and Philosophy* 9, no. 4 (October 1993): 486–502.

Chapter 2—"The Transparent Shadow: Kierkegaard and Levinas in Dialogue," *Kierkegaard in Post-Modernity,* ed. Martin Matuštík and Merold Westphal (Bloomington: Indiana University Press, 1995), 265–81.

Chapter 3—"Levinas' Teleological Suspension of the Religious," *Ethics as First Philosophy: The Significance of Levinas for Philosophy, Literature, and Religion,* ed. Adriaan T. Peperzak (New York: Routledge, 1995), 151–60.

Chapter 4—"Commanded Love and Divine Transcendence in Kierkegaard and Levinas," *The Face of the Other and the Trace of God: Essays on the Philosophy of Emmanuel Levinas,* ed. Jeffrey Bloechl (New York: Fordham University Press 2000), 200–233.

Chapter 5—"The Trauma of Transcendence as Heteronomous Intersubjectivity," *Intersubjectivité et théologie philosophique,* ed. Marco M. Olivetti (Padua: CEDAM, 2001), 87–110.

Chapter 6—"Transcendence, Heteronomy, and the Birth of the Responsible Self," *Calvin O. Schrag and the Task of Philosophy after Postmodernity,* ed. Martin Beck Matuštík and William L. McBride (Evanston, Ill.: Northwestern University Press, 2002), 201–25.

Chapter 7—"Levinas and the 'Logic' of Solidarity," *Graduate Faculty Philosophy Journal* 20, no. 2, & 21, no. 1 (1998): 297–319.

Chapter 8—"Intentionality and Transcendence," in *Subjectivity and Transcendence,* ed. Arne Grøn, Iben Damgaard, and Søren Overgaard (Tübingen: Mohr Siebeck, 2007), 71–93.

# ABBREVIATIONS

The following abbreviations will be used in text and notes.

## Levinas

BCI     "Bad Conscience and the Inexorable," in FFL

BI      "Beyond Intentionality," *Philosophy in France Today*, ed. Alan Montefiore (Cambridge: Cambridge University Press, 1983)

BM      "Martin Buber, Gabriel Marcel, and Philosophy," *Martin Buber: A Centenary Volume*, ed. Haim Gordon and Jochanan Bloch (n.p.: KTAV Publishing House, 1984)

BPW     *Emmanuel Levinas: Basic Philosophical Writings*, ed. Adriaan T. Peperzak, Simon Critchley, and Robert Bernasconi (Bloomington: Indiana University Press, 1996)

BTK     "Martin Buber and the Theory of Knowledge," in LR

CPP     *Collected Philosophical Papers*, trans. Alphonso Lingis (Dordrecht: Nijhoff, 1987)

DEH     *Discovering Existence with Husserl*, trans. Richard A. Cohen and Michael B. Smith (Evanston, Ill.: Northwestern University Press, 1998)

DEL     "Dialogue with Emmanuel Levinas," in FFL

DF      *Difficult Freedom*, trans. Seán Hand (Baltimore: Johns Hopkins University Press, 1990)

EE      *Existence and Existents*, trans. Alphonso Lingis (Dordrecht: Kluwer, 1978)

EF      "Ethics as First Philosophy," in LR

EL      "Emmanuel Levinas," *French Philosophers in Conversation*, ed. Raoul Mortley (London: Routledge, 1991)

EN      *Entre Nous: On Thinking-of-the-Other*, trans. Michael B. Smith and Barbara Harshav (New York: Columbia University Press, 1998)

ET      "The Ego and the Totality," in CPP

FC      "Freedom and Command," in CPP

FFL     *Face to Face with Levinas*, ed. Richard A. Cohen (Albany: SUNY Press, 1986)

# Abbreviations

| | |
|---|---|
| GCM | *Of God Who Comes to Mind,* trans. Bettina Bergo (Stanford, Calif.: Stanford University Press, 1998) |
| GP | "God and Philosophy," in CPP |
| HB | "Hermeneutics and Beyond," in EN |
| II | "Ideology and Idealism," in LR |
| IOF | "Is Ontology Fundamental?" in BPW |
| LP | "Language and Proximity," in CPP |
| LR | *The Levinas Reader,* ed. Seán Hand (Oxford: Basil Blackwell, 1989) |
| MB | "Martin Buber and the Theory of Knowledge," in LR |
| MS | "Meaning and Sense," in CPP |
| NI | "No Identity," in CPP |
| NTR | *Nine Talmudic Readings,* trans. Annette Aronowicz (Bloomington: Indiana University Press, 1990) |
| OB | *Otherwise Than Being or Beyond Essence,* trans. Alphonso Lingis (Dordrecht: Kluwer, 1991) |
| OS | *Outside the Subject,* trans. Michael B. Smith (Stanford, Calif.: Stanford University Press, 1994) |
| PE | "Phenomenon and Enigma," in CPP |
| PII | "Philosophy and the Idea of Infinity," in CPP |
| PN | *Proper Names,* trans. Michael B. Smith (Stanford, Calif.: Stanford University Press, 1996) |
| PWD | "Prayer without Demand," in LR |
| RJT | "Revelation in the Jewish Tradition," in LR |
| RR | "The Ruin of Representation," in DEH |
| S | "Substitution," in LR |
| Si | "Signature," ed. Adriaan Peperzak, *Research in Phenomenology,* Vol. VIII (1978) |
| TD | "Truth of Disclosure and Truth of Testimony," in BPW |
| TH | "Transcendence and Height," in BPW |
| TI | *Totality and Infinity,* trans. Alphonso Lingis (Pittsburgh: Duquesne University Press, 1969) |
| TIH | *The Theory of Intuition in Husserl's Phenomenology,* trans. A. Orianne (Evanston, Ill.: Northwestern University Press, 1973) |
| TO | *Time and the Other,* trans. Richard A. Cohen (Pittsburgh: Duquesne University Press, 1969) |
| TrI | "Transcendence and Intelligibility," in BPW |
| TrO | "The Trace of the Other," *Deconstruction in Context,* ed. Mark C. Taylor (Chicago: University of Chicago Press, 1986) |
| WO | "Wholly Otherwise," *Re-Reading Levinas,* ed. Robert Bernasconi and Simon Critchley (Bloomington: Indiana University Press, 1991) |

## Kierkegaard

CI     *The Concept of Irony,* trans. Howard V. Hong and Edna H. Hong
       (Princeton, N.J.: Princeton University Press, 1989)

CUP    *Concluding Unscientific Postscript,* 2 vols., trans. Howard V. Hong
       and Edna H. Hong (Princeton, N.J.: Princeton University Press,
       1992)

E/O    *Either/Or,* 2 vols., trans. Howard V. Hong and Edna H. Hong
       (Princeton, N.J.: Princeton University Press, 1987)

FT     *Fear and Trembling/Repetition,* trans. Howard V. Hong and Edna H.
       Hong (Princeton, N.J.: Princeton University Press, 1983)

GA     "The Difference between a Genius and an Apostle," in *Without
       Authority,* trans. Howard V. Hong and Edna H. Hong (Princeton,
       N.J.: Princeton University Press, 1979); also found in *The Book on
       Adler,* trans. Howard V. Hong and Edna H. Hong (Princeton, N.J.:
       Princeton University Press, 1998)

JP     *Søren Kierkegaard's Journals and Papers,* 7 vols., trans. Howard V.
       Hong and Edna H. Hong (Princeton, N.J.: Princeton University
       Press, 1967–78); numbers are entry numbers, not page numbers

PC     *Practice in Christianity,* trans. Howard V. Hong and Edna H. Hong
       (Princeton, N.J.: Princeton University Press, 1991)

PF     *Philosophical Fragments/Johannes Climacus,* trans. Howard V.
       Hong and Edna H. Hong (Princeton, N.J.: Princeton University
       Press, 1985)

SLW    *Stages on Life's Way,* trans. Howard V. Hong and Edna H. Hong
       (Princeton, N.J.: Princeton University Press, 1988)

SUD    *Sickness unto Death,* trans. Howard V. Hong and Edna H. Hong
       (Princeton, N.J.: Princeton University Press, 1980)

TA     *Two Ages: The Age of Revolution and the Present Age, A Literary
       Review,* trans. Howard V. Hong and Edna H. Hong (Princeton, N.J.:
       Princeton University Press, 1978)

WL     *Works of Love,* trans. Howard V. Hong and Edna H. Hong
       (Princeton, N.J.: Princeton University Press, 1995)

Levinas and Kierkegaard in Dialogue

# Introduction

This volume is the result of the circumstances under which I first began reading Levinas. I had already been working on Kierkegaard for more than twenty years when, in the spring of 1989, Martin Matuštík and Patricia Huntington asked to do a tutorial on Kierkegaard with me. I agreed and asked them to give me a list of what they wanted to read. The list included the usual suspects and, as the last item, a book called *Totality and Infinity*. Their excuse was that they were looking for an opportunity to read Levinas and figured this was as good a place as any. Since I was in the same situation, I agreed. So we spent the last two (!) weeks of that semester reading *Totality and Infinity*.

Thus I began reading Levinas immersed in Kierkegaard. What struck me like a bolt of lightning was not so much their differences as their agreements. The latter were formal and structural, leaving plenty of room for substantive disagreement. But in the light of their divergences, the convergences were all the more striking, especially in the way they together formed a radical challenge to main strands of the western philosophical tradition, a challenge very different from the critiques of Nietzsche, or Husserl, or Heidegger.

Ever since then I've been exploring the profound and surprising relation between these two thinkers, seeking to learn from both, to read each in the light of the other, and to ask what each needs to learn from the other. The first essay to emerge was "Levinas, Kierkegaard, and the Theological Task."[1] Written in the heat of discovery, it is more a research agenda than anything else, and I have not included it here. I have included eight subsequent essays, revised so as to make a more nearly linear argument. If the Alpha of the sequence is the notion of revelation and the Omega the notion of inverted intentionality, the whole can be seen as an attempt to think through the most important fact about ourselves: we are addressed. Epistemology, metaphysics, and ethics are not neatly separated here as distinct regions of reflection but supervene upon one another as inseparable from each other.

Material has been added to make relationships more fully explicit; and material has been dropped, primarily to avoid duplication. But I have not tried to eliminate all duplication. After all, Levinas especially keeps coming back to the same themes again and again, though the difference of context keeps him from mere repetition. Cross-references will lead the reader from sketchier to more extensive treatments of a given theme. The goal has been to blend the chapters into a coherent whole while not precluding the possibility of fruitfully reading each chapter on its own. This will be especially true of those chapters whose Levinas portion focuses on a single essay: chapter 2 on "Phenomenon and Enigma," chapter 4 on "God and Philosophy," and chapter 6 on "No Identity."

More space is devoted to Levinas than to Kierkegaard. This is the result of two contingencies: the venues in which the chapters were originally presented and the fact that I have been playing catch-up, trying to bring my understanding of the large and complex Levinas corpus up to par with my understanding of the equally large and complex Kierkegaardian corpus. I have treated the Levinas corpus as essentially simultaneous, since whatever differences there may be between Levinas I (*Totality and Infinity* and the essays that gather around it) and Levinas II (*Otherwise Than Being* and the essays that gather around it) don't seem especially important for my argument. Chronology is more important in my treatment of Kierkegaard on at least one point. To emphasize that his treatment of ethics cannot be restricted to *Fear and Trembling*, as Levinas seems to suppose, I have noted the need to include later writings, especially *Works of Love,* along with other writings I call "Religiousness C." There is a significant shift of emphasis from the God relation worked out in hidden inwardness to the God relation worked out in visible works of love. Without ceasing to be the Paradox to be believed, Christ becomes the Prototype to be imitated in "the only thing that counts . . . faith working through love" (Gal. 4:5). While not ignoring the difference between Kierkegaard and his pseudonyms, I have been fairly relaxed about it, sometimes using 'Kierkegaard' to refer to ideas he presents for our consideration, whether pseudonymously or in his own name.

Levinas is self-consciously a phenomenologist and Kierkegaard is often a literary writer; so it is not surprising that their accounts of the moral authority of the Other should find literary confirmation. I refer here to two such texts. The first is from Faulkner's *Light in August,* quoted by Sartre in his analysis of the Look in terms of "Concrete Relations with Others." The Negro, Christmas, having been castrated by a white mob, is dying.

> But the man on the floor had not moved. He just lay there with his eyes open and empty of everything save consciousness, and with something, a shadow, about his mouth. For a long moment he looked up at them with peaceful and unfathomable and unbearable eyes. Then his face, body, all, seemed to collapse, to fall in upon itself and from out the slashed garments about his hips and loins the pent black blood seemed to rush like a released breath. It seemed to rush out of his pale body like the rush of sparks from a rising rocket; upon that black blast the man seemed to rise soaring into their memories forever and ever. They are not to lose it, in whatever peaceful valleys, beside whatever placid and reassuring streams of old age, in the mirroring face of whatever children they will contemplate old disasters and newer hopes. *It will be there, musing, quiet, steadfast, not fading and not particularly threatful, but of itself alone serene, of itself alone triumphant.*[2]

Since, as Levinas says, "The face speaks" (TI 66), these murderers have indeed heard the commandment, "You shall not commit murder" (TI 303). They have been addressed, undeniably, unceasingly, and inescapably addressed.

Something similar happens in Erich Maria Remarque's *All Quiet on the Western Front.*[3] Here is how I presented it in that first essay:

The ethical impossibility of killing the Other is written in the Other's face. . . . On a foray between the trenches, I have become separated from my comrades and have found refuge in a crater filled with water and mud. Suddenly a question occurs to me. "What will you do if someone jumps into your shell-hole? Swiftly I pull out my little dagger, grasp it fast and bury it in my hand once again under the mud. If anyone jumps in here I will go for him . . . stab him clean through the throat, so that he cannot call out; that's the only way; he will be just as frightened as I am; then in terror we fall upon one another, then I must be first" (184).

As suddenly as the question arises, a body falls on top of me. "I do not think at all, I make no decision—I strike madly home, and feel only how the body suddenly convulses, then becomes limp and collapses. When I recover myself, my hand is sticky and wet. The man gurgles. . . . It sounds to me as though he bellows. . . . I want to stop his mouth, stuff it with earth, stab him again, he must be quiet, but [I] have suddenly become so feeble that I cannot anymore lift my hand against him" (185).

Overcome by the desire to get away, I move as far away as possible in the shell-hole, watching and listening. Morning comes, and the gurgling continues, drawing first my unwilling gaze and then my whole body in a crawling journey to the side of the dying man. "At last I am beside him. Then he opens his eyes. He must have heard me, for he gazes at me with a look of utter terror.

The body lies still, but in the eyes there is such an extraordinary expression of fright that for a moment I think they have power enough to carry the body off with them . . . the gurgle has ceased, but the eyes cry out, yell, all the life is gathered together in them. . . . The eyes follow me. I am powerless to move so long as they are there" (187).

When I am finally able to move, I strain some muddy water from the bottom of the crater, give it to my dying enemy, and then dress his wounds as best I can. The gurgling resumes. After the passing of an eternity, the young Frenchman passes into eternity at about three in the afternoon. "I prop the dead man up again so that he lies comfortably. . . . I close his eyes. They are brown, his hair is black and a bit curly at the sides. The mouth is full and soft beneath his moustache; the nose is slightly arched, the skin brownish; it is now not so pale as it was before, when he was still alive. For a moment the face seems almost healthy;—then it collapses suddenly into the strange face of the dead that I have so often seen, strange faces, all alike" (190).

Just as the compulsion to help had followed the compulsion to flee, now the compulsion to speak takes over. "Comrade, I did not want to kill you. If you jumped in here again, I would not do it, if you would be sensible too. But you were only an idea to me before, an abstraction that lived in my mind. But now, for the first time, I see you are a man like me. I thought of your hand-grenades, of your bayonet, of your rifle; now I see your wife and your face and our fellowship. Forgive me, comrade. We always see it too late. . . . I will write to your wife" (191).

Fellowship. Forgiveness. With Levinas we might find these in the face of the neighbor, who may well be the enemy, who calls and commands us with a voice not our own, a voice Levinas will treat as divine. Or with Kierkegaard we might find fellowship and forgiveness in a voice neither ours nor our neighbor's, whose command calls us to see in the face of the neighbor, who may well be the enemy, not an abstraction we are free to deface but someone to whom we belong as God's children, to whom and for whom we are responsible.

It is the possibility of a conversation between these two powerful thinkers, at once deeply convergent and deeply divergent, that is staged, as it were, and explored in the chapters that follow. The flow of the argument goes as follows. Chapters 1 and 2 are devoted to the idea of revelation, the idea that a voice other than our own can address us so directly that it cuts through the horizons of expectation we bring with us like a turtle shell and says what it has to say on its own terms. In this event every a priori, every "already said," every basis for knowledge as recollection is neutralized, whether the power to preside over meaning and truth be interpreted metaphysically, as in Plato and Descartes, transcendentally as in Kant and Husserl, or socio-historically as in Hegel. Because these horizons define what is to count as "Reason," in going beyond and against them revelation will involve us with enigma (Levinas) and paradox (Kierkegaard).

Both Levinas and Kierkegaard attribute divinity to the voice of revelation, but they don't seem to mean the same thing by 'God.' So in chapters 3 and 4 their views of God are explored. They agree that the transcendence and alterity that deserve to be called divine are not to be found in the realm of theoretical knowledge as interpreted by major strands of the western philosophical tradition; they rather occur in the decentering of the cognitive self by a command that comes from on high. But they disagree in that Levinas insists that the neighbor is always the middle term between me and God, while Kierkegaard insists that it is God who is always the middle term between me and my neighbor. This is their fundamental disagreement; perhaps, in the final analysis, their only one. Each has his reasons, and each can be supplemented by the other. So I speak of the conversation and dialogue between them. At times, as if among siblings, it becomes a quarrel.

While emphasizing the convergence that first astonished me about these two thinkers, I do not try to minimize their divergence. Where they differ my sympathies tend to be with Kierkegaard, and I have not tried to hide this. But I offer two caveats. First, I do not see the path of thought as a one-way street leading from Levinas to Kierkegaard. I think we can and should learn from both and that each of them can and should learn from the other in the conversation I am attempting to stage. Second, I do not see the difference as essentially a Jewish-Christian debate, as I point out in several places; it rather points to issues that arise within both traditions as they seek to answer the questions Who is the God of the Bible? and Who are we? I believe some who think primarily within Christian horizons will be conceptually closer to Levinas, and some who think within Jewish horizons will be conceptually closer to Kierkegaard. The question concerns the meaning of monotheism, prior to questions about Messiah, or Incarnation, or Trinity.

In the midst of their debate over what we might call the theology of revelation, Levinas and Kierkegaard are in full agreement that the kind of transcendence experienced in the divine command is traumatic in its heteronomous character. It requires a decisive break with modernity's aspirations to both epistemic and ethical autonomy. So chapters 5 and 6 explore the link between heteronomy and transcendence. This takes us beyond the classical debate between theism and pantheism as accounts, respectively, of God's transcendence and immanence. This debate remains within causal/cosmological categories, where the question is whether and how God might be said to be *beyond the world*. By contrast, the traumatic heteronomy that is central to Levinas and Kierkegaard takes us beyond these categories to epistemic, ethical, and religious categories insofar as meaning, truth, the good, and the right come to us from *beyond us*. Instead of our presiding over these values, the voice through which these come to us presides over us—with authority and by right. In this way our *identity* is compromised in that who we are is a function of a relation to an Other we did not choose; our *authority* is compromised in that we do not preside, either individually or collectively, over the norms to which our beliefs and behavior must conform; and our very *essence* is compromised in that our *conatus essendi* is demoted to a supporting role by the call to supplant (teleologically suspend, relativize) our natural self-centered self-love in self-denial and self-sacrifice.

The shattering of the cogito and the disturbing of our *conatus essendi* are a double trauma, but they are not the "death of the self" or the "end of man." They are rather the unavoidable birth pangs that accompany the birth of the responsible self—if we are willing to let ourselves be born from above.

This birth, or rather rebirth, can also be understood as a reversal, a radical change of direction. To make room for such repentance and rebirth, for welcome rather than murder, for faith rather than offense, both Levinas and Kierkegaard wage relentless war on the dominant logos of the western philosophical tradition and the ontology it presupposes. They are not intimidated by the fact that it calls itself "Reason" with a capital R. They unite in saying, "I have found it necessary to deny 'Reason' in order to make room for responsibility." So in chapters 7 and 8, we find their epistemic critiques in the service of neither knowledge nor skepticism but of the becoming of the self that knows itself to be authoritatively addressed. The "logic of solidarity" that each presents, however sketchily, requires a decisive break with the dominant logos.

Levinas makes it clear that the difference between the realist version (Hegel, yes Hegel) and the transcendental idealist version (Husserl, and Heidegger, yes Heidegger) is a distinction without a real difference. So in chapter 7 Levinas calls for a "radical reversal" from cognition, on either interpretation, to a solidarity not grounded in epistemic adequation. In chapter 8 he develops this reversal in phenomenological language as occurring in an inverted intentionality. Here the arrows of intentional awareness do not emanate from me toward an object but toward me from the Other. I am aware of myself, my world, and the Other not by looking but by being seen, not by naming but by being addressed.

In both chapters Kierkegaard develops the same structures, though in a different vocabulary. In the command of God I am subsumed under an authority not my own, and in the promise of God I am given an agenda not of my own devising. It is no accident that Abraham, who hears and obeys the dramatically transcendent voice of God, is a hero to both Levinas and Kierkegaard, though not, to be sure, in the same way.[4] For both, the call of God disturbs Abraham's dwelling within the topos of his people, their logos and their ethos. Only on the basis of such a disturbance can responsible individuals enter into a human solidarity that will not be the violence that Levinas calls "history" and "politics" or the complacency that Kierkegaard calls "Christendom."

So we end where we began. The face speaks. With divine authority. We are addressed, and that makes all the difference.

# PART 1. REVELATION

# Revelation as Immediacy

*The view that there is nothing external to experience—no World of Forms,*
*City of God, independent cogito, a priori category, transcendental Mind,*
*or far-off divine event to which the whole creation moves, but only the*
*mundane business of making our way as best we can in a universe shot*
*through with contingency.*

*All "homes" are in finite experience; finite experience as such is*
*homeless. Nothing outside the flux secures the issue of it.*

Just as much of American culture and society looks like a concerted effort to
refute Jesus' claim that "one's life does not consist in the abundance of posses-
sions" (Luke 12:15), so much of contemporary French philosophy (often designated by such umbrella names as poststructuralism or postmodernism) looks
like a concerted effort to refute the claim that frames the book of Revelation, "I
am the Alpha and the Omega" (1:8, 21:6, and 22:13; cf. 1:17–18).

Through loyalty to (or entrapment in) the metaphysical traditions of
which they are so sharply critical, philosophers like Derrida, Foucault, and
Lyotard prefer Greek to Hebrew. So their assault is on the notions of *arche* and
*telos*. In its search to establish the primacy of unity over plurality, univocity
over equivocity, stability over flux, and so forth, western metaphysics has regularly resorted to the notion of an ultimate origin to be the foundation of
everything or an ultimate goal to be the harmonization of everything, or,
typically, both. But there is no pure origin, divine (creator) or human (*cogito*);[1]
the only beginnings we can find are relative beginnings, themselves grounded
in that which precedes them. Nor is there any goal by which experience or
reality can be, to use the official term, totalized. All such ends represent the

wishful thinking of finite parts to be the whole, the effort of centers of force that can see that they are not the *arche* to be the *telos*. The epistemological foundationalism of which Descartes is the paradigm and the eschatological holism of which Hegel and Marx are the paradigms are so riddled with paradox and paralogism that we must eschew the comfort they provide and accept our ultimate homelessness. Neither path leads to Absolute Knowledge, but only to other paths. The earth stands on the back of an elephant and—here's the kicker—it's elephants all the way down.

This line of thought, so nicely summarized in the quotations at the beginning of this essay, can be called contemporary French negativism. It is a series of critiques of pure reason emphasizing the wounded character of reason, its situatedness and thus its particularity, its fractured character and thus its plurality. Reason is always indebted, both to the past, by which it has been constituted, and to the future, which holds all its unfulfilled promissory notes. A number of observations can be made about this French radicalism, whose American enthusiasts sometimes bill themselves as intellectual terrorists.

1. Only the details of its critique are distinctive. For example, the two quotations at the beginning of this chapter, which the reader is no doubt quite prepared to attribute to Derrida, or Foucault, or Lyotard, are not about French postmodernism at all. The first is Louis Menand's definition of American pragmatism and the second a quotation from William James in support of it.[2] Furthermore, the repudiation of classical foundationalism with its appeal to privileged representations "which cannot be gainsaid"[3] is a staple of American philosophy from Peirce to Plantinga, and the repudiation of Hegelian holism is perhaps the only theme common to all forms of "analytic philosophy" from Moore and Russell to the present.[4]

2. French negativism refuses, persistently and explicitly, to draw the conclusion its opponents would like to foist upon it, a certain kind of nihilistic relativism. Its exponents are relativists insofar as they make the claim that *we* have access to no absolute standpoint. But they refuse to infer that every point of view or every practice is just as good as any other. They insist on making distinctions even while admitting that they have no absolute criteria for doing so. Intellectual life is not exempted from the riskiness of life in general.

For example, Lyotard argues that moral judgments can never be grounded or justified. Ought can never be derived from is, that is, prescriptions expressive of justice can never be "derived from other propositions, in which the latter are metaphysical propositions on being and history, or on the soul, or on society."[5] This repudiation of justification by derivation can be fruitfully compared with the critique of evidentialism found in the Reformed epistemology of Plantinga and Wolterstorff.[6] But just as they do not draw nihilistic conclusions from the failure of a particular, exorbitant scheme of justification, so Lyotard does not repudiate the responsibility of being just and of making moral judgments. He rather asks how to exercise this responsibility in the absence of the kinds of grounding that philosophers have traditionally sought to provide.

3. The secularism of French negativism rests upon a rather blatant non sequitur. Its proponents often sound like Nietzsche's Zarathustra, who says, "*if* there were gods, how could I endure not to be a god! *Hence* there are no gods.''[7] They often talk as if from their own confessed inability to embody an absolute standpoint, to see the world *sub specie aeternitatis*, it follows that there is no such standpoint. Had they looked back behind Nietzsche to either Kierkegaard or Kant they would have discovered another possibility, the more plausible suggestion that from the impossibility of our own finite temporality's ever seeing the world from the perspective of infinite eternity, nothing whatever follows about the possibility that God might be able to see the world from such a divine point of view. Thus Kierkegaard, for whom the phrase 'humanly speaking' is important rather than redundant, has Johannes Climacus claim that reality is a system for God even if never for us as existing individuals, and Kant converts the distinction between the human perspective we embody and a possible divine perspective we do not into the central distinction of the critical philosophy, that between appearances and things in themselves.[8]

Against Hegelian monism, French negativists untiringly insist on the irreducible plurality of human meanings, perspectives, criteria, and so forth. But by never questioning the Hegelian view that the human is the measure of all things they betray how incomplete is their break with Hegel and how dogmatic is the atheistic framework in which they set their thought.

There is a double importance in noting the non sequitur underlying what I have been calling French negativism. First, it deprives these traditions of any pretensions, whether by the main characters or their followers, of having shown the preferability of atheism to theism. Second, and more important in my view, it deprives theists of an easy excuse for dismissing their thought. If there were a substantial link between this radical finitism and atheism, the plausibility of theism and French negativism would vary more or less inversely. But if there is no such link, the story is quite different. When the attempt to act as if

> A—there is no *arche* or *telos*, no pure origin or ultimate end
> followed from
> B—we do not preside over or have access to any such origin or end

is explicitly repudiated, that is to say, when B no longer has A hanging around its neck as an albatross, B can be looked at more dispassionately and less defensively by Christian philosophers. And when that happens, the case for the incorrigible finitude of human knowledge emerges, I believe, with new power and nuance. Theistic philosophers have every reason to take these critiques, as expressed in B, with great seriousness. For they clearly have theological import, and they just might be true.

That deconstructive strategies and insights are not essentially linked to the secular assumptions that seem to prevail in a French negativism with deep roots in Nietzsche and Heidegger has been brilliantly argued by Kevin Hart and Jean-Luc Marion, among others.[9] In other words, if the previous observation suggests that French negativism does not obviously have the nihilistic import often attributed to it by its enemies, this observation suggests that it does not have the atheistic import often attributed to it by both its fans and its foes.

4. French negativism can be fruitfully compared with what I shall inevitably have to call German positivism, though it has nothing to do with positivism in the usual sense. Two major moments in contemporary Germany philosophy, the hermeneutics of Gadamer and the critical theory of Jürgen Habermas, share with French negativism a commitment, at once anti-Cartesian and anti-Hegelian, to the ineluctable finitude of human knowledge. Both are as allergic to Descartes as any contemporary philosopher, and while both are deeply indebted to Hegel, they are both closer to Kantian finitism than to Hegelian absolutism. We might call them Hegelians without the Absolute.

There is a good deal of bad blood between French negativism and both of these German traditions.[10] But looked at closely, the ongoing debate seems to be between two parties who are in essential agreement about how much water is in the glass, but who insist, on the one hand, that it is half empty, and on the other hand, that it is half full. While hermeneutics and critical theory share with French postmodernism a repudiation of both strong foundationalism[11] and totalizing holism, their tendency is to emphasize what we can have and not to linger as long on what we cannot. Hence the phrase 'German positivism.' For both Gadamer and Habermas the concept of *Verständigung*, of coming to an understanding with others, is important. Of course, no such understanding is final, beyond challenge and revision; but then, neither is it nothing. The homes created by tradition, consensus, and even compromise may be, as James suggests above, themselves homeless; but, insist Gadamer and Habermas, people live in them nevertheless, finding in them whatever meaning and truth is available to them.

\* \* \*

What I have called French negativism does not exhaust the scene in contemporary French philosophy. Two major figures, Ricoeur and Levinas, have much in common with Gadamer and Habermas in the sense that they, too, can be called the-glass-is-half-full philosophers. Both share the anti-Cartesian, anti-Hegelian stance of their French colleagues, but, like their German colleagues, they also insist that philosophical thought can be constructive as well as deconstructive. Perhaps it is not surprising that these two philosophize out of a deep sympathy rather than a deep hostility toward religion. As we turn our attention to Levinas and to his surprising relation to Kierkegaard, we will want to keep his "yes, but" relationship to French negativism in mind.

The Preface to *Totality and Infinity* opens with the following sentence: "Everyone will readily agree that it is of the highest importance to know whether we are not duped by morality" (TI 21). In the next paragraph we find politics presented as "opposed to morality" but tightly wedded both to war and to reason; and before we get past the first page we read, "The visage of being that shows itself in war is fixed in the concept of totality, which dominates Western philosophy."

Since politics is defined as "the art of foreseeing war and of winning it by every means" (TI 21), it is not surprising that politics is opposed to morality. But the linkage of politics, so construed, to reason and western philosophy is, as it is meant to be, shocking. The clue to the linkage is the notion of totality. In concert with his French negativist colleagues and against the background of Nietzsche and Heidegger, Levinas will develop his own critical narrative of western philosophy as the will to power dressed up as the Logos. Its attempts to totalize the world and our experience of it, to make everything fit within its conceptual schemes, are seen as a series of attempts to make the world safe for a Self unimpeded by any Other that is not its own other, that is, the necessary condition for its own possibility, something to be used, possessed, enjoyed. While metaphysics is the desire "toward *something else entirely,* toward the *absolutely other*" (TI 33), western ontology has systematically reduced the Other to the Same.

After Heidegger, the name for what is bad about the western philosophical tradition has usually been 'metaphysics' (in its onto-theological mode) or the metaphysics of presence. Levinas makes 'ontology' his whipping boy and reserves the name of metaphysics for the ethical posture he affirms. The reason for this terminological reversal is twofold. First, he wants to preserve the connection between metaphysics and transcendence, and he believes that what we usually call western metaphysics has largely been the attempt to eliminate or at least domesticate transcendence. Second, he believes that giving primacy to the category of being has played a major role in this project that has turned "reason" into the ally of war. Being is epistemologically problematic insofar as being is understood as that which gives itself to human understanding to be thought, making human horizons the measure of meaning and truth; and being is ethically problematic in that as *conatus essendi* it is the measureless self-assertion of the same over against any other, natural, human, or divine.

Whereas Nietzsche aims his critique of the western logos at Christianity and Platonism, and Heidegger aims his at Nietzsche himself, as the one who culminates these traditions by simply reversing their valuations, Levinas directs his critique especially at Husserl and Heidegger, the most powerful recent expressions of the totalizing tendencies of western ontology.

I shall not give separate attention to Levinas's critique of western philosophy, which will emerge quite naturally as we focus on his constructive themes. But it is this critique that is the common ground between Levinas and the French postmodernists. In the aftermath of their critiques, the increasingly pressing question has become How is ethics possible if reason is so deeply wounded? It is just this question that is posed by the opening sentence of *Totality and Infinity* in 1961, prior to the postmodern corpus of Derrida, Foucault, Lyotard, and others.[12]

As his colleagues will do later, Levinas gives a special twist to this question. In the context of the Enlightenment project, the question would be parsed something like this. For an increasingly secular modernity, God cannot be the source and guarantor of moral norms, so reason—make that Reason—will have to take over those responsibilities. But if Reason is deeply wounded, if it turns out to be merely reason, or worse, your reason, my reason, their reason, and our reason, each of which is a bundle of unfulfilled promises, what is to keep the moral life from lapsing into nihilistic cynicism? Or, to use Levinas's own language, what is to keep ethics from degenerating into politics and Reason from becoming the ideological name for the rationales of violence?

Reason is supposed to be the ally of the Right and the Good. But, as we have already seen, Levinas challenges the assumption that what calls itself Reason actually is. The ethical life presupposes the ineliminable otherness of the Other, while the western logos, which calls itself Reason, has consistently sought to reduce alterity to what can be "reabsorbed into my own identity as a thinker or a possessor" (TI 33). Thus the wounding of Reason that I have been referring to as negativism is for Levinas not merely the humility that acknowledges that human reason is human, all too human; it is also a necessary moment in making the modern world safe for the moral life. Only when the totalizing assault of Reason on the Other has been withstood is the way open for a genuinely reasonable ethics.

But even if the wounding of reason is seen in a positive rather than a negative light,[13] the question remains, How, now that the framework within which Kantians debated utilitarians has collapsed, is ethics possible? In this context the question is an epistemological question. At issue is how I can know the Good, not how I can become good by bringing my actions and feelings into conformity with it.

Levinas's answer, put in a vocabulary not his own, is that our most fundamental moral beliefs are properly basic. He agrees with Lyotard that an evidentialist justification of them is not possible. Not only can the imperatives of the moral life not be derived from theoretical knowledge of any kind, but the attempt to do so puts us within the very (totalizing) framework that makes ethical transcendence impossible by reducing the neighbor to a moment in our conceptual scheme.

But Lyotard's prescriptivism goes farther than this. It claims that "the 'you must' is an obligation that ultimately is not even directly experienced," that "the 'you must' is something that exceeds all experience."[14]

Levinas bases his ethical cognitivism on a diametrically opposite claim. Not only is obligation directly experienced; it is the only thing that is directly experienced, and, as such, it is (or deserves to be) the most fundamental element in all our language games and conceptual schemes.

In spite of his sustained critique of Husserl and Heidegger, Levinas insists, "I remain to this day a phenomenologist," defining phenomenology as "a way of becoming aware of where we are in the world" (DEL 14–15; cf. GCM xi–xv). The claim that we have a direct experience of the "you must" is a phenomenological claim that has, for purposes of the present analysis, five moments.

1. The first is the claim that "the absolutely other is the Other" (TI 39; cf. 71, II 245). By invoking the difference in French between *autre*, the other that may be either a person or a thing, and *autrui*, the Other who may only be another person, Levinas situates his phenomenological claim in the domain where instead of being a subject representing objects we are a subject confronted by another subject, one who makes claims on us.[15] Since a phenomenological claim is always an invitation to look and see for ourselves, this first moment tells us where we should be standing when we do our own looking.

2. Second, it is the face of the Other that expresses this absolute otherness of the Other as an infinity that surpasses all attempts to relativize it by representing it. The face overflows the concept and thereby all my attempts to possess, to use, or to enjoy the Other. It is face to face with the Other that I experience the claim that puts my project of being the center of the world in question. The immediacy of the ethical relation is not that of intuitionism, for I am not gazing at an object or proposition but am the one looked at, spoken to. This is the infinity of another person incarnate in a face. Thus violence consists in seeing the Other not as a face but merely as a force (FC 19).[16]

3. The next moment concerns the content of the claim placed upon me as I encounter the Other face to face. The "primordial *expression*" of the face of the Other, his or her "first word" to me, is "you shall not commit murder" (TI 199; cf. 216, 262, 303). This has the advantage of being very specific, but it seems a bit limited in scope. Have I really satisfied the claim of the Other, whose otherness regularly leads Levinas to use the term 'infinite,' so long as I manage not to kill him or her?

Levinas provides glosses on his basic formula designed to steer us away from such a reading. It is "the face of the other who asks me not to let him die alone, as if to do so were to become an accomplice in his death. *Thus* [emphasis added] the face says to me: you shall not kill" (DEL 24; cf. BCI 38). If indifference to the suffering of the Other compromises my obedience to the command You shall not kill, it is clear that there is no short and simple way to fulfill it. The concept of infinite obligation returns dramatically.

But Levinas pushes further and suggests that morally speaking I find myself a hostage, "responsible for what [others] do or suffer" (S 101). Being a hostage is "like kinship, it is a bond prior to every chosen bond . . . a responsibility for the other, and hence a responsibility for what I have not committed, for the pain and the fault of others" (LP 123). In making the claim that I am responsible for the deeds, even the fault, of the Other, and not just the suffering and pain, there is not a hint that any paternalistic privilege attends this answerability. The point is simply that prior to any free choice by which I might assume, and perhaps in so doing set limits to my responsibility for the life of the Other, I find myself the bearer of an unlimited obligation (see NTR 98–100).

Perhaps the best clue to the meaning of my responsibility for what the Other does or suffers is found in Levinas's preoccupation with Pascal's notion of "my place in the sun" and his commentary, which Levinas italicizes, *"That is how the usurpation of the whole world began"* (from *Pensées*, Sec. 295). He adds (in the same paragraph that presents the face as "the other who asks me not to led him die alone"), "In ethics, the other's right to exist has primacy over my own" (DEL 24). But if the Other's right to exist is the right to a place in the sun, then killing, in the literal sense, is the ultimate but not the only violent violation.

Levinas makes this clear when he returns to the same theme in another essay. "My being-in-the-world or my 'place in the sun,' my being at home, have these not also been the usurpation of spaces belonging to the other man whom I have already oppressed or starved, or driven out into a third world; are they not acts of repulsing, excluding, exiling, stripping, killing?" Correspondingly, the ethical relation consists in a very specific fear, "the fear of occupying someone else's place with the *Da* of my *Dasein*" (EF 82). There are many forms of repulsing, many forms of excluding, many forms of stripping, each of which denies to the Other that kind of a place in the sun where he or she has the human support needed to act well by all but the superheroes of the human race. I am responsible for what others do as well as for what they suffer, not because I am their moral guardian and supervisor, but because I am responsible for their place in the sun, its mere existence, yes, but also its quality.

4. The fourth dimension of the Other's claim on me is its double asymmetry. First of all, the Other is radically above me. The Other's claim comes as a command from "the Most High" (TI 34) whom I encounter as my lord and master (TI 72, 75, 101, 213). This is a phenomenological, not a theological, assertion. Levinas is not invoking God as the one who commands us to love our neighbor. He is claiming that the face of the neighbor confronts us not as a contractual proposal to be negotiated but as an unconditional obligation. It is unconditional in that its validity depends in no way either upon our agreeing to accept it or in the Other's doing something to evoke or merit our compliance. Levinas's complaint against Buber is that he overlooks this dimension of height in the ethical relation and makes reciprocity primordial (TI 68–70; MB 70–72; DEL 31).

At the same time, the Other is as far below me as above me. Levinas stresses the nakedness of the face, the helplessness of the one who has nothing but a face upon which to base such a radical challenge to my own instincts of self-preservation and self-assertion. The Other has nothing to offer me, "no beauty, no majesty to catch our eyes, no grace to attract us to him" (Isa. 53: 2). So Levinas insists that the Other is the stranger, the widow, and the orphan with whom the Bible is so concerned (TI 74–78, 215).

Majesty in misery, divinity in destitution. This is the double asymmetry of the ethical relation. It may seem contradictory to attribute majesty to the face immediately after having denied it. But the majesty denied is what usually counts as such, beauty and sex appeal, power and strength, wealth and acclaim, and so forth, whereas the majesty affirmed is the majesty of the face as such, the naked face, a majesty possessed by even those faces that lack all those other 'majesties.'[17]

\*\*\*

5. Finally, and most importantly, not only do we experience this "you must," we have *direct* experience of the face and its claim. "The notion of the face . . . finally makes possible the description of the notion of the immediate. . . . The immediate is the face to face" (TI 51–52).

The Hegelian-Heideggerian claim, against Descartes and Husserl, respectively, that nothing is immediate and that everything is mediated was, in 1961, when Levinas wrote this and has been ever since, *the* Shibboleth of continental philosophy from existential phenomenology, hermeneutics, and critical theory through structuralism to the varieties of poststructuralism.[18] Especially in France, to be radical has meant to give unquestioning allegiance to this orthodoxy, which has long since passed from sect to church status. Levinas's heresy could hardly be bolder or more dramatic.

"The face of the Other at each moment destroys and overflows the plastic image it leaves me. . . . It does not manifest itself by these qualities, but καθ αὐτό. It *expresses itself*" (TI 50–51; cf. FC 20). In Plato and Aristotle καθ αὐτό (*per se*, through or by means of itself ) often designates the ontological immediacy of forms or substances that are self-sufficient with regard to their existence. But it can refer to an epistemic immediacy, as in *Republic* 476b.[19] Here knowledge and opinion are being distinguished in terms of the difference between the philosophical few who can apprehend Beauty itself, and the lovers of sights and sounds who never get beyond "beautiful sounds and colors and shapes." The former must be able not only to apprehend Beauty itself (αὐτὸ τὸ καλὸν), as distinct from beautiful things; they must also apprehend it directly, through itself (καθ αὐτό) and not through the mediation of those things.[20] It is clearly this epistemic sense to which Levinas appeals.

In the face, he claims, we have "an essential coinciding of the existent and the signifier. Signification is not added to the existent," as in language where the connection between meaning on the one hand and phoneme or grapheme on the other is arbitrary. Its signification, we might say, is built right into this sign. But this means that what this sign signifies is itself. Hence the emphatic use of the concept of expression above. In this case, "to signify is not equivalent to presenting oneself as a sign, but to expressing oneself, that is, presenting oneself in person" (TI 262).

This notion of being present "in person" lies at the heart of Husserl's phenomenological theory of evidence. For Husserl the *"principle of principles"* is this: *"that every originary presentive intuition is a legitimizing source of cognition, that everything originarily* (so to speak, in its 'personal' actuality) *offered* to us *in 'intuition' is to be accepted."* Statements expressing such evidence provide "an *absolute beginning* called upon to serve as a foundation, a *principium* in the genuine sense of the word."[21] For Husserl perception (ultimately in all its modes) is "the essential possibility of [something] being simply intuited as what it is and, more particularly, of being perceived as what it is in an adequate perception, one that is presentive of that existent itself, 'in person,' *without any mediation by 'appearances.'*"[22]

There are unmistakably Husserlian overtones to the claim that "knowledge in the absolute sense of the term, the pure experience of the other being, would have to maintain the other being καθ αὐτό" (TI 65). And yet the claim that the face presents itself with this immediacy is presented as a critique of Husserlian phenomenology, which is built on immediacy, as well as of Heideggerian phenomenology, which is built on its denial. Levinas treats these two as an either/or he declines to accept. The one gives a foundationalist, idealist account of representation, the other an anti-foundationalist, anti-idealist account (which Levinas treats as stand-in for the whole anti-immediacy orthodoxy mentioned above, including French poststructuralism).

But for Levinas the task is to get beyond the structure of representation that they share. Vis-à-vis the Other, consciousness "does not consist in equaling being with representation, in tending to the full light in which this adequation is to be sought, but rather in overflowing this play of lights—this phenomenology" (TI 27). Or again, "Here, contrary to all the conditions for the visibility of objects, a being is not placed in the light of another but presents itself in the manifestation that should only announce it; it is present as directing this very manifestation" (TI 65).[23] In short, in the call of the Other I experience an "intelligibility before the light" (OB 78). This is because the metaphysical/ethical relation "can not be properly speaking a representation, for the other would therein dissolve into the same. . . . To be sure . . . usage objects, foods, the very world we inhabit are other in relation to us. But the alterity of the I and the world inhabited is only formal; as we have indicated, in a world in which I sojourn this alterity falls under my powers" (TI 38).[24]

The expression of the Other καθ αὐτό represents, contra Husserl, a "meaning prior to my *Sinngebung* and thus independent of my initiative and my power" (TI 51; cf. S 89–90). This notion of meaning that "does not refer to its constitution" and is "prior to all *Sinngebung* . . . describes the very structure of a created being." Here "beings have a meaning before I constitute this rational world along with them. Creation is the fact that intelligibility precedes me. . . . This is not a theological thesis; we reach the idea of creation out of the experience of a face" (FC 22).

This same point can be expressed in other language. Ethics involves true transcendence "because the essential of ethics is in its transcendent intention,

and because *not every transcendent intention has the noesis-noema structure*"
(TI 29, emphasis added; cf. 49 as cited in note 23).

Levinas does not accept the Husserlian notion of a transcendental ego
outside the worlds of both nature and history that can be an absolute origin of
meaning. But in these passages he does not challenge such a notion. He
concedes it for the sake of argument in order to point out that this theory of
meaning is but a variation of reducing the other to the same, or, to be more
specific, of reducing the Other to the meaning I give him or her. **Like war,
Husserlian phenomenology defaces the Other.**

Levinas associates Platonic, Kantian, and Hegelian idealism with the
Cartesian-Husserlian variety and arraigns them on similar charges. The passages just cited about light can be read as referring to Plato as well as to
Husserl. The Platonic doctrine of the kinship of the soul to the forms and the
corresponding notion of knowledge as recollection replace transcendence
with immanence. By contrast Levinas insists that "the conversion of the soul to
exteriority, to the absolutely other, to Infinity, is not deducible from the very
identity of the soul, for it is not commensurate with the soul" (TI 61). If the
Other is truly incommensurable with my own self-identity, then to welcome
the Other is to learn something I didn't already know. Hence the sustained
polemic against the Socratic reduction of teaching to maieutics (TI 43–44, 51,
126, 171, 180, 204). Proximity, the ethical relation is "older than every past
present" (OB 76). **In the doctrine of knowledge as recollection, as in war, the
Other is defaced.**

The neo-Kantians assimilated Plato's recollection thesis with the Kantian
notion of the a priori, and Levinas thinks they are, unfortunately, right on
target. In the face as the trace of the Other, we encounter something "'older'
than the a priori" (OB 101–102; cf. 86, S 90, PII 59). Levinas extends this from
the theoretical to the practical, so that obligation is also "prior to any commitment" I may have made as well as being "older than the plot of egoism woven
in the *conatus* of being" (OB 92). Or, if we assimilate the a priori to the
linguistic turn, the Other expresses itself prior to the "already said" (OB 35–
37). All this explains the running polemic against the transcendental unity of
apperception, according to which all meaning has to be "mine" (OB 140–41,
148, 151–52, 163–64, 171). The responsible self is "older than the ego" (OB
117). **In the Kantian version of the recollection doctrine, as in war, the
Other is silenced, and thus defaced.**

Unlike the Platonic soul or the transcendental ego in either its Kantian or
Husserlian versions, Hegelian spirit is in history, or better, is history. Here
idealism is the very opposite of escapism. But when Levinas looks to see
whether there is room in this inn for the Other, he finds an all encompassing
mediation that excludes the possibility of the face καθ αὐτό. So, against Hegel
(and Marx, for that matter) he writes, "When man truly approaches the Other
he is uprooted from history. . . . Interiority is the very possibility of a birth and a
death that do not derive their meaning from history" (TI 52, 55). In the

Hegelian context, this is equivalent to claiming that the face of the Other "*is* by itself and not by reference to a system" (TI 75; cf. OB 69–70, 78), that "the interlocutor appears as though without a history, outside of systems" (ET 43). That the systems in question are practical as well as theoretical, social as well as semantic, we find in the claim that "invocation is prior to the community" (ET 41).[25] Since Hegel cannot grant the face this primacy over history, system, and community, Spirit becomes, in one of philosophy's most tragic ironies, the Other's nemesis. Although it is only ink and not blood that is spilled, at least in the first instance, **when soul and transcendental ego are made more worldly as spirit, once again, as in war, the Other is defaced.**

Heidegger's phenomenological destruction of the history of metaphysics puts him in direct conflict with the idealisms of Plato, Kant, Hegel, and Husserl. In Levinas's eyes he represents the most powerful alternative account of representation; but at the same time he remains equally deaf to the call of the Other. "Since Husserl the whole of phenomenology is the promotion of the idea of *horizon*, which for it plays a role equivalent to that of the *concept* in classical idealism" (TI 44–45). This is a surprising interpretation, for post-Husserlian phenomenology (not to mention structuralism and poststructuralism) have waged a sustained assault on idealism's Concept, whether Plato's ειδος, Kant's categories, Hegel's *Begriff*, or Husserl's *Wesen* under the banner of the Horizon and its numerous cousins. In fact, it can be said to be Husserl's own development of this notion that causes his quest for philosophy as rigorous science to unravel before his very eyes, especially in *The Crisis of European Sciences and Transcendental Philosophy*.

The theme, developed in endless variations, is quite simple. Meaning is neither atomistic nor fixed. Therefore it is never immediate nor complete. This is because every focus of cognitive attention occurs against a background or in a context to which it is relative but that can itself never be fully thematized or turned into foreground. To put the point in terms of physical vision, one can never look at the boundary of one's visual field. Thus the concept can never have the clarity and distinctness that all forms of idealism require of it, or, to put it in a different idiom, experience can never be totalized in the concept. Neither as an intuitionistic foundationalism nor as a dialectical holism can Absolute Knowledge be achieved.

Since Levinas knows all this, why does he say that since Husserl (meaning most especially Heidegger) "the idea of *horizon* . . . plays a role *equivalent to* that of the *concept* in classical idealism"? (emphasis added). It is because he asks whether the difference between Husserl and "after Husserl" makes any difference to the widow, the orphan, and the stranger. The post-Husserlians, including Heidegger and the French negativists, agree that cognition is always horizonal, incorrigibly contextual. But this is no help to the Other. The "ontological imperialism" (TI 44) of the horizon consists in the fact "to recognize truth to be disclosure is to refer it to the horizon of him who discloses. . . . The disclosed being is relative to us and not καθ αὐτό." This is because "we disclose only with respect to a project" and in disclosure we make the Other into a "theme for interpretation," whereas manifestation καθ αὐτό "consists in a being telling itself to us independently of every position we would have taken in its regard, *expressing itself*" (TI 64–65; cf. OB 91, S 89–90). Where disclosure is horizonal, "the possibility of a *signification without a context*" (TI 23; cf. PE 65) becomes impossible. But this is the most important possibility of all, for this is precisely what is meant by καθ αὐτό. By insisting on its possibility, Levinas renders himself a heretic in the eyes of the post-Husserlian church.

As the previous paragraph suggests, 'disclosure' (*erschliessen, Erschlossenheit*) is the key term through which Heidegger expresses his orthodoxy on the question of context.[26] Levinas's sustained polemic against Heidegger takes the form of contrasting disclosure with the καθ αὐτό of the Other's face, which in this context he regularly names revelation (TI 27–28, 61–67, 71–78). **Because disclosure excludes revelation, it defaces the Other as much as the idealism it so deeply opposes.**

* * *

Although he regularly links the notions of transcendence and revelation, Levinas remains clear that these are phenomenological and not theological claims and that they refer to bearers of the human face. What he calls "the Metaphysical" dimension of life is "an ethical behavior and not theology, not a thematization, be it a knowledge by analogy, of the attributes of God" (TI 78). A fuller exploration of the religious significance of Levinas's usage of religious language will have to await chapters 3 and 4. For the present, what is important is the striking structural agreement between the immediacy claimed in Levinas's contrast between revelation and recollection (in all its various forms) and that to which Kierkegaard makes appeal.[27] In neither case is there a denial that normally meaning and truth are mediated by the "already said," by metaphysical, transcendental, or historical criteria that are the conditions of possible experience in that by being always already within us they enable us to recognize whatever claims to be meaningful or true as such. The claim is rather that there is an exception to the sovereignty of these a priori's, an immediacy that cuts through them, traumatically calling us (along with these defenses, for that is how both Levinas and Kierkegaard view them) into question and taking us hostage. This exception is the immediacy called revelation.

We encounter this notion in *Fear and Trembling*, where faith, as the response to the immediacy of divine revelation, is itself designated as an immediacy. It is, of course, mediated by the word of God, but this encounter is not itself mediated by human horizons.

> The God of Abraham is a God who speaks.
> Now the Lord said to Abram, "Go from your country and your kindred

> and your father's house to the land that I will show you. I will make of you a
> great nation, and I will bless you, and make your name great, so that you will
> be a blessing. I will bless those who bless you, and the one who curses you I
> will curse; and in you all the families of the earth shall be blessed." (Gen.
> 12:1–3)

There are two differences from Levinas that should be noted. First, this is not the voice of the widow, the orphan, or the stranger. Second, just for this reason it is able to be a voice of promise as well as of command.[28] But at present the focus is on a crucial structural similarity between the two thinkers. So we remember that for Levinas, not only is the face of the widow, the orphan, and the stranger the immediate but also that "The face speaks" and that it is in the call of the interlocutor that revelation takes place (TI 66–67).

Of course, *Fear and Trembling* focuses our attention on a subsequent command, the command to offer Isaac, the son of promise, as a sacrifice. Following the Genesis narrative, the pseudonym Silentio presents this command as a revelation in the sense of a speech act performed by God. What is distinctive about his account is the immediacy he attributes to it. God expresses the divine will καθ αὑτό, and the message cuts through all of Abraham's defenses. No version of the a priori, the "already said," whether metaphysical as in Plato, transcendental as in Kant and Husserl, or historical as in Hegel,[29] enables Abraham to be the condition for the possibility of the authority of this command. So Silentio describes the whole situation as paradoxical, absurd, and sheer madness.[30] It is "unreasonable," not in and of itself, but "humanly speaking" relative to "worldly understanding" and "human calculation" (FT 17, 35–36, 46).

In the Preliminary Expectoration, where the knight of faith is contrasted with the knight of infinite resignation,[31] Silentio presents the latter's faith as a leap by contrast with mediation, "*a chimera, which in Hegel is supposed to explain everything*" (FT 42n). It is a leap because by faith Abraham locates himself beyond and outside the human horizons (language games) that otherwise mediate his identity and provide justifications for his action. In the three Problemas, where the contrast is with the tragic hero,[32] we get a fuller account of the contrast between the immediacy of faith as a response to revelation and the mediacy of reason as merely human understanding. Readers will recall that the three Problemas revolve, respectively, around the notions of a teleological suspension of the ethical, of an absolute duty toward God, and of Abraham's inability of explain himself to his family. In each case faith is the site where immediacy prevails over mediation.

The ethical that is teleologically suspended (*aufgehoben*, relativized in a larger whole of which it is not the organizing principle) is not the eternal truths of reason laid claim to by philosophers such as Plato or Kant, but what Hegel calls *Sittlichkeit*, the laws and customs of one's people (FT 54–55), and what Nietzsche calls the morality of mores. It is the universal not as an abstract principle of which actions are instances but as a social whole, a concrete network of norms, to which individuals belong as parts and from which they derive their identity. Each of the three tragic heroes who are introduced, Agamemnon, Jephthah, and Brutus, actually killed one of his own children. But they were comforted by mediation in the universal, which Silentio identifies as the nation, the state, society (FT 58–59, 62). They were members of a social order, a language game if you like, which in each case provided justification for their act. While their families and fellow citizens could no doubt in varying degrees feel their pain, they also understood why they did what they did and that it was right to do it. Abraham does not have this comfort and must be a murderer in his own eyes as well as those of his family and friends unless there is an immediacy that cuts through and trumps the prevailing rules of the social order.

The second Problema clarifies the meaning of a teleological suspension of the ethical in two ways. On the one hand, it means simply that for faith there is an absolute duty to God. On the other hand, it means that the ethical, the laws and customs of one's people, are not invalidated or rejected but rendered relative (FT 70–71). While they have substantial authority, only God is the absolute authority for the knight of faith. The paradox is that the individual (in relation to God) is higher than the universal and obviously cannot be mediated by the universal, which is now identified not only as the state but also as the church and even the sect (FT 70–71, 74, 79). Since Hegel is the immediate target of this analysis, it is not the metaphysical or the transcendental but the socio-historical a priori, the already said of a prevailing morality of mores whose rationality faith cannot take as ultimate over against the voice that in addressing it calls this ultimacy into question. Abraham's socially constructed identity is invaded and deeply wounded by the immediacy of this voice.

The third Problema repeats the refrain that Abraham's conduct cannot be justified by means of mediation in and through the universal. But the resultant immediacy, the isolation of the knight of faith in an individuation derived from a unique, nontransferable, nonshareable responsibility, is a second, later immediacy, not the first immediacy that belongs to the aesthetic stage.[33] The aesthete is an atomistic self who stands outside all obligation to God (the religious) or to neighbor (the ethical). The other is never an end but always a means to the aesthete's own satisfaction, here as in *Either/Or* presented as the interesting rather than the pleasant. This individual stands outside of and thus unmediated by the ethical universal. But this immediacy is that of the "sensate, and psychical" (FT 82) the sphere of feeling, mood, and personal idiosyncracy (FT 69). Now we understand the significance of the fact that faith takes the individual outside the universal only "after" having been socialized into the universal, after recognizing its legitimate authority over aesthetic, that is, premoral, interests and desires (FT 55–56, 99; cf. 69). Unlike aesthetic immediacy, religious immediacy gives us an essentially relational individuality, rendered unique by the relative obligations derived from society and the absolute obligations derived from God. In the context of the sustained insistence that

Hegelian Reason is incompatible with biblical faith, the point is that Hegel has collapsed the difference between society and God, making the former absolute and the latter otiose. This is why each of the three Problemas begins with the claim that if Hegel is right, Abraham is lost and can only be considered a murderer.

The third Problema also thematizes a motif that has been mentioned all along but not developed, namely, that Abraham has no language in which to make himself understood to his family and servants (FT 10, 21, 60, 67, 71, 76, 79–80). So we read, "Speak he cannot; he speaks no human language . . . he speaks in a divine language, he speaks in tongues" (FT 114). Of course, there is no shortage of people with the linguistic competence to understand such a statement as "I am going to Mount Moriah to sacrifice Isaac at the Lord's command." Rather, "Abraham *cannot* speak, because he cannot say that which would explain everything (that is, so it is understandable): that it is an ordeal such that, please note, the ethical is the temptation. Anyone placed in such a position is an emigrant from the sphere of the universal" (FT 115). Silentio has taken the linguistic turn, recognizing that social norms are themselves linguistically mediated and only thus able to mediate individual members of society.[34] The language Abraham lacks is the language game in terms of which, unlike the tragic hero, he could justify his action to his family. None of the "already saids" available to him will do the job. The tragic hero can turn to Habermas and his conception of dialogical reason. Agamemnon has "the consolation that every counterargument has had its due, that he has given everyone an opportunity to stand up against him" (FT 113) but that even his family sees that he is doing the right thing. Iphigenia can turn to Gadamer and his conversational conception of reason, in terms of which she and her father have reached "a mutual understanding" (FT 115). But for Abraham the immediacy of revelation overflows the norms contained within these linguistic dikes, leaving him not alone (that would be the aesthete) but, as with Levinas, alone before the traumatic alterity of divine revelation.

* * *

The issue in *Fear and Trembling* is epistemic, not motivational. That it was God who told him to sacrifice Isaac provides all the motivation Abraham needs, and Silentio simply stipulates, "He knew it was God the Almighty who was testing him" (FT 22). But how? We are left gasping for an epistemology of divine revelation, and, as if Kierkegaard felt this need as strongly as we do, eight months later he had another pseudonym, Johannes Climacus, suggest an answer. In the first two chapters of *Philosophical Fragments* we are offered a thought experiment that contrasts recollection and revelation.

The point of departure is taken from Plato's *Meno*, where Socrates helps a slave boy to discover the Pythagorean theorem. He insists that he doesn't teach the boy anything, that the boy already has the truth in him and needs but to recollect it, and that he, Socrates, only performs a maieutic function, providing an occasion for recollection. This role is accidental to the learning, for the slave boy could have gotten help from another or, if he were a budding mathematical genius, he might have discovered the truth all by himself.

Climacus's thought experiment poses the question, What would have to be true *if* there were to be an alternative to Socrates' account of knowledge as recollection, *if* the teacher were really to teach so that the relation to the teacher would be essential rather than accidental, a mere occasion?[35]

The name for this alternative to recollection will be revelation. So we are not entirely surprised that in working out the details of the thought experiment, Climacus introduces a whole series of Christian themes: creation, sin and bondage to sin, a savior, a deliverer, a reconciler, a judge, the fullness of time, a new person, repentance, rebirth, offense, incarnation, and atonement through the suffering and death of an innocent immortal for guilty mortals. For his troubles he is accused of plagiarism, to which he responds by saying that he makes no claim to have invented the story and that he doubts anyone else would make such a claim. It is not the kind of story one would make up (PF 15–36).

This specifically Christian package is important to Kierkegaard, for its point is that anyone who confuses Christian faith with Platonic recollection in any of its versions is confused and guilty of a serious category mistake. There may be something within the limits of philosophical reason that deserves to be called religion, but it does not deserve to be called Christianity. Here, as is so often the case, the immediate target is Hegel and his Danish followers.

But in the present context, where the point is to notice a structural convergence between Kierkegaard and Levinas, the revelation hypothesis can be stated much more briefly. First, it is necessary that the learner does not already have the truth within, is in untruth (PF 13). Second, it is necessary that the teacher give the learner the truth *and* the condition for recognizing it as the truth, "for if the learner were himself the condition for understanding the truth, then he merely needs to recollect" (PF 14), and we are back to Socrates.

It is clear that Climacus is extending the notion of recollection beyond the realm of eternal or a priori truth. It applies to empirical truth as well insofar as the knower already has within the condition for recognizing it as such. It is this condition that is the a priori element, the "already said," whether it be construed metaphysically, transcendentally, or historically. Just as revelation for Levinas is immediate, that is, independent of such conditions, so for Climacus revelation means not merely that the teacher presents the learner with some knowledge not already possessed, but most importantly, also the condition for recognizing it as truth. Only when the teacher gives the truth in this double sense does the relation to the teacher become essential.

We can see the difference between the shallow sense (presenting) and the deeper sense (enabling) of giving the learner the truth. Suppose I ask myself, What was the name of that little girl I had a crush on in second grade? I know it and need but to recollect it. I'm pretty sure it began with an L, so I get one of those lists of girls' names and go through the Ls. When I get to Linda, I remember. Yes, it was Linda. The list gave me the answer that I could not (at least for the moment) produce on my own. But I had the condition for recognizing it as the truth for which I was looking; the list was only the occasion for recollecting, and an accidental one at that. I might have just remembered a little later on, or I might have been reminded by seeing the name Linda in a newspaper story. But suppose I ask *you*, What was the name of that little girl I had a crush on in second grade? and suppose I make it a multiple choice question: Laura, Linda, or Lucy. I have given you the truth. It is staring you in the face, but you don't have the condition; so you are not able to recollect, that is, recognize the truth as such. Presentation falls short of enablement.

For both Kierkegaard and Levinas the knowledge that deserves to be called revelation is independent of the "already saids" that are the condition for our recognition of the truth as such. It is neither derivable from nor validated by what we already know. This is why Levinas writes, "This primacy of the same was Socrates's teaching: to receive nothing of the Other but what is in me, as though from all eternity I was in possession of what comes to me from the outside—to receive nothing, or to be free (TI 43). Over against this, he insists that to welcome the face that expresses itself καθ αὐτό "is therefore to *receive* from the Other beyond the capacity of the I, which means exactly: to have the idea of infinity. But this also means: to be taught. . . . Teaching is not reducible to maieutics; it comes from the exterior and brings me more than I contain" (TI 51).

In the case of Linda, if you are to learn the name of the girl in question, you will have to take it on my authority. Both Levinas and Kierkegaard link the notion of revelation to that of authority. For Levinas, the voice of the Other calls my freedom and spontaneity into question, but when he notes that it does so by virtue of my "recognizing in the Other a *right* over [my] egoism," he calls it religion (TI 43, 40). In his own name Kierkegaard contrasts the genius with the apostle. "**The genius is what he is by himself, that is, by what he is in himself; an apostle is what he is by his divine authority.** . . . *Authority* is what is qualitatively decisive. Or is there not a difference, even within the relativity of human life, although it immanently disappears, between a royal command and the words of a poet or a thinker?" (GA 94, 97). Thus he speaks of impertinence and rebelliousness on the one hand, faith and obedience on the other.

It will surely be noticed that there is a difference between the widow, the orphan, and the stranger on the one hand and the apostle on the other. Point well taken. But for both Levinas and Kierkegaard the basis of the ethical and religious life is an authoritative revelation that in its immediacy comes to us from beyond our own powers of recollection, whether they be interpreted metaphysically, transcendentally, or historically. The latter do not provide us with the criteria by which we can judge; rather we, along with them, are placed under judgment by a voice older than any human a priori and higher than any human horizon.

Both Levinas and Kierkegaard take the dominant strands of the western tradition in philosophy to be variations on the theme of knowledge as recollection. But revelation, as they understand it, not only differs from recollection but disrupts, disturbs, and deconstructs this tradition. For further clarification of this difference and for the expression of this disturbance as enigma (Levinas) and paradox (Kierkegaard), we turn to our next chapter.

# Revelation as Enigma
# and Paradox

> *For how transparent is the shadow that troubles the clarity of coherent speech!*

—(PE 71)

## Can Two Walk Together . . .

In his splendid book *To the Other*,[1] Adriaan Peperzak presents Levinas's 1957 essay "Philosophy and the Idea of Infinity" as the best brief introduction to *Totality and Infinity* (1961). A similar case could be made for the 1965 essay "Phenomenon and Enigma" in relation to *Otherwise Than Being or Beyond Essence* (1974). It has been described as the most Kierkegaardian of Levinas's essays,[2] which gives it special interest in the present context. What makes this description apt is not merely the fact that its latter half contains four of the rather rare references to Kierkegaard in Levinas's writings; it is rather the fact that "the Kierkegaardian God" (PE 66–67) plays the role in this essay that the Cartesian God plays in the 1957 essay, the infinity that is an "inassimilable alterity" (PE 71).

The Cartesian God serves to provide a formal structure of transcendence and heteronomy over against the totality and autonomy of the ontological tradition, in terms of which the face of the human Other can be understood to address me from on high (PII 47). Levinas surprisingly finds in Descartes's God a break with the tradition of the "I think" and of reminiscence according to which truth is found "in the already-known." For Plato philosophy is atheism, or rather unreligion, negation of a God that reveals himself and puts truths into us. This is Socrates' teaching, when he leaves to the master only the exercise of maieutics: every lesson introduced into the soul was already in it. The I's identification, its marvelous autarchy, is the natural crucible of this transmutation of the other into the same. Every philosophy is—to use Husserl's neologism—an egology (PII 49–50).

By contrast, the infinity we find in Descartes's idea of God is

> exceptional in that its ideatum surpasses its idea. . . . The intentionality that animates the idea of infinity is not comparable with any other;[3] it aims at what it cannot embrace. . . . In thinking infinity the I from the first *thinks more than it thinks*. . . . [The idea of infinity] has been *put* into us. It is not a reminiscence. (PII 54)

Borrowing from Aquinas's notion of infused virtues, those implanted within us by God, we might speak here of infused truth. But the explicit contrast with the Platonic doctrine of recollection brings us even closer to Kierkegaard's notion of revelation in which God gives us both the truth and the capacity to recognize it as such. In his discussion of this aspect of Descartes, Levinas provides commentary on his own concept of revelation and its convergence with Kierkegaard's.

In "Phenomenon and Enigma," however, a further dimension of this convergence is developed. Let us not forget that just as it is a formal feature of Descartes's thought that Levinas affirms, so it is a formal aspect of the Kierkegaardian God that interests him (PE 67). Just as he abstracts from Descartes's attempt to prove the existence of God via reflections on the idea of infinity, so he abstracts from the specifically Christian "salvation drama" (PE 67) that provides the content of Kierkegaard's challenge to the speculative tradition. But this does not signify a shift of emphasis from the divine transcendence to human transcendence. For this reason, it is the shadow of God, however transparent it may turn out to be, that makes this a disturbing essay. For "absolute alterity" turns out to be an "absolute disturbance" (PE 64) to every order, semantic or social, by means of which human reason seeks to make itself lord of the earth. This disturbance is thematized on virtually every page of the essay. It signifies that to go "beyond being" (PE 62, 73) is to go "beyond reason" (PE 61). Kierkegaard's Climacus insists that reality may indeed be a system for God (CUP I, 118); but he and Levinas agree that it cannot be such for us, precisely because the infinite that is other to us continually disturbs, disrupts, and, if you like, deconstructs each totality we seek to construct, every logos into which we try to make everything fit (PE 61). Revelation stands in overt tension with reason as understood by main strands of the western philosophical tradition.

The Kierkegaardian overtones are more overt when Levinas speaks of this move "beyond reason" as a kind of madness or folly (PE 61–62).[4] But beyond this "quotation," and beyond the generic role God plays as the Great Disturber, there is an even more specific Kierkegaardian element to this essay.

Long before any explicit reference to Kierkegaard, its strategy mirrors that of Johannes Climacus in *Philosophical Fragments*. In the thought experiment that occupies his first two chapters, Climacus identifies Reason as the Socratic assumption that knowledge is recollection, meaning that the human knower has the capacity to recognize the truth, and then sets out to find what it would take to generate a genuinely different understanding of human knowledge. Without saying just what motivates his effort, other than the hints of the Preface that he is critical of the Hegelian mind-set of his contemporary culture, he devotes considerable energy to working out the details of his alternative hypothesis. He does not argue for the superiority of his alternative, just that it is truly different from the Socratic assumption.[5]

In the third chapter the two accounts of human knowledge confront each other as Reason and the Paradox,[6] and the point of the project begins to emerge. Reason is proud of having excluded the Paradox, which it considers to be absurd, since it (the Paradox) does not play the game by Reason's rules. But this "discovery, if it may be put this way, does not belong to Reason but to the Paradox," and in announcing their mutual incompatibility "Reason merely parrots the Paradox," which replies to Reason, "It is just as you say, and the amazing thing is that you think that it is an objection" (PF 50, 52). The fact that Reason excludes the Paradox only proves that it is exclusionary, not that what it excludes is by that fact discredited. The point of the apparently trivial thought experiment, looking for an alternative to the assumption that knowledge is recollection, is Augustinian. It is to raise the question whether the Platonic propagation of the Socratic suggestion is not a form of "presumption."[7] By what authority (*quid juris*) does the thinking that calls itself Reason exclude other kinds of thinking and claim for itself exclusive title to the highest truth? This question is already a form of madness, for in the return of the repressed that it represents, the calm and complacent sanity of exclusionary Reason is disturbed.

Given the linguistic turn of contemporary philosophy and Levinas's own increasingly linguistic orientation as he moves toward *Otherwise Than Being*,[8] it is not surprising that his version of the *Fragments'* thought experiment, or, if you prefer, his brilliant commentary thereon, begins under the heading "Rational Speech and Disturbance" (PE 61). Like Climacus he defines rational speech quite briefly and spends most of his time and energy seeking to clarify the disturbance that "troubles the clarity of coherent speech!" (PE 71)

> As rational speech, philosophy is taken to move from evidence to evidence, directed to what is seen, to what shows itself, thus directed to the present. The term *present* suggests both the idea of a privileged position in the temporal series and the idea of manifestation. The idea of being connects them. . . . Being is a manifestation in which the uncertain memory and the aleatory anticipation are moored; being is a presence to the gaze and to speech, an appearing, a phenomenon.
>
> As speech directed upon the present, philosophy is an understanding

of being, or an ontology, or a phenomenology. In the order of its speech it encompasses and situates even what seemed first to contain this speech or overflow it, but which, when present, that is, discovered, fits into this logos. . . . To utter a speech that would not be anchored in the present would be to go beyond reason. (PE 61)

This linguistic account of philosophy as Reason makes it clear (1) how the target of Levinas's critique[9] can be designated more or less equivalently as the metaphysics of presence, logocentrism, ontology, or onto-theology, (2) why he describes this style of philosophy as the reduction of the other to the same, (3) how he takes the phenomenologies of Husserl and Heidegger to belong to this tradition rather than to be its overcoming,[10] and (4) how nothing short of the enigma that disturbs this logos can turn ontology's world of phenomena into the merely phenomenal world and the God of onto-theology into an idol. By contrast "with the indiscreet and victorious appearing of a phenomenon," what he calls enigma is "this way of manifesting himself without manifesting himself" (PE 66), that which "signifies itself without revealing itself" (PE 73).

Like Climacus's paradox, Levinas's enigma signifies that revelation involves mystery. The latter's engagement with enigma is a form of critique directed, like the earlier critiques by Augustine and Kant, against the hubris of a human reason that would be autonomous and self-sufficient.[11] It is motivated in part by the sense that logocentric Reason is dogmatically atheistic, that it arbitrarily excludes God from its world or, what is worse, domesticates God by transforming the divine into a (visible or intelligible) phenomenon, a process in which "the divinity of God dissipates" (PE 62). "Phenomena, apparition in the full light, the relationship with being, ensure immanence as a totality and philosophy as atheism" (PE 70).[12]

It is also motivated by the sense that the transcendence thus reduced to immanence properly belongs to philosophy. In pursuit of enigma Levinas takes as his guide "the notion of God, which a thought called faith succeeds in getting expressed and introduces into philosophical discourse." To affirm this thought requires that one "endure the contradiction between the existence included in the essence of God and the scandalous absence of this God . . . [and] to suffer an initiation trial into religious life which separates philosophers from believers" (PE 62).

But this thought that faith manages to introduce into philosophical discourse is not entirely eccentric to the latter. In the first place it is a thought, not simply an image or a feeling. There is no hint that what distinguishes this thought from the thoughts of logocentric ontology or phenomenology is that it is an undergraduate *mythos* that has not yet learned the doctoral-level language of the *logos*, a minor league *Vorstellung* not yet good enough to join the Big Show and its superstar *Begriffe*. The distinguishing mark of this thought is simply that it radically disturbs the thoughts by which we construct the worlds of nature and history so as to make them fully our own in theory and in practice.

Second, "to think more than one thinks, to think of what withdraws from thought, is to desire, and with a desire that, unlike need, is renewed and becomes ardent the more it is nourished with the desirable" (PE 72).[13] It is precisely this desire that Levinas takes to be, rather than either wonder or doubt, the origin of philosophy. That is why, when he speaks of "the contradiction between the existence included in the essence of God and the scandalous absence of this God" (PE 62), he presents it as what separates philosophers from believers "unless the obstinate absence of God were one of those paradoxes that call to the highways."[14] It is the affirmation of this possibility with which Levinas concludes his essay, speaking of "the antecedence of God relative to a world which cannot accommodate him" as involving "the One, which every philosophy would like to express, beyond being" (PE 73).

In *Philosophical Fragments*, Climacus's critique has the same dual motivation. On the one hand, it is directed against what is perceived to be a dogmatic and arbitrary exclusion without which human understanding could not absolutize itself as Reason. In his case the God whom the world cannot accommodate is the specifically Christian God become human in Jesus of Nazareth. What his thought experiment (PF, chs. 1–2) is designed to show is that the Socratic assumption that knowledge is recollection excludes this possibility a priori (as Lessing clearly saw).[15] An incarnation is not the sort of reality available to recollection.

At the same time, Climacus thinks human understanding has a built-in desire for an absolute that will relativize it. He says that "the thinker without the paradox is like the lover without passion" and that "the ultimate paradox of thought [is] to want to discover something that thought itself cannot think" (PF 37, emphasis added).[16] The human understanding, when not deluding itself into thinking it is Reason, has a "paradoxical passion that **wills** the collision . . . and, without really understanding itself, **wills** its own downfall." *Concretely speaking*, God incarnate is "this unknown against which the understanding in its paradoxical passion collides and which even **disturbs** man and his self-knowledge" (PF 38–39, emphasis added). *Abstractly speaking*, the unknown against which human understanding in its paradoxical passion continuously collides, is "the absolutely different. . . . Defined as the absolutely different, it seems to be at the point of being disclosed, but not so, because the understanding cannot even think the absolutely different" (PF 44–45).

Levinas's own account has its concrete side in the theory of the neighbor as the face that commands us from on high. But in the essay before us, he speaks more abstractly in a theory of enigma as semantic alterity. Phenomena signify, that is, they enter into the domain of human meaning, by appearing.

> To appear, to seem, is forthwith to resemble terms of an **already familiar order**, to **compromise** oneself with them, to **be assimilated** to them. Does not the invisibility of God belong to another play, to an approach which does not polarize into a **subject-object correlation** but is deployed as a drama

with several personages? . . . Everything depends on the possibility of vibrating with a meaning that is not synchronized with the speech that **captures** it and cannot **be fitted into** its order. (PE 62–63, emphasis added)[17]

The semantic disturbance Levinas has in mind is

the entry into a given order of another order which does not **accommodate** itself with the first. Thus we exclude from disturbance the simple parallelism of two orders that would be in a relationship of sign to signified, of appearance to thing in itself, and between which, as we have said, the relationship would reestablish the simultaneity of one single order. (PE 67, emphasis added)

Since the Other cannot appear "without renouncing his radical alterity, without entering into an order" (PE 64), only that will be transcendent (and thus disturbing) that can show itself without appearing. It cannot allow itself to be tied down to the "unbreakable chain of significations" (PE 64) that make up the "triumphant, that is, primary truths" (PE 70) of a given cultural order if it would signify as enigma rather than phenomenon. It must "tear itself" free from "the public order of the disclosed and triumphant significations of nature and history" (PE 70).[18]

It would seem to follow that the gods who play key roles in these humanly created orders of intelligibility, natural and historical, are phenomenal and not enigmatic, onto-theological and not truly transcendent. This is why a God like Kierkegaard's, who is quite thoroughly enigmatic, is "essential in a world which can no longer believe that the books about God attest to transcendence **as a phenomenon** and to the Ab-solute **as an apparition. And without the good reasons atheism brings forth, there would have been no enigma**" (PE 67, emphasis added). In other words, the "atheisms" of Hume or Kant or Feuerbach or Marx need not be seen as the vindication of dogmatic secularism but can be construed as a kind of prophetic protest against every project of domesticating the divine.[19] They can be read as opening the question whether the absence of God from self-evidence and the "scandalous absence" of God from "the moral conduct of the world" (PE 62) points to the abyss or to revelation as disturbance.

Levinas takes his semantics of the enigma, his answer to the question "How could such a disturbance occur?" (PE 63), to be at odds with the traditional theory of the sign.[20] As we have already seen, he sees the orders of sign and of signified as being parts of a larger whole in which the play between them is undisturbed by any real difference (PE 67). (There is always an ambiguity when speaking of the signified, for writers often slide between the strict meaning, *Sinn* (concept), and the looser meaning, *Bedeutung* (object referred to by the concept and thus by the sign as grapheme or phoneme). It seems to be the latter notion that is primary in Levinas, but since his concept of phenomenon is one of a kind of Kantian adequation between thing and concept, the difference may not be too important.)

The problem with the sign, according to Levinas, is its re-presentational character. It assumes that the signified has been present, has appeared, and serves to recall that appearance to mind. By definition, the enigma cannot be such a signified.

> But how refer to an irreversible past, that is, a past which this very reference would not bring back, like memory which retrieves the past, like signs which recapture the signified? . . . But in a face before signifying as a sign it is the very emptiness of an irrecuperable absence. The gaping open of emptiness is not only the sign of an absence . . . but the very emptiness of a passage. And what has withdrawn is not evoked, does not return to presence, not even to an indicated presence. (PE 65–66)

In place of the sign Levinas would put the trace, giving the following correlations: sign : phenomenon = trace : enigma. What is distinctive about the trace is its temporality, since it refers to "an irreversible, immemorial, unrepresentable past" (PE 65), or to a past "which no memory could resurrect as a present" since "the past of the other must never have been present" (PE 68).

This notion of a past that has never been present is by no means an easy one. But one thing is clear—it precludes, as it is intended to preclude, the notion that knowledge is recollection.[21] In his semantics of the trace Levinas is on the side of Climacus as he seeks an alternative both to the recollection theory (PF, chs. I and II) and to its existential correlate, the notion that one can back out of temporal existence into eternity by means of such knowledge (CUP 207–10, 217, 226).[22] This is why it is possible to read "Phenomenon and Enigma" as one of the most insightful and illuminating commentaries on the *Fragments* and *Postscript* ever written.

Recollection presupposes the essential kinship or likeness of subject and object. Thus Kierkegaard, referring to the *Phaedo*'s doctrine of the divinity of the soul, speaks of how "Socrates so beautifully binds men firmly to the divine by showing that all knowledge is recollection" (CI 30). The goal of philosophical ascesis is the "pure knowledge" we gain when we "get rid of the body and contemplate things by themselves with the soul by itself" (*Phaedo* 66e). On the recollection theory this sheer presence, the linkage of total manifestation with total presentness, is a future possibility because it has been a past actuality. Knowledge as re-presentation (the classical theory of the sign) is possible and deserving to be called knowledge, if not Knowledge, because its Alpha is a past presence and its Omega a future presence. The wound of each present presence, in which representation signifies absence as much as presence, is healed by its archeological and teleological linkage to sheer presence.[23]

It is this immanence and totality that Kierkegaard and Levinas seek to deconstruct with their notions of divine transcendence and infinity. The closeness of their thought on this point is especially clear in one form of Levinas's complaint about the atheism of what he calls the ontological tradition. "Philosophy is atheism, or rather unreligion, negation of a God that reveals himself and puts truths into us" (PII 49). The God Levinas has in mind is precisely the God whom Climacus presents in the *Fragments* as giving to the learner not just the truth, but the very condition for recognizing the truth (PF 14). (For what the slave boy in the *Meno* had within him was not the truth of the geometrical theorem Socrates "teaches" him, but the ability to recognize its truth once it is set before him, however that may be occasioned.) This is the God whose self-revelation is the antithesis to the situation where "self-knowledge is God-knowledge" (PF 11).

If Climacus describes such an act of revelation as the decisive Moment of Conversion and Rebirth (PF 18–19), the transition from "not to be" to "to be" that can only be grasped as Wonder or Miracle (PF 30, 36), it is to signify the radical disruption of ordinary time that is involved. However, since he calls the Moment *"the fullness of time"* (PF 18), it may seem as if he has something in mind quite difference from the trace, which Levinas describes in terms of "the withdrawal of the indicated" and "the very emptiness of an irrecuperable absence" (PE 65). But the fullness of time is not the Husserlian filling in intuition of a previously empty intention; it is rather the kairotic moment that disturbs the continuity of quotidian chronology. Like Kant before him and Heidegger after him, Climacus insists on temporality as the horizon of human thought. It is just because the Moment of revelation disturbs the temporality of recollection so deeply that the God who "appears" in it is the unknown (PF 39, 44), the absolutely different (PF 44–46).

It is not that God is simply absent from the world of human experience. It is rather that in every self-presentation, God remains incognito, like Jesus to the disciples on the road to Emmaus (Luke 24:13–35). Levinas writes, "For how transparent is the shadow that troubles the clarity of coherent speech!" (PE 71). Except that it is cast in terms of speech rather than thought, this might easily have been a comment on Climacus's paradox rather than Levinas's own enigma. Here is how Levinas describes it: "A God was revealed on a mountain or in a burning bush, or was attested to in Scriptures. And what if it were a storm! And what if the Scriptures come to us from dreamers! . . . It is up to us, or, more exactly, it is up to *me* to retain or to repel this God . . . this way of manifesting himself without manifesting himself, we call enigma" (PE 66).[24]

In the *Fragments* Climacus focuses on God incarnate as the paradox, the transparent shadow that shows itself while remaining invisible. But he talks of God as being incognito in the created world as well. Can I prove God's existence from the works of creation? Yes, but only if I have already decided to retain rather than to repel God's presence in the world, to interpret it as revelation and not, to return to Levinas, as a storm. "Therefore, from what works to I demonstrate [God's existence]? From the works regarded ideally— that is, as they do not appear directly and immediately. But then I do not demonstrate it from the works, after all, but only develop the ideality [inter-pretation] I have presupposed; trusting in *that* I even dare to defy all objec-tions, even those that have not yet arisen" (PF 42). The argument of chapter IV that the eyewitness follower of Jesus has no advantage over those of subsequent generations because "the god cannot be known directly" (PF 63) or because "the teacher of whom we speak could not be known immediately" (PF 68) is an argument a fortiori. Simply to watch him at work is not to eliminate the possibility, to return to Levinas again, that he is a dreamer.

### . . . Unless They Be Agreed?

Up to this point I have focused on the agreements between Kierkegaard and Levinas, which I take to be both extensive and deep. Along the road they travel together two dialogues take place. The first is between the two of them and thinkers like Nietzsche, Heidegger, Foucault, and Derrida,[25] who operate on the assumption that a serious critique of metaphysics can occur only outside the framework of Judeo-Christian faith,[26] either on the soil of some pagan cult or in the ether of a radical secularism. Together Kierkegaard and Levinas challenge the identification of these faith traditions with the onto-theologies often embraced within them, and they expose as a non sequitur the often presupposed but rarely stated assumption that to offer a critique of logocentrism is to legitimate the exclusion of the voices of these traditions from the domain of serious thought, to absolve philosophy from any need either to listen to them or to listen for the voice they purport to have heard. Together, Kierkegaard and Levinas raise the question whether prominent forms of the postmodern challenge to the Enlightenment project are simply variations of the same theme of excluding radical alterity so as to make philosophy (human reason in its reflective mode) the final arbiter of truth. The quarrel over whether truth should be spelled with an uppercase or lowercase t appears, from their perspective, to be a domestic dispute among those who have excluded any truly personal transcendence. They raise the possibility of a challenge to the Enlightenment project and the larger philosophical tradition to which it belongs from within "a tradition at least as ancient" (PII 53), which also spells (human) truth with a lowercase t, but in order to signify a divine reality that disturbs postmodern as well as modern philosophy.[27]

The other dialogue that takes place on the road I have been trying to map is the one between Kierkegaard and Levinas themselves. It is, I have been suggesting, the kind that takes place in half sentences and partially expressed thoughts. The deep inner kinship between the two makes it possible for each to anticipate what the other will say, and at times to complete the other's sentence, saying even better what the other was trying to say.

But this is true only up to a point, and the agreement between these two thinkers is limited in such a way as to make each the other's Other. They can walk together only so far, and then their paths diverge. I want now to turn to two of the places where this happens and the dialogue between them becomes debate.

Levinas writes, "The infinite is a withdrawal like a farewell which is signified not by opening oneself to the gaze to inundate it with light, but in being extinguished in **the incognito in the face that faces**" (PE 72, emphasis added). Although he immediately reaffirms the importance of Kierkegaardian subjectivity vis-à-vis the infinite, a subjectivity embodied in "someone who is no longer agglutinated in being, who, at his own risk, responds to the enigma and grasps the allusion" (PE 72), the two part company at this point.

To begin with, for Kierkegaard it is first and foremost "the face of Jesus Christ" (2 Cor. 4:6) in whom God "appears" incognito. This cannot be "the face that faces" for Levinas, who has abstracted "from the salvation drama whose play in existence Kierkegaard, a Christian thinker, fixed and described" (PE 67), and it is both obvious and unsurprising that Levinas has in mind the face of the human neighbor.

But there is a deeper divergence here than this most obvious difference between a Jewish and a Christian thinker. For Levinas, recognizing the infinity of the neighbor is an essential prior condition to recognizing the infinity of God, while for Kierkegaard it seems to be the other way around (WL 26–27). Whereas Kierkegaard would repeat Jesus' summary of the Torah, that the first commandment is to love God and the second to love one's neighbor as oneself (Mark 12:28–34), Levinas reverses the order.[28] For him ethics is first, then religion, and the neighbor always stands between me and God, while for Kierkegaard religion is first, then ethics, and God always stands between me and my neighbor. To be sure, in the theory of the stages of existence we move from the ethical to the religious, but this is in order to discover the ultimacy of the latter and the relativity of the former.

Which must be given primacy, the relation to God or the relation to the neighbor? Both Kierkegaard and Levinas seek to develop a non-Marxian form of ideology critique, and it is their difference on this point that primarily distinguishes their respective strategies. So politics is at issue, along with personal ethics and piety. I shall here address only the one aspect of it that comes especially into view in the essay before us, what Levinas calls illeity.

"We hear this way to signify—which does not consist in being unveiled nor in being veiled, absolutely foreign to the hide-and-seek characteristic of cognition . . . —under the third person personal pronoun, under the word *He [Il]*. The enigma comes to us from Illeity" (PE 71). Why is this? An enigma "is a plot with three personages: the I approaches the infinite by going generously toward the you, who is still my contemporary, but, in the trace of illeity, presents himself out of a depth of the past, faces, and approaches me" (PE 72). For the human face can appear as such "only if it enigmatically comes from the infinite and its immemorial past. And the infinite . . . solicits across a face, the term of my generosity and my sacrifice. A you is inserted between the I and the absolute He." Because of this triangle it is "vain to posit an absolute you" (PE 73).

We know why Levinas wants to keep the human neighbor between God and the religious self. He believes this is the only protection against religion becoming ideology, the ally of a dehumanizing violence that desecrates in one and the same moment the infinity of both divine and human persons, reducing both to mere means in the service of some individual or community will to power.[29] History becomes war, and war all but inevitably becomes holy war.

The denial of an absolute You raises the question of prayer. If God is an absolute He but not an absolute You, if, in other words, I can speak to you about Him but not to Him, as another You, about you, what happens to prayer?[30] Here are some of the questions Kierkegaard, who so often in his writings addresses God in the second person, will want to ask. Does it make sense to insist on the personal character of divine infinity and then restrict it to the third person? Is there not some other way to work against idolatry and inhumanity, given the high price of this strategy? Surely the Jewish scriptures know no such qualms against addressing God in the second person. Does Levinas want his distinction between his "Greek" and his "Hebrew" writings to become the gap between the God of the philosophers and the God of Abraham, Isaac, and Jacob? Is he, in this respect, much closer to the ontological tradition than he realizes? Has he made the world safe for ethics by sacrificing something utterly essential to religion, at least to the biblical traditions that Jews and Christians share? It is not that Levinas either repudiates or ignores prayer, which he acknowledges to be "one of the most difficult subjects for a philosopher" (DF 269). But in one of his "Hebrew" writings he says, "the Judaism of reason must take precedence over the Judaism of prayer: the Jew of the Talmud must take precedence over the Jew of the Psalms" (DF 271).

What is the nature of this must? If it is that religion must not be too offensive, too disturbing to the modern Zeitgeist to make assimilation, and thus sociological survival possible, then Kierkegaard, who makes the offense of faith an essential part of it,[31] will ask, What is the point of insisting on the disturbing role of infinity only to give priority to the Talmud over the Psalms because it is less disturbing to modern sensibility? Is it sufficient, or even possible, to challenge the violence of ontological totality without challenging its prayerlessness? Or, to put it just a little differently, can the community of faith be a light to the nations (Isa. 42:6) without grounding its life in the prayerfulness of the Psalms?

In another essay, Levinas approaches the problem of prayer differently. We begin, as we might expect, with ethics. "This responsibility for others therefore comes to be for man the meaning of his own self-identity. His self (*son moi*) is not originally *for itself* (*pour soi*)." The *conatus essendi* of our egoistic self-assertion must be inverted or converted until we become "*the one for the others*" that forgets itself in "'fear and trembling' for the other" (LR 230–32). The conclusion is that "prayer means that, instead of seeking one's own salvation, one secures that of others." Levinas summarizes the treatise he is expounding quite categorically. "True prayer, then, is never for oneself, never 'for one's needs'" (LR 233).

Here Kierkegaard will have two questions. First, does not the Torah command me to love my neighbor *as myself* (Lev. 19:18, 34)? The self-concern of my natural *conatus essendi* is to be the measure of my "fear and trembling for the other." But if I cannot pray for my own needs, how can I pray for my neighbor's? Second, leaving myself aside and focusing just on my neighbors, how can I pray for their needs, material or spiritual, if I cannot address God in the second person, if the only legitimate speech about God is that which mentions Him to some human you?

A second point at which the dialogue between Kierkegaard and Levinas turns into debate involves the notion of the trace. While phenomena are signified by signs, that which indicates the enigma is the trace. What is essential to the trace is that it "signifies" a past that has never been present (PE 68, 73). Levinas is fond of the story in Exodus 33 of Moses' being allowed to see God only from behind. He uses it here (PE 69) to suggest that what makes the enigma enigmatic is that we always arrive too late to encounter it face to face. If we catch a glimpse of it, it is always already departing, withdrawing. For us it never is (here), but always has been (here). The spatial image for this temporal definition of the trace is the transparent shadow.

The trace "signifies" what is beyond being, "a beyond borne by a time different from that in which the overflowings of the present flow back to this present across memory and hope. Could faith be described then as a glimpse into a time whose moments are no longer related to the present as their term or their source?" (PE 62). Such a faith, it would seem, is cut off from hope just as much as it is cut off from memory. Just as we cannot access transcendence through recollection, since its past has never been present, so we cannot await transcendence in hope, since its future will never be present either. That is why the infinite cannot be given to desire "as an end . . . cannot be incarnated in a desirable, cannot, qua infinite, be shut up in an end" (PE 72–73).

By contrast, the Climacus writings link faith tightly to hope. The whole problematic of faith is portrayed in terms of the hope for eternal happiness. Although he does not put it just this way, Climacus's critique of speculation is a continuous meditation on the Pauline reminder that for now "we see in a mirror, dimly" (1 Cor. 13:12), while the orientation of faith to eternal happiness expresses its hope that "then we will see face to face." The critique of the metaphysics of presence in *Fragments* and *Postscript* is intended to open the door to such a hope, not to preclude it, as Levinas seems to do.

If we go back and take a closer look at the two respective critiques of recollection, we will find the difference that underlies this disagreement. Levinas writes, "The impossibility of manifesting itself in an experience [that defines enigma] can be due not to the finite or sensible essence of this experience, but to the structure of **all thought,** which is correlation. Once come into correlation, the divinity of God dissipates" (PE 62, emphasis added), or, in other words, God ceases to be disturbingly different. "An enigma is beyond not finite cognition, but **all cognition**" (PE 71, emphasis added).

On the surface these claims appear to be dogmatically Hegelian; for they make human thought in its present capacity the ultimate measure of thought as such. This, I believe, is how Climacus would see them. His lack of enthusiasm for them stems both from his anti-Hegelianism, which one would have expected Levinas to share, and from his giving a different diagnosis of why we are cut off from recollection. The paradox (enigma) is the unknown because it is "absolutely different" and "the understanding cannot even think the absolutely different. . . . But if the god is to be absolutely different from a human being, this can have its basis not in that which man owes to the god (for to that extent they are akin) but in that which he owes to himself or in that which he himself has committed. What, then, is the difference? Indeed, what else but sin. . . . We stated this in the foregoing by saying that the individual is untruth and is this through his own fault" (PF 44–47; cf. 28, 31, 34).

Climacus agrees with Levinas that the flaming sword east of Eden that bars any recollective return to the presence of paradise (Gen. 3:24) does not bear the name of creaturely finitude. Creation may generate absolute dependence, but not absolute difference, since "to that extent they are akin." But on his view it is not "all thought" or "all cognition" that are cut off from the presence of God, but sinful thought and sinful cognition. Radical alterity is not to be found in an ontological interpretation of finitude vis-à-vis infinity, but in a moral interpretation of evil vis-à-vis goodness.

This has important consequences for the possibility of presence. If there were to be a "salvation drama" in which sin and its consequences were eliminated from our experience, restoring us to what was intended in creation, the hope of seeing God face to face would not be unrealistic. It is to such a drama that Climacus refers when he describes the Paradox as manifesting itself "negatively, by bringing into prominence the absolute difference of sin and, positively, by wanting to annul this absolute difference in the absolute equality" (PF 47).

Climacus might put his critique of speculation this way. Ontology is the utopian moment of human thought, the longing for salvation. The trouble with ontology, from Plato to Hegel, is that by insisting prematurely on replacing faith with sight it converts utopia into ideology, claiming to possess now a presence for which we have only the right to hope. But the critique of ontology that responds by eliminating even the hope of sight, thereby reducing ontological utopianism to political utopianism, is a counsel of despair. Is not this despair, that is to say, political utopianism, devoid of both the sense of sin and the hope of divine salvation, the major source of the violence of our most recent history?

It now appears that Levinas has abstracted not just from the specifically Christian "salvation drama" of Kierkegaard, but from any drama that gives to God a decisive agency in human affairs and envisages a fundamental alteration of experience as we now endure it. He seems to share with Hegel and with the secular postmodernists the conviction that "it doesn't get any better than this."

Ironically, on one point Levinas is closer to Kierkegaard in "Philosophy and the Idea of Infinity" than in his "most Kierkegaardian" essay, "Phenomenon and Enigma." There, too, he is concerned with radical alterity. But there he links the idea of infinity with "the collapse of the good conscience of the same" and repeatedly describes the experience of the otherness of the Other as one of guilt and shame in which I know myself to be wicked and unjust (PII 50–53, 57–59). Just as for Climacus it is sin that generates absolute difference, in this context what makes the absolutely other absolutely other is fault, not the conditions of "all thought" or "all cognition." Most immediately this is fault in relation to my neighbor. But if the human face has its moral appeal "only if it enigmatically comes from the infinite and its immemorial past" and if the absolute He "solicits across a [human] face" (73), then injustice toward my neighbor is sin against God as well.

Taking the two essays together, we might say that Levinas has a philosophy of sin without salvation. Of course, the reality of sin is no guarantee of divine deliverance. But to exclude such a possibility from philosophic reflection at the outset by restricting reflection ("all thought . . . all cognition") to the domain of what is conceivable (and achievable) in the circumstances of our present fallenness—is that not to reduce the other to the same? Is it not to abandon "the original antecedence of God [as Savior] relative to a world which cannot accommodate him" (PE 73), compelling him to accommodate himself to that world so as to fit in to the conditions of our present experience?

It is not surprising that epistemological talk about revelation should lead to metaphysical talk about God as its source.[32] Although there remain formal, structural agreements between Levinas and Kierkegaard, it is here the material, substantive disagreements break out. I want to suggest that we not read them as essentially a Jewish-Christian debate, however obvious and important it may be that Levinas is a Jewish thinker and Kierkegaard a Christian thinker. The reason is that the questions posed by Kierkegaard in response to Levinas's idea that it is "vain to posit an absolute you" (PE 73) can be posed from the Jewish scriptures alone and need not appeal to Jesus as the Christ or to God as triune. When the question revolves around prayer, the issue is whether God is a speaker to whom we can speak in the second person and who speaks to us with a voice that is neither ours, nor our society's, nor that of the widow, orphan, and stranger. When the question revolves around hope and salvation, the issue is whether God is an agent distinct from ourselves, our society, and our neighbor. It seems to me that the God of the Hebrew Bible is a fully personal God in these senses: a speaker and an agent different from every human speaker and agent, individual or collective. To put it differently, I think Levinas would be a better Jewish thinker if his God were more nearly like Kierkegaard's in these respects, just as I think that Christian thinkers who find themselves closer to Levinas than to Kierkegaard on these issues would be better Christian thinkers if the reverse were the case.

That being said, it is time to turn in the next two chapters to further exploration of the divine source of revelation as understood by our two passionate thinkers.

PART 2. GOD

# Teleological Suspensions

*Everyone will readily agree that it is of the highest importance to know whether we are not duped by morality.*

—(TI 21)

*Philosophy, for me, derives from religion. It is called into being by a religion adrift, and probably religion is always adrift.*

—(NTR 182)

Unlike the positivists, postmodernists have not taken their critique of metaphysics to mean the end of ethics. They act as if philosophy continues to play a morally significant critical role in a postmodern world and even say things like "Nothing seems to me less outdated than the classical emancipatory ideal."[1] On the other hand, they have not been very eager to give an account of how this is possible, and what little they have had to say has not seemed entirely satisfactory. For this reason, the first epigraph above seems to many more urgent than when Levinas used it in 1961 to open *Totality and Infinity*.

No doubt the most conspicuous difference between Levinas and such thinkers as Derrida, Foucault, and Lyotard is that he accompanies his powerful critique of ontology as the sustained attempt to reduce the other to the same with an at least equally developed account of how ethics is possible after the collapse of the Enlightenment Project. At first he sounds very much like his secular contemporaries (whose critique of metaphysics, incidentally, comes after his).[2] But then he goes decisively beyond anything they have offered as an account of how ethics is possible.

The second epigraph above points to a second difference between Levinas and major French postmodernists. They are all more or less united in their irreverence toward the Greek *logos*. But in place of the secular irreverence (à la Aristophanes) that has been the hallmark of French poststructuralism,[3] Levinas offers a prophetic irreverence (à la Amos) rooted in "a tradition at least as ancient" as the Greece to which Heidegger appeals (PII 53), going back to Parmenides (TO 42–43, 85; cf. TI 269). Or, as Derrida puts it, Levinas offers us a thought "for which the entirety of the Greek logos has already erupted, and is now a quiet topsoil deposited not over bedrock, but around a more ancient volcano."[4] Levinas's assault on Athens comes from the direction of Jerusalem, or, to be more precise, from the direction of Sinai.

"Philosophy," he tells us, "derives from religion." But anyone turning to Levinas with the expectation of finding a theological foundation for ethics to replace the philosophical foundations whose cracks have been found to be irreparable will be immediately and permanently disappointed. There is no direct appeal to Sinai, and Levinas is no Jewish version of Karl Barth or Dietrich Bonhoeffer. At the same time he tells us that philosophy derives from religion, Levinas forswears such a direct appeal. For how could theology be the foundation of ethics if "religion is always adrift"?

So what, then, is the relation between religion and "Ethics as First Philosophy"? When speaking about ethics Levinas employs a vocabulary so deeply religious as to awaken even the sleepiest reader to the fact that something unusual is going on. But at the same time he seems to be as allergic (in his "Greek" writings) to describing God as a distinct reality as traditional ontology is allergic, on his view, to radical alterity in any form. At times it almost seems as if he wants to reduce religion to ethics.

Some readers of Levinas would welcome such an outcome,[5] while others would think it a great loss. But in either case it is important to be as clear as possible about the role God plays in his thought. How are we to interpret such statements as these? "It is only man who could be absolutely foreign to me" (TI 73). "God commands only through the men for whom one must act" (PII 59). " 'Going towards God' is meaningless unless seen in terms of my primary going towards the other person" (DEL 23). "The invisible but personal God is not approached outside of all human presence. . . . There can be no 'knowledge' of God separated from relationship with men. . . . It is our relations with men . . . that give to theological concepts the sole signification they admit of. . . . Without the signification they draw from ethics theological concepts remain empty and formal frameworks" (TI 78–79). "[God] is neither an object *nor an interlocutor*. His absolute remoteness, his transcendence, turns into my responsibility—non-erotic par excellence—for the other. And this analysis implies that God is not simply the 'first other,' the 'other par excellence,' or the 'absolutely other,' but other than the other . . . transcendent to the point of absence, to the point of a possible confusion with the stirring of the *there is*" (GP 165–66, first emphasis added; cf. OB 148, 158). And what are we to make of the sustained polemic against any "world behind the scenes" (OB 4–5, 8, 45, 154, 185)?

It is clear that Levinas's God is not the God of the Bible. For the God of creation and of covenant is not restricted in these ways. The God of the Bible is clearly an interlocutor, and if there is an unseen God who is both creator and covenant maker, then there is surely a "world behind the scenes."[6]

In his Talmudic writings Levinas contextualizes such allergic reaction to theological discourse with qualifiers such as "since Maimonides" and "at least for the Talmud" (NTR 14–15). Are we dealing here with a postbiblical Jewish reduction of religion to ethics, one that would rescue ethics from bankruptcy in a postmodern world by returning to Feuerbach and transferring all assets of the divine bank account to the human account? Or is this rather an extreme Jewish version of the Christian warning "Those who say, 'I love God,' and hate their brothers or sisters are liars; for those who do not love a brother or sister whom they have seen, cannot love God whom they have not seen. The commandment we have from him is this: those who love God must love their brothers and sisters also" (1 John 4:20–21).

I want to suggest that the primary relation between philosophy, conceived by Levinas as the metaphysics of transcendence or the ethical relation, and religion is best expressed in Kierkegaardian language. For Levinas, the ethical is the teleological suspension of the religious. One advantage of this formula is that by appearing to be exactly the opposite movement to the one Kierkegaard presents, it invites comparison with the nineteenth century's most powerful critic of the philosophical reduction of the other to the same, a thinker whose relation to Hegel strongly resembles that of Levinas to Husserl and Heidegger.

A teleological suspension is not a reduction. It does not say that X is nothing but Y. It is rather an *Aufhebung*. It says that X can only be properly understood in relation to Y, that X is not a substance in Spinoza's sense, something that "is in itself and is conceived through itself" (*Ethics* I, Def. 3). Its being, and thus its comprehension (objective genitive), is relational. Thus a teleological suspension does not eliminate; it relativizes. The object of a teleological suspension is negated in its claim to autonomy, to self-sufficiency and completeness; but it is affirmed in relation to that which is higher, that which draws it into a larger whole of which it is not the first principle. The highest card in its suit will take many tricks, but it can always be trumped.[7]

There is a triadic structure in *Totality and Infinity* that moves from Enjoyment to Dwelling to Transcendence. Like the movement in Aristotle from the vegetative soul to the animal soul to the rational soul, this movement can be interpreted along the lines of Kierkegaard's movement from the aesthetic to the ethical to the religious, that is, as a sequence of teleological suspensions. In all three triads, Aristotle's, Kierkegaard's, and Levinas's, the second transition is the crucial one, the one that brings us to what each author views as the heart of what it means to be human. For Levinas the rationality and intelligibility that accompany Enjoyment and Dwelling (whose roots are in need) are to be teleologically suspended in the rationality and intelligibility of Transcendence (whose roots are in desire). In his claim "The Other is the first intelligible" (Si 185; cf. TI 201–19), Levinas teleologically suspends a whole tradition that culminates, for him, in Husserl's account of intentionality and Heidegger's of disclosure, a tradition dominated by the metaphor of vision. He insists that his irreverence toward the *logos* of their phenomen*ologies* is not a flight into mysticism or a lapse into irrationalism, but the ascent to a higher rationality.[8]

Against the Enlightenment's claim that knowledge is corrupted by interest and can only truly be knowledge if it is objective in the sense of being disinterested, Levinas argues (1) that all knowledge is interested, (2) that desire (in his technical sense of the term as desire for the Infinite, for the Other), is a higher form of interest than is need, since "this desire for the non-desirable . . . is the subjectivity and uniqueness of a subject" (OB 123), and (3) that the forms of knowledge rooted in need (and analyzed in terms of intentionality) are therefore not fully rational but need to be teleologically suspended in the genuinely rational knowledge rooted in desire, the knowledge that accompanies the ethical relation. The "object" of this "knowledge" is "the stranger in the neighbor" (OB 123).

This has an immediate and very interesting correlate. If I want "to see things in themselves," I must transcend both "enjoyment and possession." But this does not mean the suspension of interest in a neutral (and neuter), impersonal objectivity. To know things as they truly are, "I must know how *to give* what I possess. . . . But for this I must encounter the indiscreet face of the Other that calls me into question. The Other—the absolutely other—paralyzes possession, which he contests by his epiphany in the face. He can contest my possession only because he approaches me not from the outside but from above." It is only in the context of welcoming precisely this Other and opening myself to the teaching she addresses to me that I am able to fulfill philosophy's aspiration for the *Sache selbst* (TI 171). The ethical relation is the key to the meaning of the world. It is the philosopher's stone that changes opinion into Knowledge and understanding into Reason. Of course, these traditional ways of speaking will be misleading unless we notice that when the Other becomes the philosopher's stone, the highest goal of thought ceases to be *episteme* or *Wissenschaft* as traditionally conceived.

This means that contemplative rationality, which belongs to the order of enjoyment, and instrumental rationality, which belongs to the order of possession, represent Reason adrift unless and until they are teleologically suspended in the welcoming, teachable, infinitely responsible rationality that belongs to the order of transcendence.

A similar movement, I believe, relates the religious to the ethical in Levinas's thought. So perhaps by "religion adrift" Levinas means religion understood primarily as enjoyment and as dwelling. Religion is no exception to the claim that we are never disinterested. It follows that the religious life is in the service either of the egoism of need or of the decentering transcendence of desire. For this reason both religious orthodoxy and religious orthopraxy must submit to interrogation by the ethical, which stands above them as it stands above enjoyment and dwelling (including its extension in labor and possession), refusing to accept their rationality and their intelligibility at face value and asking insistently, Yes, but is it good for the widow, the orphan, and the stranger? Just as Levinas has no respect for "that Reason which is capable of considering as ordered a world in which the poor man is sold for a pair of sandals" (LR 238; cf. Amos 2:6), so he opposes any religion capable of considering such a world sacred.

Levinas is more than nervous about any theology understood as "an indication or a monstration of the signified in the signifier, according to the **facile** itinerary in which pious thought **too quickly** deduces theological realities" (LP 124, emphasis added). Part of the reason why he seeks to replace, or perhaps supplement, semiotics with talk about the trace is to make the move to theological realities at once less facile and less quick. "The trace in which a face is ordered is not reducible to a sign for the simple reason that a sign and its relationship with the signified are already thematized. But an approach is not the thematization of any relationship; it is this very relationship" (LP 124). Structuralism and poststructuralism think all but exclusively in terms of the relation of signifier and signified, and for this reason can neither diagnose nor prescribe adequately in the present crisis.

If the face is not to be construed as a sign, then "the crisis of meaning, which is evident in the dissemination of verbal signs that the signified no longer dominates . . . is opposed by the meaning that is prior to the 'sayings,' which spurns words and is unimpeachable in the nudity of its visage, which is felt in the proletarian destitution of another and in the offence he suffers" (II 246). In other words the decentering of the subject that occurs in structuralist and poststructuralist semiotics is teleologically suspended in the decentering of the subject that occurs in the ethical relation.

In the Talmud this meaning is expressed in the claim that some prayers "cannot penetrate to heaven, because all the heavenly gates are closed except those through which the tears of the sufferers may pass" (II 246). For Levinas it becomes the claim that the semantic crisis of our time, including its religious version (the crisis in theology), is, to use Hegelian language, partly *Schein* and partly *Erscheinung*, whose *Wesen* in either case is a crisis in welcoming the Other. Is it possible that Levinas's closest kin are the liberation theologians of Latin America and South Africa rather than either the Jewish or secular intellectuals of Paris?[9]

There is no mystery about how Levinas intends to resist "the **facile** itinerary in which pious thought **too quickly** deduces theological realities." Since it is the directness of the movement from signifier, whether it be the world or the data of biblical revelation and religious tradition, to deity as the signified that renders that movement both too easy and too fast, Levinas will insist on making it indirect. He will interpose the human Other into the middle of any situation in which I purport to find God, forbidding the sign to be a direct link, however hermeneutically hesitant, between myself and the absolute. "I approach the infinite insofar as I forget myself for my neighbor who looks at me. . . . [The infinite] solicits across a face, the term of my generosity and my sacrifice. A you is inserted between the I and the absolute He" (PE 72–73).[10]

In a polemical state of mind, he puts the point this way: "The direct encounter with God, *this* is a Christian concept. As Jews, we are always a threesome: I and you and the Third who is in our midst. And only as a Third does He reveal Himself" (II 247).

Levinas appears to compromise this "trinitarian" moment in his thought when he tells us elsewhere that "the absolute is a person," because only that which supports justice could be absolute, and such an absolute would have "the absolute status of the interlocutor." He immediately insists, "This is not at all a theological thesis; yet God could not be God without first having been this interlocutor" (ET 33). The argument would go like this:

1. Levinas makes it clear that this interlocutor is the human Other.
2. But he also identifies this interlocutor with God.
3. Therefore, he collapses the difference between the divine and the human and thereby reduces religion to ethics. The apparent threesome is an actual twosome.

But this would be a wooden and uncharitable reading. In other texts he makes it clear that he intends no *simple* identification of the human and divine, perhaps just as Spinoza intends no *simple* identification of God and the world. "The Other is **the very locus** of metaphysical truth, and is indispensable for my relation with God. He does not play the role of mediator. The Other is not the incarnation of God, but precisely by his face, in which he is disincarnate, is the manifestation of **the height in which God is revealed**" (TI 78–79, emphasis added). The point is that the ethical relation is the scene, the clearing, the only horizon within which the true God is truly revealed.[11] "It is in this ethical perspective that God must be thought, and not in the ontological perspective of our being-there . . . it is only in the infinite relation with the other that God passes (*se passe*), that traces of God are to be found" (DEL 20, 31). We might put it this way: the only horizon in which I can be truly open to the true God is the horizon in which all my horizons are relativized by the ethical claim of the Other.

This is not to say that humans do not think they find God elsewhere. Nor is it to say that concepts of deity originating elsewhere are vague, formal, and empty. Levinas himself seems to suggest the latter when he says (see above), "It is our relations with men . . . that give to theological concepts the sole signification they admit of. . . . Without the signification they draw from ethics theological concepts remain empty and formal frameworks" (TI 78–79). But it is clear from the larger context of his writings that this emptiness is not final, but a standing invitation to evil. We are reminded of the situation Jesus describes of an unclean spirit, having left a person but having found no new home. "Then it says, 'I will return to my house from which I came.' When it comes, it finds it empty, swept, and put in order. Then it goes and brings along seven other spirits more evil than itself, and they enter and live there; and the last state of that person is worse than the first" (Matt. 12:44–45).

Religion that is not bound to the scene of the ethical relation consists of "empty and formal frameworks" in just this sense. However rich it may be in images, narratives, concepts, theories, practices, and institutions, it is utterly devoid of anything that would prevent it from being the home, the shelter, the base, the legitimizer of the various evils that deface the Other. Thus, when Levinas speaks of "the very name 'God' [as] . . . subject to every abuse" (NTR 14), when he suggests that the "degeneration" of religion is more dangerous than its disappearance (NTR 152, 159), when he joins Plato in the struggle against "tyrannical religion" (FC 23), when he warns of the danger of the move from the Other to divinity (II 246), and when he distinguishes the holy from the sacred, (NTR 140–60), in short, when he speaks of religion being always adrift (NTR 182), he is echoing Freud, who writes, "It is doubtful whether men were in general happier at a time when religious doctrines held unrestricted sway; more moral they certainly were not."[12]

The teleological suspension of the religious in the ethical provides, in the perceptive words of Derrida, "the premises for a non-Marxist reading of philosophy [including philosophical theology] as ideology." Religious representation easily becomes the "alibi" for historical oppression of every sort.[13] If Levinas is willing at times to risk sounding as if he wants to reduce religion to ethics, it is because he knows how easily religion drifts into defacement.

Levinas offers something of a catalog of dangerous, degenerate religion. It suggests some strange bedfellows. (1) First, he expresses a strong mistrust "of everything in the texts studied that could pass for a piece of information about God's life . . . these apparent news items about the beyond . . . a pretentious familiarity with the 'psychology' of God and with his 'behavior' " (NTR 14, 32). This project of knowing the inner secrets of God without any linkage to our infinite responsibility in the face of the human Other he calls theosophy, alluding no doubt to certain forms of both Jewish and Christian mystical metaphysics.

(2) But it is not easy to distinguish theosophy from more "sober" forms of philosophical theology. Levinas treats discussions of God as the Supreme Being or the creator or cause of nature as if they were theosophy (NTR 14; DEL 24, 32). He is equally hard on discourses that thematize the divine in terms of attributes (TI 78; DEL 31), as if the content of theology did not come from the "dimension of height" that constitutes the ethical relation (MB 70) but belonged to the realm of that which is objectifiable and representable in terms of consciousness as intentionality (EF 77; PWD 228). The genius of Kant's Copernican revolution consists in the fact "that immortality and theology could not determine the categorical imperative," but the movement goes

in just the opposite direction (OB 129; cf. RJT 206 and IOF 10). In these contexts Levinas makes no distinction between natural and revealed theology. The question concerns the form and the content of discourse about God, not the mode of its justification.

If the assimilation of traditional discussions of the "metaphysical attributes" of God to theosophy causes distress in certain theological quarters, as it is intended to, and signals the disruption of many familiar modes of theological discourse, the same is true of Levinas's critique of (3) the myth of participation. This is his name for those religious contexts, so powerfully described by Eliade, where human society and human action are but microcosmic imitations of a macrocosmic order that is, as sacred, the epitome of a totality immune to any interrupting infinity.[14] When Levinas calls for a "break with participation" and a "faith purged of myths" (TI 58, 77) many will no doubt congratulate their own discourse on the divine for effecting a sufficient linkage between Athens and Jerusalem to have made a decisive move from *mythos* to *logos* and to deserve the name theo*logy*.

Levinas does not deny this move, only its significance in the present context. In his view, the ancient move from *mythos* to *logos* in Plato and Aristotle and its modern, Enlightenment, and Hegelian reenactments serves to distinguish logocentric philosophical theologies from the myths of participation only as two species of the same problem, religion adrift in a discourse that at best marginalizes the discourse in which I and we are decentered by the face of the Other, who commands, judges, and takes us hostage from on high.

In short, the philosophical theologies that purport to be the triumph of the concept over primitive myth and esoteric theosophy are indeed just that. But unless the shadow of the Other dramatically dims even the uncreated light in which God would shine as directly present to my intellect, Levinas suspects that my theology is adrift; and even if I have a humble theology that neither identifies representation with sheer presence nor theology with the beatific vision, if the grounds for my caveat are the finitude of my intellect rather than the face of the Other, I will end up abusing "the very name 'God' " (NTR 14), or, to speak biblically, taking the name of the Lord my God in vain.

Derrida suggests that Levinas's true target is "the complicity of theoretical objectivity and mystical communion."[15] This is true but incomplete, for Levinas applies the same teleological suspension to religious practices as well as to religious representations. Thus he condemns (4) "the impure stratagem of sorcery" or magic as the reduction of the sacred to a power in the service of profit (NTR 141–42). Then, in a move now familiar to us, he describes what takes itself to be quite different from this as being only superficially different. Just as traditional forms of philosophical theology were assimilated to theosophy and myth, here (5) private personal piety is assimilated to sorcery. Levinas has in mind the devotional life in which God is "the correlate of the ego in an amorous and exclusive intimacy" (ET 32). He finds in the prophet Ezekiel a critique of "the righteousness of the righteous who save their own selves, who think of their own selves and their own salvation. The existence of evil people by their side attests, in fact, to the defect in their righteousness. They are responsible for the evil that remains. . . . Saints, monks, and intellectuals in their ivory tower are the righteous subject to punishment. They are the Pharisees, in the non-noble meaning of the term, which the Jewish tradition is the first to denounce" (NTR 188). "Watch out," he warns, "for the peace of private worship! . . . the artificial peace of synagogues and churches!" (NTR 193).

From the point of view of the suffering it matters little whether religion becomes the magical pursuit of private material benefits or the liturgical and devotional pursuit of private spiritual benefits. In either case, the faithful have ears to hear, but do not hear the cries of human anguish. **When the Other does not get in the way of my seeing God, God will end up getting in the way of my hearing the Other. That is what the teleological suspension of the religious is all about.**

\* \* \*

It may seem as if the disparity between this view and the one presented in *Fear and Trembling* consists in the reversed positions of the ethical and the religious. For Levinas the ethical trumps the religious, while for Kierkegaard the religious trumps the ethical. But before we conclude that we are dealing with a simple contradiction and begin to ask whether we have located some fundamental difference between Judaism and Christianity, we need to notice the massive equivocation that confronts us on the term 'ethical' when we talk this way. The difference between what Levinas means by the term and what Silentio means could hardly be greater. In *Fear and Trembling* the ethical is *Sittlichkeit*, the laws and customs of one's people, the morality of mores. The primary target is Hegel.[16] But this is what Levinas calls "politics" "history," "totality," and "the ontology of war" (TI 21–22). What he calls the ethical is clearly meant to be at the very least the teleological suspension of this domain and its rationality. He and Kierkegaard are in agreement in appealing to a transcendence that interrupts and calls into question the human, all too human language games that purport to express the highest norms for human life.

The most extensive presentation of "the ethical" in the Kierkegaardian corpus is the letters of Judge William in volume II of *Either/Or*, filled with references to God. The pious worldview he presents is precisely what constitutes Christendom as Christendom. It is, in Kierkegaard's view but in Levinas's language, religion adrift. It identifies as divinely authorized a social totality humanly constructed so as to be immune to any intrusions of any infinite.

For Kierkegaard, then, as for Levinas, philosophy "is called into being by a religion adrift, and probably religion is always adrift" (NTR 182). The same prophetic sense that there is no sacrilege as dreadful as that of the "faithful" motivates the hermeneutics of suspicion they both practice, a hermeneutics dramatically different from that of Marx, Nietzsche, and Freud just because of its different motivation.

In other words, both Levinas and Kierkegaard appeal to an immediacy that trumps all social mediation. Both call for revelation, the expression καθ αὐτό of an infinite that will puncture the ontological and sociological totalities in which the same prevails over every other.[17]

But they appeal to different immediacies. Silentio protests that in Christendom the human relation with God is too mediated by social contingency to allow for the faith of Abraham.[18] He looks for that mediation to be suspended in a direct encounter with God, one not constrained by merely human horizons. When there is an absolute duty to God and the ethical is, to repeat, not "invalidated" but "reduced to the relative," then the ethical receives "a paradoxical expression, such as, for example, that love to God may bring the knight of faith to give his love to the neighbor—an expression opposite to that which, ethically speaking, is duty" (FT 70). Levinas protests that the human relation with God is too direct in such a context, and he looks for the suspension of both social morality and theology in the face of the human Other that cuts through both.

Immediacy in this context is an *epistemological* term. It refers to the ability the voice of the Other, whether the God of Abraham or the widow, the orphan, and the stranger, to get through with divine authority unfiltered by horizons of the "already said." *Ontologically* speaking, individuals are anything but immediate, self-standing and self-sufficient. For both thinkers they are doubly mediated: first by the socialization process, and then by the voice that in addressing them from on high relativizes and overrides that first mediation. There is no disagreement here. Where Levinas and Kierkegaard disagree is on the nature of this second ontological mediation. Levinas says, "As Jews, we are always a threesome: I and you and the Third who is in our midst" (II 247). Kierkegaard agrees that we are always a threesome, but insists that it is God who is always the middle term between me and my neighbor (WL 58, 67, 77, 107, 119, 121, 142). For Levinas, as we have seen, it is always the neighbor who is the middle term between me and God.

In one respect the two positions need not be mutually exclusive. Is it not possible that the voice of the visible human face and the voice of the invisible God are in agreement? Is that not exactly what we should expect if, as the Genesis story found in both Jewish and Christian Bibles tells us, the neighbor is created in the image of God? Indeed, would it not be the deepest grace of all if in our violent world we could learn to hear the harmony of their hope for the widow, the orphan, and the refugee?

## You Shall Not Commit Murder

We have already seen why Levinas takes the stand he does.[19] He knows that religion can take the name of the Lord God in vain,[20] and in the tradition of the prophets he seeks to guard against giving legitimacy to defacing the neighbor by means of theological discourse. Kierkegaard doesn't have this worry as much as he should, and this is perhaps the most basic lesson he can learn from Levinas.

But he, too, stands in the prophetic tradition,[21] even if for him religion adrift is primarily a matter of bourgeois complacency. We need to enquire why he insists of making God the middle term between me and my neighbor, why he says, "Ultimately, love for God is the decisive factor; from this originates love for the neighbor . . . the Christian love commandment commands loving God above all else, and then loving the neighbor" (WL 57; cf. 108, 140). In other words, while he knows that the commandment to love the neighbor as oneself is of Jewish origin (WL 24; see Lev. 19:18), he insists on following Jesus' teaching that this is the second commandment and that it is not the same as the "first and greatest" commandment, "You shall love the Lord you God with all your heart, and with all your soul, and with all your mind" (Matt. 22:34–40). It is not that we should turn our attention to God and forget the neighbor. Rather, "Shut your door and pray to God—because God is surely the highest . . . when you open the door that you shut in order to pray to God and go out the very first person you meet is the neighbor, whom you *shall* love" (WL 51).

In other words, Kierkegaard agrees with Levinas when he writes, "There can be no 'knowledge' of God separated from relationship with men." But he does not agree when Levinas writes, "It is our relations with men . . . that give to theological concepts the sole signification they admit of" (TI 778–79). The God relation is not separable from the neighbor relation;[22] but it is distinct and it is first. Why?

In *Works of Love,* where Kierkegaard in his own name gives us the ethics that belongs to faith and is not teleologically suspended by the religious, he gives us three reasons.[23]

First, ontologically speaking, God is the source and origin of love. Thus the text begins with a prayer:

> How could one speak properly about love if you were forgotten, you God of love, source of all love in heaven and earth; you who spared nothing but in love gave everything; you who are love, so that one who loves is what he is only by being in you! (WL 3)

The prayer is followed by a parable:

> Just as the quiet lake originates deep down in the hidden springs no eye has seen, so also does a person's love originate even more deeply in God's love. If there were no gushing spring at the bottom, if God were not love, then there would be neither the little lake nor a human being's love. Just as the quiet lake originates darkly in the deep spring, so a human being's love originates mysteriously in God's love. Just as the quiet lake invites you to

contemplate it but by the reflected image of darkness prevents you from seeing through it, so also the mysterious origin of love in God's love prevents you from seeing its ground. (WL 9–10)

Kierkegaard's emphasis is on the commanded character of neighbor love and the divine authority behind that command. But by contrast with Levinas, who gives us a "theology" of law without grace, Kierkegaard, like Luther, Augustine, and Paul before him, links law and grace, commandment and enablement. Ontologically speaking, neighbor love is grounded in the mysterious God relation without which it would be impossible.

Second, at the level of consciousness there is the closely linked issue of motivation. Since everyone is my neighbor, the commandment to love my neighbor as myself becomes the commandment to love my enemies (see Matt. 5:38–48). Why on earth would I want to do that? Because of "the kinship of all human beings—because the kinship is secured by each individual's equal kinship with and relationship to God in Christ; because the Christian doctrine addresses itself equally to each individual, teaches him that God has created him and Christ has redeemed him" (WL 69).[24]

There is a double motivation here. First, I am the one who owes to God an infinite debt of gratitude. God loved me first, not only in creation but also in redemption, and my efforts to love others are a striving that grows out of gratitude (WL 101–3).[25] Second, God has shown the same love of creation and redemption to my neighbor, even my enemy. If God somehow finds my neighbor, even my enemy, loveable, maybe I can follow suit.

Finally, almost as a corollary to this second point, there is the "as yourself" of the love command. Kierkegaard regularly insists that love is self-denial and self-sacrifice in opposition to self-centered self-love. But he also emphasizes that there is a proper self-love that goes with love for God and neighbor (WL 18, 22, 107, 130). The logic is the same. If God loves me I can love myself, and just as God's love for me doesn't place me at the center with everyone else a means to my ends, so my own proper self-love will be modeled on God's love for me. Perhaps the reason why there seems no place for proper self-love in Levinas's thought is that in his fear of "religion adrift" he has shortchanged the God relation.

Here once again, while Kierkegaard appeals to the manifestation of God's love in Christ, I see no reason why there shouldn't be a structural agreement between him and Levinas in terms of God as the lover whose love enables and motivates us to love God, to love our neighbor (even the enemy), and to love ourselves. It seems to me that the God of Abraham, Isaac, and Jacob, of Moses and David, of Isaiah, Jeremiah, Ezekiel, and Amos is not only personal enough to be a speaker (uttering promises as well as commands) and to be an agent (effecting salvation and deliverance), but also to be a lover. If the deepest motivation is to be sure that the widow, the orphan, and the stranger are not defaced by "religion adrift," is there any need to be as nervous about a fully personal God as Levinas seems to be, especially in his philosophical writings?

In fairness to Levinas, we can now turn our attention to an essay in which he purports to challenge the philosophical discourse of the West from the standpoint of the God of the Bible.

# Commanded Love and
# Divine Transcendence

Levinas's essay "God and Philosophy" is contemporaneous with *Otherwise Than Being or Beyond Essence* and develops theological implications of the argument left largely unthematized in what we might call the magnum opus of Levinas II.[1] He purports to set the God of the Bible over against "the philosophical discourse of the West" and its interpretation of rationality; and he taunts "rational theology" for accepting "vassalage" to philosophy's claim to be "the amplitude of an all-encompassing structure or of an ultimate comprehension" that "compels every other discourse to justify itself before philosophy" (GP 153–54).[2] We are reminded of Heidegger's critique of onto-theology.

In an earlier essay, Levinas had evoked that critique by speaking of "the notion of God, which a thought called faith succeeds in getting expressed and introduces into philosophical discourse" (PE 62). In onto-theology, on Heidegger's account, "the deity can come into philosophy only insofar as philosophy, of its own accord and by its own nature, requires and determines that and how the deity enters into it."[3] For theology to seek the imprimatur (censorship?) of onto-theologically constituted metaphysics would be to sell its soul and its birthright simultaneously. For the "god of philosophy" is religiously useless. "Man can neither pray nor sacrifice to this god. Before the *causa sui,* man can neither fall to his knees in awe nor can he play music and dance before this god."[4]

The scenario sketched by Levinas in which it is *faith* that introduces the notion of God into philosophy suggests the interruption of the latter's complacent hegemony by a double alterity. First, faith is presented as a thought, challenging the notion that philosophy has a monopoly on meaning and intelligibility. Second, the God who is introduced into philosophical discourse by this interloping outsider has come to the party uninvited. This God is not at the beck and call of philosophy's project of *episteme* or *Wissenschaft* in accord with the *principium reddendae rationis.* So it is not surprising that throughout the essay, this God (along with the human face we always find between ourselves and deity) is presented as a disturbance to philosophical thought, even the "absolute disturbance" of "an absolute alterity" (PE 64). This God is the philosopher's stone, to be sure, but "a stone of stumbling, and a rock of offense" (Isa. 8:14, 1 Peter 2:8 KJV) rather than the keystone or the cornerstone of the temple of Being as Presence.

But (to return to "God and Philosophy"), while the taunt that rational theology stands in vassalage to philosophy again evokes Heidegger's critique, it does not merely echo it. In the first place, the problem with rational theology is not its *Seinsvergessenheit.* "If the intellectual understanding of the biblical God, theology, does not reach to the level of philosophical thought, that is not because it thinks of God as *a being* without first explicating the 'being of this being,' but because in thematizing God it brings God into the course of being. But, in the most unlikely way . . . the God of the Bible signifies the beyond being, transcendence" (154). The issue is transcendence, not the ontological difference.[5]

Second, rational theology tries to take divine transcendence into account "with adverbs of height applied to the verb being; God is said to exist eminently or par excellence." For Heidegger, to speak of God as the Highest Being is the first step toward onto-theology. But Levinas asks, "And does not the modality which this adverb . . . expresses modify the verbal meaning of the verb to be to the point of excluding it from the thinkable as something inapprehendable, excluding it from the *esse* showing itself, that is, showing itself meaningfully in a theme?" (GP 154; cf. 159). In other words, does not the metaphor of height deconstruct the ontological totality rather than constitute it onto-theologically?[6]

What is the ontological totality that needs to be deconstructed if transcendence is to prevail over immanence, if the other is to avoid reduction to the same, if the God of the Bible is to escape the vassalage that rational theology accepts? In this essay Levinas describes it in terms of four themes against which he wages a sustained polemic: (1) being as manifestation, (2) meaning as thematization, (3) the present as the time when being becomes manifest as thematized meaning, and (4) transcendental subjectivity or the I think as both the agent and location of this event (*Ereignis?*).

*1. Being as manifestation.* Levinas speaks of "the coinciding of being with appearance in which, for Western philosophy, meaning or rationality lie" (GP 161). Philosophy derives its cultural hegemony from

> the strict coinciding of thought, in which philosophy resides, and the idea of reality in which this thought thinks. *For thought*, this coinciding means not having to think beyond what belongs to 'being's move' [*geste d'être*]. . . . *For the being of reality*, this coinciding means: to illuminate thought and the conceived by showing itself. . . . Rationality has to be understood as the incessant emergence of thought from the energy of 'being's move,' or its manifestation, and reason has to be understood out of this rationality. (GP 153–54, emphasis added)[7]

In other words, "meaning is equivalent to the manifestation of being, and manifestation equivalent to being's *esse*" (GP 173), or, more briefly, "being *is* manifestation" (GP 155).

*2. Meaning as thematization.* The meaning that arises from the manifestation of being (subjective and objective genitive) is not just any old meaning. It is thematized content. For western philosophy "meaning or intelligibility coincide with the manifestation of being, as if the very doings of being led to clarity, in the form of intelligibility, and then became an intentional thematization in an experience. Pressing toward or waiting for it, all the potentialities of experience are derived from or susceptible to such thematization. Thematic exposition concludes the business of being or truth" (GP 155). Where 'being' and 'truth' are thus placed in apposition, "spirit is taken to be coextensive with knowing" (GP 155) and theory is primary.

*3. Presence.* But thematization is representation, and re-presentation ties meaning to the present. "As rational speech, philosophy is taken to move from evidence to evidence, directed to what is seen, to what shows itself, thus directed to the present. The term *present* suggests both the idea of a privileged position in the temporal series and the idea of manifestation" (PE 61). Nothing can remain hidden; everything must be brought to presence, "which is the time of the same" (GP 154).

The same? How so? Perhaps the point is best put in Aristotelian language. Knowledge is the immaterial reception of the form in the intellect, which means that the form in the intellect and the form in the thing are identical. Not numerically, of course, but the one is the perfect mirror image of the other. Like Heidegger before him and Derrida after him, though in different ways, Levinas seeks to undermine the infatuation with presence that undergirds the notion of philosophy as the mirror of nature and the corresponding requirement that everything, even God, be squeezed into the Procrustean bed of correspondence and adequation.

*4. The I think.* References to now are always token reflexive, and it is the I think to which they are relative. "Transcendental subjectivity is the figure of this presence; no signification precedes that which I give to myself" (GP 157).

For Levinas what is at issue here is not just the "I think" of Descartes, Kant, and Husserl, but the "we think" of Hegel, the "Dasein cares" of Heidegger, and the knowledge as recollection theme in Plato.[8] The view that bothers Levinas can be realistic as well as idealistic. We can return to Aristotle. The claim that "no signification precedes that which I give to myself" does not mean that, empirically speaking, the form of the hundred-year-old oak tree was not in the tree before it was in my intellect. It means that since I can re-present the tree by bringing that form to presence, nothing about this meaning is *essentially* prior (transcendent) to my thinking. Being as essence and intellect as representation are contemporaneous, honeymooning, as it were, in an eternal now.[9]

Levinas does not deny that there is a dimension of human experience to which these notions are appropriate; what he denies is the totalizing claim that this is the whole story, or, if not the whole story, the most basic story. As early as 1951 he embarks on the "reckless undertaking" not just of asking, "Is Ontology Fundamental?" but of making it a rhetorical question with a negative answer (IOF 2); in 1965 he defines the Other as enigma in terms of "this way of manifesting himself without manifesting himself" (PE 66) and the infinite as "not a cognition but an approach, a neighboring with what signifies itself without revealing itself" (PE 73); and in 1984 transcendence and intelligibility signify not two mutually exclusive domains but an intelligibility of transcendence "Otherwise Than According to Knowledge" (TrI 154).

So we should not be surprised to find "God and Philosophy" insisting on an intelligibility and rationality that transcend the immanence of ontology, where (re)presentational thought and being are identical twins. "The intelligibility of transcendence is not something ontological. . . . But the break between philosophical intelligibility and the beyond being . . . does not exclude God from signifyingness" (GP 172). Indeed, we can ask

> whether the meaning that is equivalent to the *esse* of being, that is, the meaning of philosophy, is not already a restriction of meaning. Is it not already a derivative or a drifting of meaning? . . . We must ask if beyond the intelligibility and rationalism of identity, consciousness, the present, and being—beyond the intelligibility of immanence—the signifyingness, rationality, and rationalism of transcendence are not understood. Over and beyond being does not a meaning whose priority, translated into ontological language, would have to be called *antecedent* to being, show itself? (GP 154–55)[10]

This makes it clear why Levinas can't find a dime's worth of difference between rational theology (by which we can understand the attempt to establish the existence and nature of God by rational argument independent of specific religious experiences or divine revelation) and those theologies that appeal precisely to religious experience or revelation (GP 158–59, 168, 171). To him they are three variants on the vassalage of God-talk to the discourse of immanence. Since being is manifestation, God must shine forth. God is real only to the degree that God shows Godself to human understanding, whether this be by reason, experience, or revelation.[11]

We can also see now why Levinas wishes to distinguish his critique of onto-theology, not only, as we have already seen, from Heidegger's, but also from Pascal's and that of Pseudo-Dionysius.[12] He makes it clear that in going beyond being he does not intend to relapse "into speaking of opinion or faith. In fact, in staying or wanting to be outside of reason, faith and opinion speak the language of being. Nothing is less opposed to ontology than opinion and faith" (GP 155). He explicitly identifies Pascal's contrast between the God of Abraham, Isaac, and Jacob and the God of the philosophers with this relapse. He assumes, mistakenly I believe, that Pascal locates religious faith within the framework of Plato's divided line, on which *pistis* (faith, belief) is the second level up from the bottom and still a mode of *doxa* (opinion), the bottom "half" that falls short of *dianoia, noesis,* and *episteme.* So construed, Pascal would belong not just to ontology but, more specifically, to rational theology, when, "for the benefit of religion, it reserves a domain from the authority of philosophy . . . [which] will have been recognized to be philosophically unverifiable" (GP 153). Levinas sees in a recent book that denies that 'God' is a concept at all a continuation of Pascal's refusal "to accept the transcendence of the God of Abraham, Isaac, and Jacob among the concepts without which there would be no thought. What the Bible puts above all comprehension would have not yet reached the threshold of intelligibility!" (GP 154).[13]

Pseudo-Dionysius is quite willing to place the God of the Bible above all comprehension, and, indeed, explicitly beyond being. For like Levinas, he sees such a strict correlation between human thought and being that it would be irreligious not to find God otherwise than being or beyond essence.[14] But when Levinas writes that the "transcendence of God cannot be stated or conceived in terms of being, the element of philosophy, *behind which philosophy sees only night*" (GP 172, emphasis added), he suggests that negative theology is other to philosophy only on the latter's terms.[15] What Pascal and Dionysius have in common, on Levinas's reading, is that while they refuse to constrict faith within the bounds of ontology, they accept philosophy's claim to have a monopoly on meaning. Rather than posit a rationality of transcendence, they leave faith outside the pale of intelligibility. But, then, whether they say it is found below or above the privileged realm of evidence and presence is of little import.

If the break with the onto-theological mode of ontological immanence is not made by the appeal to religious experience or divine revelation, where is it to be found? This question generates no suspense. We know Levinas finds it in the experience of responsibility for the Other.[16] Put in terms of language, the (rhetorical) question is: "can discourse signify otherwise than by signifying a theme?" (GP 159). This question also generates no suspense. We know, for example, from an earlier Talmudic study, that for Levinas

> speech, in its original essence, is a commitment to a third party on behalf of our neighbor: the act *par excellence*, the institution of society. The original function of speech consists not in designating an object in order to communicate with the other in a game with no consequences but in assuming toward someone a responsibility on behalf of someone else. . . . Responsibility would be the essence of language. (NTR 21; cf. TI 39–40, 50–51)

But language is ethically constituted when we are addressed as well as when we speak. "The epiphany of the face is wholly language" (PII 55) and "The face is a living presence; it is expression. . . . The face speaks. The manifestation of the face is already discourse" (TI 66; cf. 193). The saying that the face is can be without words. "The enigma extends as far as the phenomenon that bears the trace of the *saying* which has already withdrawn from the *said*" (PE 69).

It is this last theme that Levinas picks up in "God and Philosophy." Part of what the nakedness of the neighbor's face signifies is that it does not always have access to forums where its empirical voice can be heard. It must "be heard like cries not voiced or thematized, already addressed to God. There the resonance of silence—*Geläut der Stille*—certainly sounds. . . . My responsibility . . . is the hearing or understanding of this cry" (GP 167–68).

The use of the phrase *Geläut der Stille* is intended to distance Levinas even further from Heidegger. It is the latter who first uses this phrase to signify a silence at the origin of language. But, in the first place, it is language that speaks and not the neighbor. "The peal of stillness is not anything human."[17] Second, Heidegger's interest in this silence belongs to the project of linking language more closely to the thinking of Being. For him, *"The essential being of language is Saying as Showing."*[18] This showing that is heard in silence is prior to language as signs, but in Levinasian perspective it is just another version of Being as manifestation.

The very different saying that Levinas wants us to hear in the silence interrupts the language of manifestation, thematization, and representation. "Language understood in this [ethical] way loses its superfluous and strange function of doubling up of thought and being. Saying as testimony precedes all the said. Saying, before setting forth a said, is already the testimony of this responsibility [for the neighbor]—and even the saying of a said, as an approach to the other, is a responsibility for him" (GP 170).[19]

In the language of speech act theory, constative, assertive, indicative speech acts belong to immanence. It is commanding, ordering, imperative speech acts that awaken to transcendence. What awakens is not just a demand (GP 161) but "a demand that no obedience is equal to, no obedience puts to sleep" (GP 156). Perhaps that is why the image of being awakened is the mildest way Levinas has for speaking about the "disturbance" (GP 156, 158; also his favorite term in PE) that ontological complacency undergoes. It is a "devastating" (GP 162–64), "jolting" (GP 159), "breaking up" (GP 159–61,

173) of consciousness as governed by the I think, which is "interrupted" (GP 160) by an "exposedness" (GP 157) to the Other that can only be described as a "trauma" (GP 161, 163, 166, 173). This awakening is the moral equivalent of reveille at boot camp.

And God is the drill sergeant! For transcendence not to be absorbed in immanence

> it is necessary that the desirable or God remain separated in the desire; as desirable it is near but different: holy. This can only be if the desirable orders me to what is the non-desirable, the undesirable par excellence—the other. The reference to the other is an awakening, an awakening to proximity, and this is a responsibility for the neighbor. . . . We have designated this way for the Infinite, or for God, to refer, from the heart of its very desirability, to the non-desirable proximity of others, by the term 'illeity'. . . . Through this reversal the desirable escapes desire. The goodness of the Good—the Good which never sleeps or nods [Ps. 121:4?]—inclines the movement it calls forth, to turn it from the Good and orient it toward the other, and only thus toward the Good; through this separation or holiness it remains a third person, the *he* in the depth of the you. He is good in just this eminent sense: He does not fill me up with goods, but compels me to goodness, which is better than goods received. (GP 164–65)[20]

This sounds very much like the biblical God who commands "You shall love your neighbor as yourself." And Levinas, invoking the classic distinction between eros and agape, makes it clear that it is neighbor love that he has in mind. "Love is only possible through the idea of the Infinite . . . which devastates and awakens" (GP 164). Suggesting that any love that arises from the lover's need is an attempt to reduce the other to the same, to make the other part of me as the object of my enjoyment, Levinas boldly says No to Plato's Diotima. "The celestial and the vulgar Venus are sisters." Both are "concupiscence in Pascal's sense of the term, an assuming and an investing by the I" (GP 164). But there is a "love without Eros" (GP 165) precisely when I rise and shine to the rude awakening by the God who deflects my need love for Infinite Goodness "to the non-desirable proximity of others" and thus "compels me to goodness" (GP 165).[21]

This is the overcoming of onto-theology, for "in this strange mission that orders the approach to the other, God is drawn out of objectivity, presence and being. . . . His absolute remoteness, his transcendence, turns into my responsibility—non-erotic par excellence—for the other" (GP 165).

At the outset of "God and Philosophy," Levinas promised to oppose the God of the Bible to the God of the philosophers and of rational theology, in this case the Beautiful Itself of erotic Platonism. He has done so by contrasting the transcendence of the God who commands neighbor love to the immanence of the God who is the obscure object of indigent, needy desire. As "the desirable escapes desire" (GP 165) in this way, divine transcendence is defined, not in cosmological terms, but in ethical terms. God is "high and lofty" (Isa. 6:1) not by being outside the world but by resisting my project of making the whole of being, including God, into satisfactions of my needs, means to my ends.

So it is a bit surprising that Levinas returns to "Philosophy and the Idea of Infinity" and develops much of his argument in relation to Descartes's Third Meditation, since Descartes's God is not famous for commanding neighbor love. Actually, it is not Descartes's God that interests Levinas so much as the idea of God as infinite, an idea whose innateness means not simply that it is a priori but that it has been put into us. This is a *Sinngebung* of which the I think is not the subject. Levinas calls this a passivity to be sharply distinguished from the receptivity of knowing that, as "an assembling of a dispersed given in the simultaneity of presence, in immanence" (GP 166), "assumes what affects it" (GP 172; cf. 160, 163).

In his critique of Understanding, Hegel identifies receptivity as surrender. "Instead of entering into the immanent content of the thing, [the Understanding] is forever surveying the whole and standing above the particular existence of which it is speaking. . . . Scientific cognition [philosophy as system], on the contrary, demands surrender [*sich übergeben*] to the life of the object, or what amounts to the same thing, confronting and expressing *its* inner necessity."[22]

Similarly Heidegger, speaking of the natural and humanistic sciences, in distinction from metaphysics, speaks of the "submissive attitude [*Dienststellung*] taken up by scientific theory" such that "the distinction of science lies in the fact that . . . it and it alone explicitly allows the object itself the first and last word. In this objectivity of questioning, definition and proof there is a certain limited [N.B.] submission [*Unterwerfung*] to what-is, so that this may reveal itself."[23] Later on Heidegger will portray the thinking that is "releasement [*Gelassenheit*] toward things and openness to the mystery" as "a kind of passivity" in which there is present a "higher acting [that] is yet no activity" and is thus "beyond the distinction between activity and passivity."[24]

Levinas has no quarrel with these analyses. He only insists that they belong entirely to the rationality of immanence. The traumatic passivity of the command to love the undesirable is of a wholly different order. The primacy of ethics over ontology is Kantian only to a point;[25] for here it means not the autonomy of the rational will but the heteronomy of the will taken hostage, for "to be one's brother's keeper is to be his hostage" (168).

But it is precisely this ethical dimension that is not present in Descartes's notion of the idea of Infinity as prior to the cogito. Levinas develops the notion that the idea of God is "put into" us into a conception of creation that opens into his an-archic notion of time and the trace. To be created means to be subject to an idea that is essentially prior to me, that exceeds every horizon of my thought and cannot be gathered into the present of my I think (161; cf. OB 122). But nothing in Descartes suggests that creation signifies a demand or a call to be obeyed; and when Levinas adds that ethical dimension, it looks a bit like a transplanted organ in danger of being rejected by the Cartesian immune system (161; OB 110, 113).

Wouldn't he have done better to appeal to Augustine and Kierkegaard, for whom commanded neighbor love does not need to be added on to the idea of a God who disturbs the ontological sleep of Plato and Hegel, respectively, but belongs to that idea essentially?[26] To be sure, their notions of God are "contaminated" by biblical faith in ways that those of Plato and Descartes are not. So they cannot support the deconstruction of western philosophy from within in quite the same way in which Levinas hopes Plato's *epikeina tes ousias* and Descartes's idea of God as the idea of Infinity will be able to (TI 48–52, 102–103). But Levinas acknowledges that it is only "the *formal* design" of Descartes's analysis that is of use to him (PII 53), and we have just seen that the omitted content is precisely the ethical demand that is absolutely central to Levinas's project.

The same can be said in regard to Plato, as can be seen from Levinas's assimilation of the celestial and vulgar Venuses to one another and to philosophy's immanence. Yes, Plato's Good is otherwise than being and beyond essence. But it is also the Beautiful that attracts without diverting desire to the undesirable. Plato and Descartes can disturb the soul's sleep and the cogito's complacency, but they are not the rude awakening that is needed really to overcome ontology and establish "ethics as first philosophy."[27]

For Augustine as for Levinas, divine transcendence is a more radical enemy of human tranquility. In both cases, we encounter it as a disturbing wake-up call. *Wachtet auf, ruft uns die Stimme.*[28] Since both are exploring the meaningfulness of the transcendence of the biblical God, it is fitting that the awakening motif is itself a biblical one. In Isaiah 52:1, for example, the prophet announces impending deliverance from captivity with these words:

> Awake, awake, put on your strength, O Zion!
> Put on your beautiful garments, O Jerusalem, the holy city.

Eschatological expectation is the typical context for wake-up calls in the New Testament as well. Thus the tragi-comic sequence in which we find Jesus urging his disciples to wakeful readiness (Matt. 24:36–44), repeating this admonition in the parable of the wise and foolish bridesmaids or virgins (Matt. 25:1–13), and, at a more immediate and mundane level, urging them to stay awake with him in Gethsemane. Whereupon they fall asleep, not once, but twice (Matt. 26:36–46). Eschatological calls to awaken or to stay awake are also found in Romans 13:11, Ephesians 5:14, 1 Thessalonians 5:1–6, and Revelation 3:2–3. Two of these show up in Augustine's *Confessions*.

Augustine's intellectual conversion takes place in Book VII. But since he is not the onto-theologian he is sometimes taken to be, it is not enough that his theoretical questions are answered to his full satisfaction. Beyond the question of truth is the question of the way. "The way—the Saviour Himself—pleased me, but I was still reluctant to enter its narrowness" (VIII, 1).[29] This reluctance turns out to be "the iron bondage of my own will," which allowed lust to become habit. Three metaphors describe this bondage: a chain, a weight (perhaps the ball at the end of the chain), and the lethargy and drowsiness of sleep. Deliverance from this slavery to his old ways begins "when you called me: *Awake, thou that sleepest, and arise from the dead, and Christ shall give thee light*" (VIII, 5).[30]

Although Augustine repeats that he is convinced of the truth of the Christian faith, he can "find nothing to say except lazy words spoken half asleep: 'A minute,' 'just a minute,' 'just a little time longer.' But there was no limit to the minutes, and the little time longer went a long way" (VIII, 5). Eventually, however, in the famous garden scene where the child's voice repeats the words "Take it and read it," Augustine is awakened. Remembering the conversion of Antony, he picks up the Bible and reads, "*Not in rioting and drunkenness, not in chambering and wantonness, not in strife and envying: but put ye on the Lord Jesus Christ, and make not provision for the flesh in concupiscence*" (VIII, 12).

Augustine quotes only the portion that was decisive for him, Romans 13:13–14. He tells us that he read no further, but not that he did not begin reading earlier. Even if he read only the verses he quotes, the words served as a wake-up call from God, which makes the two previous verses most interesting. "Besides this, you know what time it is, how it is now the moment for you to wake from sleep. For salvation is nearer to us now than when we became believers; the night is far gone, the day is near. Let us then lay aside the works of darkness and put on the armor of light" (Rom. 13:11–12). The traumas of awakening for Augustine were neither an intellectual paradigm shift not the discovery of a cognitive breakdown or dead end. They were the teleological suspension of indicative discourse in imperative discourse. He went from being the subject to being the suspect, from cogito to culprit.[31]

If we back up to the previous paragraph in Romans 13 (vv. 8–10) we find a brief discourse on commanded love including the reminder (1) that we owe love to one another, (2) that "Love your neighbor as yourself" is a summary of the commandments against adultery, murder, theft, etc., (3) and thus, that "love is the fulfilling of the law." Even if he read this portion of the text, Augustine does not mention it. For as he understands himself, his besetting sin is not indifference to others but a twofold lust expressed in an illicit sexual relation and in a career oriented toward fame and fortune rather than service (VIII, 1, 6). That is why he zeroes in on that passage about the flesh and its concupiscence; or perhaps, why it zeroes in on him.

But Augustine knows that the God who jolted him out of the key elements of his private and public life is the God of Moses in Leviticus, the God of Jesus in Matthew, and the God of Paul a paragraph earlier in Romans—the God who commands neighbor love. So when he says to God, "Blessed is the man who loves you," we have the celestial Venus; and when he adds, "who loves his friend in you," we have either the vulgar or celestial Venus, depending on how "Platonic" the friendship is; but when he adds "and his enemy because of you" (IV, 9), we see that our desire has been deflected to the undesirable by the one who "compels me to goodness" (165). This is not Venus but the Yahweh of

Leviticus 19:18 to whom Jesus appeals both when he includes "You shall love your neighbor as yourself" in his summary of the whole law (Matt. 22:34–40),[32] and when he rejects the interpretation of this that says, "You shall love your neighbor and hate your enemy," insisting rather, "Love your enemies and pray for those who persecute you, so that you may be children of your Father in heaven." To exclude enemies from the category of neighbors is to imitate, not the perfection of the heavenly Father, but tax collectors and Gentiles, who serve the vulgar Venus by restricting their love to those they find desirable (Matt. 5:43–48).

Like Levinas and Augustine, Kierkegaard understands divine transcendence in terms of commanded love. The first half of *Works of Love* includes six meditations on that theme. Three are directly on the command "You shall love your neighbor as yourself." Three others are on related texts: "Love is the fulfilling of the law" (Rom. 13:10); "But the sum of the commandment is love out of a pure heart and out of a good conscience and out of a sincere faith" (1 Tim. 1:5); and "Owe no one anything, except to love one another" (Rom. 13:8).[33] The other two essays affirm that God is the source and origin of love and that love of God is inseparable from love of neighbor. "If anyone says, 'I love God,' and hates his brother, he is a liar; for how can he who does not love his brother, whom he has seen, love God, whom he has not seen?" (1 John 4:20).

Although he works exclusively from New Testament texts, Kierkegaard knows that commanded love first appears in Judaism (WL 24). If he regularly identifies it as Christian love, it is because his target is Christendom, whose paganism he seeks to expose (WL 47–50, 59, 109, 120, 128, 146, 198–201). He draws a sustained contrast between commanded love and celebrated love, which turns out to be a variation on the contrast of agape and eros. Recognizing the distinction between the vulgar and celestial Venus, Kierkegaard presents two species of celebrated love, erotic love in the narrow, sexual sense, and friendship. Since he lumps these together, it is clear that the problem with celebrated love is not sensuality but selfishness (WL 52; cf. E/O II, 49, 91).

The argument that erotic love and friendship are forms of self-love revolves around the preferential and spontaneous character of these relations. The beloved and the friend are selected from among the others, preferred above the others. There is something essentially exclusionary about both forms of love (WL 52). To be preferred, the beloved and the friend must be attractive **to me.** They must satisfy **my** drives and inclinations (WL 44, 49–52, 56). Sexual attraction is just one mode of this relation. Kierkegaard notes that cultural affinity, for example, is another (WL 60). It is because **my** drives and inclinations, whether vulgar or celestial, are the basis of the preferential, exclusionary relationship that both modes of celebrated love can be called spontaneous. I am the origin of both relationships; both loves reach out from my erotic or educated nature toward that which pleases me.

Levinas might say that erotic love and friendship are the reduction of the Other to the Same.[34] Kierkegaard would understand immediately, for he tells us that "'the neighbor' is what thinkers call 'the other,' that by which the selfishness in self-love is to be tested" (WL 21). Commanded love of neighbor is the end to preference. In order to be my neighbor you need not be attractive to me sexually, culturally, or in any other way; indeed, you may be more than a little repulsive. Like Augustine, Kierkegaard notes that the enemy is also the neighbor, and points to the radical equality that the command introduces, since there is no basis to exclude anyone.[35] The love that is deflected by the command to the undesirable is no longer spontaneous. Its basis is nothing within me but a divine authority that is thoroughly heteronomous (WL 96–97). Not only does the command come from outside of me; it is there prior to any act on my part. In relation to God I begin with an infinite debt. Thus, like Levinas, Kierkegaard links the notion of creation to that of an obligation that precedes the I think (WL 102, 115; cf. 69).[36]

The depth of the affinity between Kierkegaard and Levinas can be seen if we push the analysis a radical step further. A feature of "God and Philosophy" that clearly marks it as belonging to Levinas II has barely been mentioned to this point. In speaking about the obligation I bear toward the Other, he uses the images of substitution, accusation, hostage, and expiation (164–71). Along with the notions of obsession and persecution, these are central to the argument of the central chapter of *Otherwise Than Being*, "Substitution."[37] Of the many important themes expressed by this cluster of ideas, one is especially significant in the present context. It is the answer they give to the question What does the face of the Other say? What said comes closest to catching the meaning of its *Geläut der Stille*?

In *Totality and Infinity*, the answer given by Levinas I is simply enough, "You shall not commit murder" (TI 199, 216, 262, 303). In other writings, this gets translated as "You shall not usurp my place in the sun" (DEL 24; BCI 38; EL 19; EF 82) and as "You shall not let me die alone" (DEL 24; BCI 38; EL 15; BI 112).[38] This latter formulation goes dramatically beyond anything to be found in liberal natural rights theory (where rights tend to reduce to the right to be left alone).[39] But in explicating substitution and the notions that cluster around it, Levinas goes even farther. In the trauma of substitution I am taken hostage for the other and find myself responsible for "the misfortunes *and faults* of a neighbor . . . [this responsibility] is something completely astonishing, a responsibility that even extends to the obligation to answer *for another's freedom, to be responsible for his responsibility*" (166–67, emphasis added; cf. LP 123; II 245). Substitution means expiation, responsibility "for the other—for his distress *and his freedom*" (169, emphasis added). Right after the dedication of *Otherwise Than Being* to the victims of the Holocaust, Levinas gives us a page of quotations, the first of which is from Ezekiel 3:20. When a righteous man goes bad, "he shall die: because you did not warn him, he shall die for his sin, and the righteous deeds which he has done shall not be remembered, *but his blood will I require at your hand*" (emphasis added). The gloss on this in the text, again in terms of substitution and being taken hostage, tells us that we stand "accused of *what the others do* or suffer, or responsible for *what they do* or suffer" (OB 112, emphasis added).

This is not paternalism, which says (1) I have superior wisdom in relation to the Other and (2) the Other has a duty to be guided by my wisdom. The Levinasian text knows nothing of superior wisdom, nor of a duty the Other has to submit to my guidance. It knows only my responsibility for the Other's use or misuse of her freedom. It is my job, not to make the Other just like me, but to help the Other to become good.

Perhaps not many will agree with Levinas on this point, but Kierkegaard does. His formulation of this awesome responsibility, however, is quite specific. I am commanded to love my neighbor, but "truly to love another person is to help that person to love God" (WL 130; cf. 107, 120–21). It is at this point, where perhaps the deepest kinship between Levinas and Kierkegaard is to be found, that we find ourselves face to face with their sharpest divergence. Kierkegaard insists that God is always the middle term in my relation to the neighbor (WL 58, 67, 107, 119–21, 142). While we could conceivably use this language to express the Levinasian notion that it is God who deflects desire toward the undesirable, Levinas is more in the habit of placing the neighbor between me and God.

This is not just a question of imagery. Kierkegaard writes, "Ultimately, love for God is the decisive factor; from this originates love for the neighbor." For this reason, the commandment "commands loving God above all else, and *then* loving the neighbor" (WL 57–58, emphasis added). Love for God comes first (WL 108, 112–13), and Kierkegaard is eloquent about the beauty and importance of this prior rendezvous that takes place in hidden inwardness (WL 3–10).[40]

Levinas is very skittish about any private relation to God prior to my relation to my neighbor. One reason is that he fears that religion in such a mode can encourage indifference to my neighbor or even legitimize oppression of my neighbor. But this can hardly be an objection against Kierkegaard, who includes an essay on 1 John 4:20 and the impossibility of loving God without loving the neighbor and who presents the God who is to be loved first precisely as the God who tells me I must love my neighbor. "Shut your door and pray to God—because God is surely the highest . . . when you open the door that you shut in order to pray to God and go out the very first person you meet is the neighbor whom you *shall* love" (WL 51).

But perhaps another reason Levinas will not allow love of God to be prior to love of neighbor comes to light in "God and Philosophy." The God who deflects desire toward "the non-desirable proximity of others" does so as the Good that "inclines the movement it calls forth, to turn it from the Good and orient it toward the other, and only thus toward the Good" (GP 165). Kierkegaard will agree, nay insist, on this "only thus." It is only as loving our neighbor that we can also love God; but Levinas is not comfortable with this "also." He introduces the term "illeity" for the God who is "the *he* in the depth of the you.

He is good in just this eminent sense; He does not fill me up with goods, but compels me to goodness, which is better than goods received" (GP 165).

This sounds like a theology of law without grace. But there is a prior and deeper issue. Is this a theology without God? If God is only "the *he* in the depth of the *you*," does this mean that God is not a distinct personal being but rather the depth dimension of the human person? Does Levinas persuasively re-define 'God' to mean simply the trans-empirical moral significance of the neighbor?[41] Levinas writes, "[God] is neither an object *nor an interlocutor.* His absolute remoteness, his transcendence, turns into my responsibility—non-erotic par excellence—for the other. And this analysis implies that God is not simply the 'first other,' the 'other par excellence,' or the 'absolutely other,' but other than the other . . . transcendent to the point of absence, to the point of a possible confusion with the stirring of the *there is*" (GP 165–66, first emphasis added).[42] The reason for this possible confusion is clear. By refusing to let this "he" be another "you," Levinas makes it all but impossible to distinguish "him" from some "it." It seems that 'he' is only apparently a personal pronoun, or that its personal character is entirely derivative from the human "you" behind which it stands.

By contrast, Kierkegaard's God is unambiguously personal, an interlocu-tor who would never be confused with the *there is*, who is other than the human other precisely by being the 'first other,' the 'other par excellence,' or the 'absolutely other.' Thus at the outset of *Works of Love* the following prayer, "How could one speak properly about love if *you* were forgotten, *you* God of love, source of all love in heaven and on earth; *you* who spared nothing but in love gave everything; *you* who are love, so that one who loves is what he is only by being in *you*" (WL 5, emphasis added).

We cannot ask philosophy to resolve this difference, for both Levinas and Kierkegaard are engaged in the task of interrupting the dominant discourse of western philosophy with reference to the biblical God, of awakening the com-placency of immanence with the trauma of transcendence. It could be argued, however, that Kierkegaard's is the more genuinely biblical God. Neither when the issue is posed in terms of law and grace nor when it is posed in terms of whether or not God is a distinct, personal interlocutor should it be thought that the issue concerns the differences between Judaism and Christianity. For the argument would be that the God of the Jewish Bible and not just of the New Testament is (1) a God of grace as well as of law, and (2) a personal being who speaks and to whom we speak (and only as such the ground of the moral significance of the neighbor). The question, at least for Jews and Christians, is whether to stick with the biblical portrayals of God as a fully personal inter-locutor or to allow oneself to be pulled toward something less personal than the God of Abraham, Isaac, and Jacob. But by whom? For what "reason"?

There is a psychological and motivational issue here. Levinas and Kierke-gaard agree in emphasizing that neighbor love runs counter to our natural self-love. But if it is indeed a heteronomous call to self-denial and self-sacrifice, if it overrides our spontaneous preferences, if it is contrary to our *conatus essendi*, how, if at all, is it possible, even imperfectly?

Our psychological knowledge, both formal and informal, gives a clear answer. Only by being loved do we develop the capacity to love, and Kierkegaard's God is fully personal enough for his answer to be "We love because he first loved us" (1 John 4:19). He gives us a moral transcription of God as *mysterium tremendum et fascinans*. God is *mysterium* by remaining hidden even within the piety of hidden inwardness,[43] *tremendum* by commanding the subordination of self-love to neighbor love, and *fascinans* by being the fountain of forgiving love that gives us both our own sense of worth and our capacity to love others. Levinas's God is the *mysterium tremendum*; but where is the *fascinans* in the Good that gives no goods but only compels to goodness? When the command to love is unaccompanied by the love that enables obedience to the command, is this not a recipe for despair and even cynicism?

Of course, the need for Kierkegaard's kind of God does not guarantee the reality of such a God. The world may be as Sartre portrays it, a Godless world in which love can never be more than the demand to be loved. But Kierkegaard's analysis gives us a powerful rationale for hoping rather than fearing that there is a truly personal God, one who first loves and then commands love. If philosophy, as disinterested, pure reason, had brought to clear and distinct presence either the unreality of such a God or the unwarranted nature of belief in such a God, we might feel obliged simply to disregard hope in a kind of epistemic Stoicism. But both Levinas and Kierkegaard (and a host of others) have given us compelling reasons not to accept this self-portrait of philosophy (sometimes called Modernity).

But isn't it dangerous to let reason be guided by hope? Yes, indeed. The danger is that reason will either find God conveniently unreal or will find a convenient God, one who is all *fascinans* and no *tremendum* (and who usually ceases to be *mysterium* in the process). That is what Kierkegaard saw in the God of Hegel and the God of Christendom. But he tries his best to rescue the biblical God both from philosophy and from the middle class, and it is not just Climacus in *Concluding Unscientific Postscript* but Kierkegaard throughout the entire authorship who is devoted to making the life of faith more difficult, not easier. And beyond Kierkegaard, both Augustine and Levinas stand ready to provide insights that can be helpful in guarding against a piety of convenience.

One of the insights we can gain from all three is that in the final analysis it is not a matter of insight, as if we eliminate the danger simply by understanding it. Just as for Kierkegaard love is always the works of love, so here faith is the work of faith, a 'belief that' which is but an abstract moment in a "belief in" that involves trust, gratitude, repentance, and obedience. There is no reason why it should be easier to love God than to love the neighbor. "But all things excellent are as difficult as they are rare."[44]

PART 3. HETERONOMY

# The Trauma of Transcendence as Heteronomous Intersubjectivity

The question of the transcendence of God is utterly fundamental to any philosophical theology. Some would even say it is the most basic issue.[1] In the previous two chapters we have seen that although there seems to be considerable divergence between Levinas and Kierkegaard on the meaning of 'God,' they strongly agree that God's transcendence is experienced as a traumatic heteronomy. Unintimidated by the Enlightenment's assertion of autonomy, they make no apology for insisting on heteronomy, only noting the decisive break this involves with major strands of western philosophy. The next two chapters will be devoted to exploring this heteronomy in detail. Each of them shows that the heteronomy of divine transcendence, at once epistemic and ethical, is so deep that it relativizes the very identity of the self while at the same time being essential to the birth of the responsible self.

On the other hand, the question of intersubjectivity is central not only to ethics and politics but increasingly to ontology and epistemology; but, insofar as religion is a social phenomenon and *extra ecclesiam nulla salus* has a sociological as well as a theological meaning,[2] the philosophy of religion must be added to those subdisciplines for which intersubjectivity is an important theme.

What might be the relation between these two themes, transcendence and intersubjectivity?[3] Perhaps the first thing to be said is that no such relation is necessary or inevitable. It is quite possible to pose the questions of divine transcendence and of human intersubjectivity in such a way that "never the twain shall meet."

Let us consider divine transcendence first. The classical debate is between theistic/creationist and pantheistic/emanationist accounts of the relation of the One to the many, the latter denying that God is "outside" or "beyond" or "independent of" the world in the way the former affirms. As Spinoza puts it, "God is the immanent, not the transitive, cause of all things."[4] Like Aristotle's forms, God is in the world, not above and beyond it. And Hegel carries on a sustained polemic against the *Jenseits* in any form.[5]

It is important to see that to cash in the theistic claim of transcendence it is not enough to be able to distinguish God from the world. Plotinus can distinguish the One from the many that emanate therefrom just as we can distinguish the fire, which is there, from the heat and light that emanate from it, but are here. Similarly Spinoza can and emphatically does distinguish *natura naturans* from *natura naturata*; and Hegel distinguishes the Idea as concept, which for him is "God as he is in his eternal essence before the creation of nature and a finite mind,"[6] from its actualization. Thus, for example, the first paragraph of the *Philosophy of Right* reads, "The subject-matter of the philosophical science of right is the Idea of right, i.e., the concept of right together with the actualization of that concept," and goes on to explain that the concepts of philosophy are not "mere concepts." Philosophy shows that "it is the concept alone . . . which has actuality, and further that it gives this actuality to itself."[7] Accordingly, his system is made up first of a Logic and then of a *Realphilosophie* in two parts, Philosophy of Nature and Philosophy of Spirit. The actuality of the world is the actuality of God.

Creationist theism makes the stronger claim that God and the world are not just distinguishable but separable. More specifically, they are existentially asymmetrical. There cannot be the world without God, but there can be God without the world—without this particular world, or, for that matter, any world at all. God's actuality is not the same as the actuality of the world. Moreover, God's creative activity springs not from necessity but from a free choice of the will. The world does not merely contain contingency; its very existence is contingent.[8] Thus Aquinas can claim both (1) that while the world might have been co-eternal with God (as it is for Plotinus, Spinoza, and Hegel), it need not be such and in fact is not and (2) that even if it were, its very being would still be contingent upon divine free choice.[9] This is the cash value of the claim that God is "outside," "beyond," or "independent of" the world.

So far as any theism makes this claim and goes no farther, it concerns itself with what we might call causal or cosmological transcendence; and it is clear that it can say what it wants to say without invoking the categories of intersubjectivity.

It is likewise possible to invoke such categories without implying theological transcendence. Hegel comes immediately to mind. With Descartes and Kant he sees that human consciousness is self-consciousness, but not merely as cogito or transcendental apperception. As the desire for recognition, human self-consciousness is mediated through the Other. "With this, we already have before us the concept of *Spirit* . . . this absolute substance which is the unity of the different independent self-consciousnesses which, in their opposition, enjoy perfect freedom and independence: 'I' that is 'We' and 'We' that is 'I.' "[10] In its most immediate form, this We exists as the family, to which one belongs "not as an independent person but as a member."[11] The spiritual significance of marriage thus "consists in the parties' consciousness of this unity as their substantive aim, and so in their love, trust, and common sharing of their entire existence as individuals."[12] The laws and powers of such social institutions "are on the one hand an object over against the subject" with an "absolute authority" infinitely higher than the laws of nature. "On the other hand, they are not something alien to the subject. On the contrary, his spirit bears witness to them as to its own essence, the essence in which he has a feeling of his own selfhood and in which he lives as in his own element, which is not distinguished from himself. The subject is thus directly linked to the ethical order by a relation which is more like an identity than even the relation of faith or trust."[13] I am who We are.

Clearly this powerful, noncontractual account of intersubjectivity, which Hegel applies to the state as well as to the family,[14] does not signify theistic transcendence. Thus, in the passage just cited, where he introduces spirit in terms of the I that is We, he adds that in this concept of Spirit "consciousness first finds it turning-point, where it leaves behind it the colourful show of the sensuous here-an-now **and the nightlike void of the supersensible beyond,** and steps out into the spiritual daylight of the present."[15] When, at the end of chapter 6 of the *Phenomenology*, the 'I's become a spiritual 'We' through forgiveness, Hegel calls this "a reciprocal recognition which is *absolute* Spirit. . . . The reconciling *Yea*, in which the two 'I's let go their antithetical *existence*, is the *existence* of the 'I' which has expanded into a duality, and therein remains identical with itself, and, in its complete externalization and opposite, possesses the certainty of itself: **it is God** manifested in the midst of those who know themselves in the form of pure knowledge."[16] So far from intersubjectivity implicating divine transcendence, it is rather the substitute that frees us from having to think of God as anything *Jenseits.*[17]

It is possible, as Levinas has shown us, to read Buber's philosophy of I and Thou and in dialogue as a variation on the Hegelian theme of reciprocal recognition as the essence of spirit. Thus, for all his appreciation of Buber, he insists upon a certain asymmetry in one's relation to the Other that he does not find in Buber. It "consists in going to the other without concerning oneself with his movement toward me" (OB 84). He fears that the unconditionality of responsibility is diluted in the reciprocity he finds in Buber. In responsible asymmetry, contrary to Buber, "I hardly care what the other is with respect to me, that is his own business; for me, he is above all the one I am responsible for" (EN 105; cf. 107 and PN 32–33). Thus "I must always demand more of myself than of the other; and this is why I disagree with Buber's description of the I-Thou ethical relation as a symmetrical copresence. As Alyosha Karamazov says . . . 'We are all responsible for everyone else—but I am more responsible than all the others.' And he does not mean that every 'I' is more responsible for all the others" (DEL 31; cf. OS 44). Buber's I-Thou converts the face to face into "a harmonious co-presence, as an eye to eye" (GCM 150; cf. OB 25). In this way, like Hegel, he violates the distance that is transcendence. "The I *and* You are not embraceable objectively, there is no *and* possible between them, they form no totality" (GCM 145; cf. OB 12).

Perhaps this is unfair to Buber, who notes that even a violent relation can have the I-Thou structure and that dialogue can be with the opponent, *hostis* or *adversarius*.[18] Still, he leaves himself open to this complaint with his emphasis on the move "from communication to communion" and the transformation of "discussion . . . into a bond."[19] In any case, we are alerted to the way in which reciprocal intersubjectivity can lead toward totality rather than transcendence.

But suppose one were to make intersubjectivity itself the basis for articulating divine transcendence. Augustine might well have done so, but seems not to have noticed. He remains within the boundaries of causal/cosmological transcendence even when he describes how "our Life came down to us and suffered our death. . . . He thundered, calling us to return to Him." To whom are we to return? To the one "who made all things, and He is our God . . . turn your love back from [bodies, if they please you] to their maker. . . . Return, sinners, to your own heart and cling to Him who made you" (IV, 11–12).[20] Later he tells us how he was enabled to return with the help of "an unchangeable light shining above this eye of my soul and above my mind. . . . Nor was it above my mind as oil floats on water or as the heaven is above the earth. It was higher than I, because it made me, and I was lower because I was made by it" (VII, 10). Still later, he wonders what he loves when he loves God. He asks the earth, the sea, and the living creatures in them, then the sun, the moon, and stars. He is told, "We are not your God. Look above us . . . we are not the God for whom you are looking. . . . He made us" (X, 6).

To be sure, the God of Augustine is the maker of heaven and earth. But he does not relate to God primarily as his causal origin. God is rather from start to finish his interlocutor, the one to whom he speaks and the one who speaks to him, calling him, as we have just read, to return. Augustine is too much a Platonist to be free of the metaphorics of light and vision. But God for him is so much a subject to be listened to and not merely an object to be looked at that even in those moments usually taken to be mystical "visions," he thinks of God as the One Who Speaks (VII, 10; IX, 10). The resources are there for thinking transcendence in terms of intersubjectivity, but Augustine continues for the most part to gloss "above me" in terms of "made me."

So let us turn to Levinas, who also links transcendence to height[21] but also, most decisively, to intersubjectivity. Of course, the Other is not, in the first instance, God, but the human Other (*Autrui*), the widow, the orphan, and the stranger whom I meet face to face. They are the ones of whom he says, "The absolutely other is the Other" (TI 39), "*The other qua other is the Other*" (TI 71),[22] and "it is only man who could be absolutely foreign to me" (TI 73). Still, the structure of this human transcendence may be helpful in trying to think the transcendence of God, especially since Levinas insists that it is the only site at which God legitimately comes to mind.

In *Otherwise Than Being*, Levinas often speaks of "the trauma of transcendence" (OB xlii).[23] Our exposure and vulnerability to the otherness of the Other is a bell that tolls threat, as with Sartre, rather than opportunity and hope, as with Buber and Marcel. So what is the threat? Wherein lies the trauma?

To begin with, there is an epistemic threat, a decentering of the transcendental ego, a wounding or shattering of the cogito, as Ricoeur has put it so eloquently. But this is not the mild decentering of hermeneutics, which humbles the I think by reminding it of its embeddedness in the body, in a particular language and culture, in pre-understandings and pre-judices that are prior to all our noetic acts and can never be fully transferred to the noematic side of the equation by means of reflection. In two ways Levinas's traumatic transcendence is a wilder epistemic heteronomy whose humbling effects can be experienced only as humiliation by that aspiration for autonomy that philosophy often calls modernity, but that religion calls simply calls sin ("I will be like the Most High"; Isa. 14:14), implying that contact with transcendence will be resistance and rebellion if it is not repentance, offense if not faith. And we are only at the epistemic trauma!

Its first moment is what Levinas calls the immediacy of the face.[24] Whereas hermeneutics reminds us of the concreteness and contingency of the horizons of our thought, giving rise to the specter or vertigo of relativity, the Other is precisely what does not arise within our horizons. The face represents "*signification without a context*" (TI 23). Not even with the all too human horizons in which I am constituted and that I bring with me like a turtle's shell am I the condition for the possibility of this "experience," for "to disclose, on the basis of a subjective horizon, is already to miss the noumenon" (TI 67).[25] The Other is prior to the a priori. Here I am dealing with "meaning prior to my *Sinngebung*" (TI 51) even when immersed in enough horizonal contingency to make Richard Rorty happy. In his brilliant comparison of the traumatized subject in Levinas, Freud, and Lacan, Rudolf Bernet describes trauma this way: "like a bullet that hits the mark, it makes a hole in the symbolic fabric of which the history of the subject is composed."[26]

In *Totality and Infinity* this theme is summarized in the notion that the Other is manifest καθ αὐτό.[27] The teaching that I receive from the Other can thus be called revelation (TI 62, 66–67, 73; cf. FC 20–22).[28] In *Otherwise Than Being* (35–39) the immediacy of the Other is developed in terms of a saying that is not absorbed in the *already said*. It is precisely the ability to give meaning to whatever is encountered in terms of the *already said* (a.k.a. the logos; a.k.a. the apophantic as, "a consecrating of 'this as this' or 'this as that' ") that constitutes consciousness and language in the mode of immanence.

This brings us to the second trauma to be undergone by the cogito. Not only does knowledge have limits that shatter all variations of the recollection/maieutics theme and require the self to be taught by Another if it would understand transcendence; transcendence, and, for that matter, teaching, is not at its heart a matter of knowing or understanding at all. For what refuses to be absorbed in the *already said* is not some unusual theme, a temporary anomaly, as it were, that requires a scientific revolution, a revision of the *already said* that makes possible its absorption, elsewhere called the reduction of the other to the same. Nor is it some permanent anomaly, a hyper-essence that always exceeds our *Wesensschau*-ability. Here the formula is quite simple: "Not *to be otherwise*, but *otherwise than being*" (OB 3). That is why ethics is not negative theology (OB 151). It is rather saying itself, which signifies transcendence by showing up "prior to anything said" in order to lead us "beyond the said" (OB 43, 38).

Hence the sustained polemic against the sites of thematization and adequation as the primary scene for philosophical reflection, a polemic expressed in such titles as "Is Ontology Fundamental?" (1951), "The Ruin of Representation" (1959), "Hermeneutics and Beyond" (1977), "Beyond Intentionality" (1983), and "Ethics as First Philosophy" (1984), but insistent throughout the entire corpus. The primacy of these sites is common to realism, to idealism, to phenomenology, and to hermeneutics, which Levinas lumps together under the title 'ontology.' Even where fallibilist and finitist motifs reduce adequation to a regulative ideal approximated in reflective equilibrium, 'ontology' signifies that being *is* what gives itself to thought to be adequately represented.[29] Thus "Truth can consist only in the exposition of being to itself. . . . That one could think being means, indeed, that the appearing of being belongs to its very movement of being, that its phenomenality is essential, and that being cannot do without consciousness, to which manifestation is made" (OB 61, 131). Or, in other words, Hegel was "absolutely" right when he claimed to be the *Vollendung* of philosophy.

With Levinas, by contrast, transcendence is a trauma to thought precisely because it is no longer a matter of cognition. The cogito, which proudly proclaims, "Ich bin der Geist der stets versteht [ ja, und auch erklärt]," is more radically humbled than by epistemic finitude. The Other is not a noema to which existence has been restored, not even a numinous one (TI 77). The Other is not an object to be intended and represented but a subject to be approached and welcomed, not an essence to be seen but a voice to be heard. "To hear the divine word does not amount to knowing an object" (TI 77). "The face speaks. The manifestation of the face is already discourse" (TI 66). Not disclosure but discourse![30]

Discourse or conversation, so understood, **wounds** the cogito by limiting its epistemic autonomy. But it **shatters** the cogito only when it goes beyond the domain of the epistemic, to its deepest meaning. Discourse is not constative communication, the sharing of apophansis. That is why the Other is not in the final analysis the alter ego, an intentional center alongside my own. The Other is the voice that calls me to responsibility, that asymmetrically commands from on high. Conversation is "an ethical relation." "To welcome the Other is to put in question my freedom" (TI 85; cf. TrO 353). The face of the Other is a voice that "puts the spontaneous freedom within us into question. It commands and judges it and brings it to its truth" (TI 51).[31] Here we move from the finitude of the understanding to the primacy of practical reason.[32] I have found it necessary, Levinas tells us, to deny representation in order to make room for responsibility. "Ethics is first philosophy," and the scene of meaning and truth is the one in which we are questioned, commanded, accused, and judged by the Other.

This is the meaning of the priority of the saying over the said in Levinas's later writings. To be addressed cannot be reduced to having a propositional content presented for one's assent or denial. First, the horizon of the "already said" is radically surprised, breached by a teaching that goes beyond recollection and maieutics; now the "said" as such is denied privilege of being the primal scene of meaning and truth.

We are frequently reminded that the ethical decentering of the self is more traumatic than the epistemic decentering that prepares for it and follows from it. Thus, "Subjection to the order that orders man, the *I*, to answer for the other is, perhaps, the **harsh name of love**. Love that is no longer what this compromised word of our literature and our hypocrisies expresses, but the very fact of the approach to the unique, and, consequently, to the absolutely *other*, **piercing** what merely shows itself" (EN 174, boldface added; cf. 104).

Levinas does not shy away from speaking of violence when describing our election to serve as hostage, substituted for the Other, placing us in a passivity more passive than all passivity. To be sure, responsibility is imposed on us with "a good violence" (OB 43). Because the Good "redeems the violence of its alterity" (OB 15, 123), we find our identity invaded by the Other, but without alienation (OB 112, 114–15, 118). Despite the gestation of the other in the same, which this responsibility for the other signifies," it is not a "slave's alienation" (OB 105).[33]

The formula is this: "if no one is good voluntarily, no one is enslaved to the Good" (OB 11, 138). Defying the self-evidences of ontology, responsibility is neither freedom nor alienation. "We are probably on the hither side of freedom and unfreedom" (OS 35). But even if it does not arise as alienation, responsibility arises in a heteronomy that Levinas continues to describe as a certain violence. What is this "trauma of transcendence," which denies to the self not only its role as the *arche* of knowing but also its role as *telos* of action?

Of the many ways in which Levinas describes this trauma, I will focus on only three modes of heteronomy, three ways in which the Other is the law of the same. First, my identity is compromised by the invasion of the Other into the inner sanctum of my selfhood.[34] Transcendence signifies the presence of "an alterity in me" a "having-the-other-in-one's skin." In this way "identity is inverted," and I find that "I exist through the other and for the other" and that "I am 'in myself' through the others" (OB 112–15).[35]

As Sartre so powerfully reminds us, I would like to be able to define myself, to establish my identity in a pure relation of myself to myself, and then, on the basis of an assured and autonomous identity, go out into the world and establish relations with others. Such relations, of course, will be accidental and external. I will still be my very self no matter what happens in relation to my wife, my kids, my colleagues, my students, and so forth. This is, of course, the ontology that underlies social contract liberalism.

As a trauma of identity, transcendence means that the Other is internally related to me. We find ourselves back at Hegel's notion of a relation "more like an identity than even the relation of faith or trust." I am who We are. Except that by virtue of the asymmetry of the relation we do not form a totality based on reciprocity. When in reflection I turn my intentional arrows back toward myself in order to recognize myself, to define myself, and to choose myself, in short, to say "I," I discover the Other already there between me and myself. And to make matters worse, it is not only my wife, my kids, my colleagues, and my students whom I find there. The winds blowing from that "more ancient volcano"[36] of which Derrida speaks have blown in the widow, the orphan, and the stranger as well, those whom I would just as soon not notice. There they sit, on opposite sides of my inner sanctum, perhaps, making clear by their mere presence that only as related to them, whether by irritation and indifference or by welcome and hospitality, can I be related to myself. This is not just breaking and entering. It is kidnapping. I have been taken hostage.[37]

This notion of being taken hostage, along with the notions of election and persecution, calls to our attention a second dimension of trauma. Along with my Identity, my Authority is decentered. I am called and questioned by the saying of the Other, assigned and accused, judged and found guilty. But none of these require my consent for their validity. Nor do I have any right of veto, and deep down I recognize this. As we say colloquially, I've been had. "The responsibility for the other can not have begun in my commitment, in my decision . . . the Good is not presented to freedom; it has chosen me before I have chosen it. No one is good voluntarily. We can see the formal structure of nonfreedom in a subjectivity which does not have time to choose the Good and thus is penetrated with its rays unbeknownst to itself" (OB 10–11; cf. 56–57). These are the rays of the Good, to be sure, but their mission is not to illuminate Being for Thought; it is rather to enable, or perhaps even compel, me to see the widow, the orphan, and the stranger as "the glory of transcendence" (OB 13; cf. 140–52).

Just as there is something prior to my horizons, prior to the "already said" that constitutes me as transcendental apperception, so there is something prior to my choice, consent, commitment. The neighbor is *"the first one on the scene"* (OB 86), not as a theme to be represented but as a command to be obeyed. Once again I arrive too late to be in charge. An authority has been set up whose presence I can resent, but whose validity I cannot deny. The Other as Most High is not only a source of teaching as revelation; this teaching is the law. "I am as it were ordered from the outside, traumatically commanded" (OB 87).

Finally (for the present), the trauma of transcendence is heteronomous intersubjectivity because the Other, to whom and for whom I find myself responsible, is not just a law that comes to me from outside (formal heteronomy) but a command that contradicts my *conatus essendi* (material heteronomy). Along with my Identity and my Authority, my Essence is rendered relative to something outside it, though already inside it.[38] "Beyond essence" does not merely signify the marginalization of theory as *Wesensschau*. It displaces the desires that are more basic to me than my beliefs. For "*Esse* is *interesse*. . . . Being's interest takes dramatic form in egoisms struggling with one another." The result of this conflict can be either war, as "the drama of the essence's interest," or the liberal, contractual peace of "calculation, mediation and politics . . . exchange and commerce." Without doubt, "Commerce is better than war," but because the standpoint of reciprocal egoism has not been transcended, "Transcendence is factitious and peace unstable." Essence must be constrained more radically than by "reciprocal limitation" (OB 4–5). For this reason responsibility is the continuous "break up" or "break out" of essence (OB 8, 12–14).

My *conatus essendi* is that self-assertion in which Nietzsche saw the anticipation of his own will to power. It is the other side of being, not being as that which gives itself to (human) thought to be grasped but being as the grasping that takes everything for itself. As the practical reduction of the other to the same, it is rebuked by the Good, which implies the reversal or inversion of my *conatus* (OB 70, 75, 95). This "superindividuation of the ego consists in being in itself, in its skin, without sharing the *conatus essendi* of all beings which are beings in themselves" (OB 118). The self-coincidence of myself with myself as the origin of my action is "undone by the other. . . . Already the position of the subject is a deposition, not a *conatus essendi*" (OB 127).

In other words, the call of the Other is a call from *eros* to *agape*. Described as assignation, election, persecution, hostage, substitution, expiation, accusation, and so forth, the "traumatizing blow" of this appeal "cannot be converted into an 'inward need' or a natural tendency. This response answers, but with no eroticism, to an absolutely heteronomous call" (OB 53). The *"for* of the-one-for-the-other . . . is a *for* of total gratuity, breaking with interest" (OB 96).

Responsibility is the "harsh name" for love of neighbor, love without eros, love without concupiscence (EN 103, 131, 149, 169, 186, 194, 216, 227–28).

In *Totality and Infinity*, Levinas does not speak this language. But *conatus* appears as the egoism of the psychism, which "lives from" its other in such modes as enjoyment and dwelling (see Sections IB and II). Because this egoism is a separation from the totality that is a necessary condition for hearing the language of the face, the self in conversation "cannot renounce the egoism of its existence; but the very fact of being in a conversation consists in recognizing in the Other a *right* over this egoism" (TI 40). The disinterestedness of desire for the infinite, by contrast with egoistic need, shows itself in gift, in generosity (TI 50).

In all these ways, both epistemic and ethical, Levinas portrays transcendence as the trauma of heteronomous intersubjectivity. But he is not doing philosophical theology, at least not primarily. For the *heteros*, the Thou, the Other, is my neighbor, the widow, the stranger, and the orphan, and not God. Still, Levinas insists that our only access to God is through the neighbor. "To posit the transcendent as stranger and poor one is to prohibit the metaphysical relation with God from being accomplished in ignorance of men and things. The dimension of the divine opens forth from the human face. . . . There can be no 'knowledge' of God separated from the relation with men. The Other is the very locus of metaphysical truth, and is indispensable for my relation with God" (TI 78).

In passages like these, it often sounds as if Levinas's God is as dependent on my neighbor as I am, as if the transcendence of God has been sacrificed to the glory of the face. Sorting out the ambiguities of Levinas's theology can remain a task for another day.[39] What is of interest here is Levinas's analysis of the structure of transcendence even if the Thou or the You of transcendence is not in the first instance (and perhaps never) God. For one thing, it is clearly not the structure of the causal/cosmological transcendence that emerges from the debate between theism and pantheism. For another, if we did not find otherwise than being (in Levinas's sense) and being otherwise (in a traditionally theistic sense) to be mutually exclusive but saw the former as the telos of the latter,[40] and if we were not skittish about a God behind the scenes who was our Prime Interlocutor, we could nevertheless think divine transcendence in Levinasian terms. We might speak of the teleological suspension of causal/cosmological transcendence in epistemic/ethical transcendence.

The use of a Kierkegaardian term here is not accidental, for my thesis is that this is precisely what happens in the Kierkegaardian authorship, taken as a whole. So here are five theses, possibly attributable to Kierkegaard, the difference being, of course, that the Other is now in the first instance God. But first, two observations about the God relation in Kierkegaard. First, the Kierkegaardian self is as relational as the Levinasian self. His existential individualism is badly misunderstood if seen as a kind of Nietzschean loneliness. To be sure, he and his pseudonyms work tirelessly to reflect me as an individual out of immersion in the "they," the social order into which I have been "thrown," even, yea, especially if it be Christendom. But the point is not to leave me alone but alone—with God. *Coram Deo* is the sign of an essentially relational self. Second, the single-mindedness with which this task is pursued by such pseudonyms as Silentio and Climacus could leave the impression that God is the only Other that matters, that the neighbor has been forgotten; but that would happen only if we stop reading before we get to *Works of Love* and *Practice in Christianity*. As in Jesus' summary of the law as the commands to love God and neighbor, the Kierkegaardian self is essentially related, first to the divine Other and then, just as essentially, to the human Other.

FIRST THESIS: THE COGITO IS WOUNDED BY A CRUCIAL EPI-STEMIC HETERONOMY. It is especially in *Philosophical Fragments* that Climacus develops this theme by contrasting the Socratic thesis that knowledge is recollection with an alternative, which turns out to be divine revelation. The slave boy in the *Meno* needs help in getting the truth in front of himself. He cannot simply produce it. But when confronted by it, he has in and by himself the capacity to recognize it as the truth. This is why his knowledge counts as recollection and Socrates is only a midwife whose "teaching" is but maieutics.

In his thought experiment, Climacus argues that if the Christian's knowledge of the God-man is not to be simply another instance of recollection, it will be, not just because we cannot come up with this truth on our own, but because even when confronted by the truth we do not have "the condition," the capacity to recognize it as the truth. This must be given to us by another, whose teaching goes beyond maieutics and deserves to be called revelation just as our knowledge, on the hypothesis being explored, goes beyond recollection and is properly called faith. Faith is not a lower stage on the divided line (*pistis, doxa*) but a knowing beyond the power of the autonomous cogito. This is precisely the structure of what Levinas calls the immediacy of the face, of that which gives itself to our understanding καθ αὐτό, as a signification for which none of our horizons is the condition of possibility.[41] But this time it is God (incarnate) who is transcendent.

SECOND THESIS: THE COGITO IS SHATTERED BY HAVING ITS KNOWING TELEOLOGICALLY SUSPENDED IN OBLIGATION. As with Levinas, the self as intentionality in quest of adequation, even in its receptiveness to revelation, is not obliterated; but it is subordinated to responsibility. What we could call a primacy of practical reason, remembering that reason is no longer autonomous but receptive beyond its dependence on sensibility, decenters the theoretical, apophantic project as a whole. It is not just that my truths are relative to my capacities, nor that the most important truth is beyond my capacity altogether, but the whole domain of truth is relativized to obedience in order that it may be put in the service of love.

This is already clear in *Fear and Trembling*. By a simple stipulation at the outset, Johannes de Silentio removes the question of faith from the divided line and questions about doubt and certainty, opinion and knowledge. "[Abraham] *knew* it was God the Almighty who was testing him" (FT 22, emphasis added). God is the voice who commands, not a theme to be represented nor an hypothesis to be confirmed, and the task of faith is that of an obedience unlimited by the interests that constitute my essence, that is, by the horizons of either my personal preference or my society's standards (*Sittlichkeit, Saedelighed,* our collective *conatus essendi*). When Silentio insists that he does not share Abraham's faith, it is not because he lacks Abraham's certainty but because he lacks Abraham's courage (FT 33–34, 48–49).

The other Johannes, Climacus, is in full agreement. In portraying the God-man as the distinctively Christian paradox, he looks for a thought that human thought cannot think, an unknown or an Other that is "absolutely different." But such a difference cannot be found in the ontological, causal/cosmological order of creation. For "if the god is to be absolutely different from a human being this can have its basis not in that which man owes to the god (for to that extent they are akin) but in that which he owes to himself, or in that which he himself has committed. What, then, is the [absolute] difference? Indeed, what else but sin, since the difference, the absolute difference, must have been caused by the individual himself" (PF 46–47). Absolute Difference, Absolute Paradox, in a word, transcendence, is due not to creation but to the fall, not to ontological distance but to moral disobedience. That is why the unhappy relation to the Absolute Paradox is not doubt or uncertainty but offense (PF 49–54). It is also why the happy relation to the Absolute Paradox, faith, is not *Vorstellung* in contrast to *Begriff,* which would leave us in the realm of theory and speculation, but has to be described in terms of "*conversion,*" "*repentance,*" and "*rebirth*" (PF 18–19). Correspondingly, it is why the teacher, who goes beyond maieutics, must also be "*savior,*" "*deliverer,*" and "*reconciler*" (PF 17).

Climacus pursues this analysis in *Concluding Unscientific Postscript* in the contrast between objectivity and subjectivity, the what of faith and the how of faith. Propositional content as the objectivity of the what of faith is not repudiated, as if it makes no difference what we believe; but it is subordinated to subjectivity and the how. In our relation to the Eternal, even within the immanence of Religiousness A, the epistemic adequacy of our representations is secondary to the moral adequacy of our response. Socratic piety does not go beyond recollection to epistemic heteronomy. But even in the religion of epistemic immanence there is a genuine transcendence insofar as (1) in Religiousness A I know my relation to the Eternal to involve total, qualitative guilt (CUP I, 525–55), and (2) I understand that the task of simultaneously relating absolutely to the Absolute and relatively to the relative is a transcognitive and never completed task (CUP 387, 407, 414, 422, 431).

N.B. In *Fragments,* Socrates represents the immanence of recollection. In *Postscript,* without ceasing to stand for recollection as distinct from revelation, he signifies the transcendence that is possible in that domain when attention is shifted from knowledge to action at its deepest level. It is this transcendence that enables Socrates to know an obligation that comes to him from beyond both his personal *conatus essendi* and the corporate *conatus* of the Athenian established order. Neither the I nor the We is the highest norm for his life (and death) but something beyond both.

The epistemic transcendence that enters with Christian revelation and Religiousness B presupposes as its proper scene the moral transcendence that is already to be found in Socrates. The famous definition of faith in terms of truth as subjectivity comes long before we get to the Christian paradox: "An objective uncertainty, held fast through appropriation with the most passionate inwardness" (CUP 203–204). Transcendence signifies the how of appropriation, and the first instance is Socrates.

When we get to *Works of Love* we find Kierkegaard thematizing the *Aufhebung* of knowing in doing in his own name. He imagines someone asking the apostle Paul a typically ontological "what is" question, What is love? "Paul answers, 'It is the fulfilling of the Law.' . . . Paul does not become involved with the questioner . . . with his answer he immediately points the direction and gives the impetus to act accordingly." There is something Socratic about this strategy, but it is also "essentially Christian," for

> the essentially Christian, which is not related to knowing but to acting, has the singular characteristic of answering and by means of the answer imprisoning everyone in the task. . . . The questioner [whether sophists questioning Socrates or Pharisees questioning Jesus] did indeed receive an answer, but in addition to the answer he in one sense learned too much. He received an imprisoning answer that . . . with divine authority grasped the questioner and placed him under the obligation to do accordingly; whereas the questioner perhaps wished only to remain at the protracted distance of curiosity or inquisitiveness or definitions from himself and from—*doing the truth*." (WL 96, emphasis added)[42]

As if the first two traumas were not enough, we find that once representation has been displaced by responsibility, the task that defines our new locale is itself a series of traumas, including the three Levinasian traumas to our identity, our authority, and our essence.

THIRD THESIS: MY IDENTITY IS SO DEEPLY RELATIONAL THAT MY RELATION TO MYSELF IS ALWAYS MEDIATED BY MY RELATION TO GOD. Kierkegaard never tires of telling us that God is the middle term between me and my neighbor. But it turns out that God is also the middle term between me and myself. It is Anti-Climacus who insists most vigorously that my identity is not independent of my God relation. Like Silentio and Climacus he removes the question of faith from the purely theoretical realm. The real alternative to faith is not doubt but despair and offense. It is thus a matter "of personality (the single individual) and the ethical" (PC 81, n. 18).[43] More specifically, it is a matter of sin and forgiveness (SUD, part 2), and the proper expression of faith is worship (SUD 129).

But the God relation, whether it be one of faith or of offense and despair, is internal to my very identity. This is because the self is "a relation that relates itself to itself and in relating itself to itself relates to another" (SUD 13–14). Had Hegel used such a formula, the point would have been that the other is in fact oneself, even if this is not immediately obvious. For Anti-Climacus, in agreement with Levinas, the point is just the opposite. I have no relation to myself unmediated by my relation to an Other who is decidedly not myself.

Faith gets defined in terms of this mediated self-relation: "in relating itself to itself and in willing to be itself, the self rests transparently in the power that established it" (SUD 49; cf. 82). This power is regularly identified as God, and this transparent rest is not easily won. For God is not only the one on whom I am ontologically dependent, but also the one from whom in sin I am morally estranged. Thus willing to be myself means the welcoming of an Other before whom and to whom I am not only responsible but already irresponsible; it means accepting the forgiveness of sins. God's transcendence is this ethical distance, whose overcoming is not insight, nor even the courage of which Silentio speaks (FT 33, 49), but "humble courage" (SUD 78, 85). For it involves "being helped by a superior" that the will to autonomy can experience only as "humiliation" (SUD 71).[44]

Of course, such faith is by no means inevitable. But its absence, offended despair, is just as much a mediated self-relation as is faith. Because the very structure of selfhood involves the God relation, because God is always already there between me and myself, whether that presence is welcome or not, my identity as pure self-relation, self-choice, self-definition has been compromised beyond recovery.

FOURTH THESIS: THE GOD I ENCOUNTER IN HIDDEN IN-WARDNESS SENDS ME BACK INTO THE WORLD WITH THE COM-MAND TO LOVE MY NEIGHBOR. All fears that by making the God rela-tion first, that by reflecting the individual out of the crowd and the present age so as to be alone—*coram Deo*—the human Other would be left in the lurch are removed by the First Series of *Works of Love*. It consists of meditations on commanded love. A long chapter is devoted to analysis of the commandment You shall love your neighbor as yourself. It is followed three further chapters on neighbor love as a categorical imperative: "Love Is a Matter of Conscience" (1 Tim. 1:15), "Our Duty to Love the People We See" (1 John 4:20), and "Our Duty to Remain in Love's Debt to One Another" (Rom. 13:8). The spiritual life begins, to be sure, alone with God in hidden inwardness; but that very God sends me back out to love my neighbor. "Shut your door and pray to God—Because God is surely the highest . . . when you open the door that you shut in order to pray to God and go out the very first person you meet is the neighbor, whom you *shall* love" (WL 51).

Because he is writing to an audience that thinks of itself as Christian, he speaks of commanded love as Christian. But he reminds us that it is not a Christian invention, but comes to us from Judaism. Whether on the lips of Moses or Jesus, it is "at the boundary where human language halts and courage fails" that the command arises, that "revelation breaks forth with divine origination and proclaims what is not difficult to understand in the sense of profundity or human parallels but which did not arise in any human being's heart." We are beyond recollection, which is perhaps why love "had existed also in paganism, but this obligation to love is a change of eternity—and everything has become new" (WL 24–25). As with Levinas, there is a Hebrew challenge to Hellenism; Moses and Jesus are surely Jews, and if Paul is already jewgreek, he is far more Jew than Greek.

It goes without saying that the command of God does not require my consent for its validity (WL 115). We have here a full-fledged moral heteronomy in its formal mode. The law comes to me from without. One indication of this is the nature of the language in which the command occurs. "The divine authority of the Gospel does not speak to one person about another . . . no, when the Gospel speaks, it speaks to the single individual. It does not speak *about* us human beings, but speaks *to* us human beings" (WL 14). We all say "I," but "the sign of maturity and the devotion of the eternal is to will to understand that this *I* has no significance unless it becomes the *you* to whom eternity incessantly speaks and says: *You* shall, *you* shall, *you* shall" (WL 90).

Another indication of the transcendent source of obligation, in this passage and countless others, is the reference to eternity as its origin. Where Levinas says Infinity, Kierkegaard says Eternity. Commanded love must be "consciously grounded upon the eternal," must have "undergone the change of eternity by having become a duty" (WL 31–32; cf. 37–42). But human existence, for Kierkegaard, is radically temporal. Eternity is precisely what I am not. Nor are We the Eternal, for the Present Age, the Crowd, the Established Order (in which Hegel is all too willing to find the Eternal), is just as deeply embedded in becoming as the individual. Eternity is a transcendent source of the command to love my neighbor. Neither in obedience nor in disobedience do I reduce this Other to the Same. I am addressed, accused, commanded.

FIFTH THESIS: COMMANDED LOVE REQUIRES THE REPLACEMENT OF SELF-LOVE WITH SELF-DENIAL. In *Works of Love*, Kierkegaard contrasts commanded love with celebrated love, the erotic love and friendship praised by the poets. These latter he classifies as self-love. It is because it is the overcoming of this egoism that commanded love is self-denial (WL 4, 52–56, 84, 113, 119, etc.), not because it is a form of self-hatred.[45] In fact, Kierkegaard insists that learning to love my neighbor as myself and learning properly to love myself are two sides of the same coin (WL 18, 22–23, 107).

Still, the heteronomy of this command is a trauma to my natural self-love, and as with Levinas the heteronomy is material or substantive and not merely formal. The command does not merely come from without; it runs counter to my inclinations (WL 49–50, 143), which rather are to be themselves changed. My duty is to find the neighbor lovable despite obvious imperfections. To use a culinary metaphor, it is one thing to cultivate a discriminating taste. "It is something else not merely to be able to eat the plainer foods but to be able to find this plainer food to be the most exquisite, because the task is not to develop one's fastidiousness but *to transform oneself and one's taste*" (WL 158, emphasis added).

Another way to put this is to say that my *conatus essendi*, which places me at the center and finds lovable all and only those who support my fundamental project, is to be broken up. Nor is it enough to leave my *conatus* intact and mitigate the selfishness it represents by contracting reciprocal relations: "I'll scratch your back if you'll scratch mine." For neighbor love is unconditional (WL 49, 117); it signifies an infinite debt beyond calculation (WL 102, 105, 132, 176–78, 184, 187) and is not a matter of reciprocity (WL 34, 39).

That neighbor love cannot be thought in terms of reciprocity is seen from two directions. First, the selfish self-love that is to be overcome can be collective. "We" can be the Same that reduces the Other to ourselves just as easily as "I" can be the self-centered center of the universe, whether "we" are lovers, family, gender, class, race, or nation (WL 56, 119, 123–24). Kierkegaard would have us see the impiety of that famous prayer "Dear Lord, bless me and my wife, and our two kids. Us four, no more. Amen." Second, and this may be the most traumatic trauma of all, my enemy is also my neighbor, whom I am commanded to love (WL 19, 67–68).

It is because the command of neighbor love is such a shattering blow to self-love, whether personal or collective, that it lacks two characteristics of celebrated love. Erotic love and friendship are preferential. I prefer this one over that one as my beloved or my friend. The other must have a certain "sex appeal," either literally or metaphorically, for me to be motivated toward erotic love or friendship; and this attraction must be mutual if the relation, essentially reciprocal, is to become actual. Although it seems crude to put it this way, there is always an implicit cost-benefit analysis in the celebrated loves, for if we find that we are not getting enough out of the relation we do not enter in in the first place, or we get out, in one way or another.

Erotic love and friendship are also spontaneous, on Kierkegaard's analysis. The primary meaning here is simply that celebrated loves arise from our natural inclinations; neighbor love constrains those inclinations, and therefore must be commanded. Like Levinas, Kierkegaard thinks Kant is just kidding himself when he says we command ourselves.

But there is a second sense in which neighbor love is not spontaneous for Kierkegaard, and here his difference with Levinas resurfaces. The fact that the God relation is first now becomes a difference that makes a difference. The opening prayer of *Works of Love* begins like this: "How could one speak properly about love if you were forgotten, you God of love, *source of all love in heaven and on earth*; you who spared nothing but in love gave everything; you who are love, so that one who loves is what he is only by being in you!" (WL 3, emphasis added). To speak of God as the source of all love seems to mean more that the neighbor love begins with the divine command. While the command might be a motivator, it is not an enabler. But just to the degree that, as Levinas and Kierkegaard agree, our essence is self-interest, if self-love is not merely to be condemned but transformed, teleologically suspended in neighbor love, it looks as if we need two things from beyond ourselves: the command to point us in the right direction and the capacity to obey the command. In theological language, we need law and grace. Thus Kierkegaard writes, "Suppose a person in all sincerity, humanly speaking, loves God—ah, but God has loved him first; God is an eternity ahead" (WL 101–102). This love is as anarchic and diachronous as the command. It is the grace of enabling love.[46]

For Kierkegaard it is divine grace that enables me to welcome the invasion of the Other into my identity, my authority, and my essence as self-interest. If this theme is not altogether missing in Levinas, it is certainly not very conspicuous. Perhaps it is because in the absence of a world behind the scenes and a God who is my First Interlocutor, there cannot be a God who is First Lover. Be that as it may, it is clear that Levinas is worried about any reciprocity between I and You, between Same and Other, lest it compromise the authority of the Other's voice, whose command comes from on high. This is a legitimate concern, to which we should ask Kierkegaard to reply.

To begin with, there is undoubtedly a certain reciprocity whenever and to whatever degree I love God. For God already loves me. Does this compromise divine transcendence? It would seem that in none of the five traumas we have explored is this the case. (1) It will still be the case that there is a knowing for which my capacities and horizons are not the condition of possibility, for which revelation and receptivity replace recollection. The cogito is deprived of its theoretical autonomy. Its horizons are not the measure of the real.

(2) It will still be the case that the primary scene on which the narrative of my life is played out will not be theory but practice, not speculation (mirroring) but imitation (mimesis), not representation but response and responsibility. The crucial question about me will still not be How much did he know? but How much did he love?, not How much did he understand? but How much did he undergo?, not How much truth did he gather into his transcendental unity of apperception? but How far was he willing to be dispersed and decentered in love for God and neighbor?

(3) It will still be the case that before I can relate to God in love, I will have to relate myself to myself via a middle term that is the God who has already both commanded me to love and loved me with an everlasting love. The voice of God, in choosing me before I choose God, will still be an election that gives me a uniqueness "without identity," as Levinas puts it (OB 57); for my identity will emerge only in my response to this prior uniqueness of a responsibility that cannot be transferred to anyone else.[47] The Welcome that in welcoming me requires that I welcome the widow, the orphan, and the stranger makes them

as well as itself essential to my identity. My self-relation is doubly mediated by the God and the neighbor who are on the scene of my inwardness before I arrive.

(4) It will still be the case that my moral autonomy is shattered by a command that comes from without. As every parent and every child knows, commands that issue from a loving authority do not thereby become self-legislation and lose the sting of heteronomy. The illusion of childhood, which is also the fantasy of the Enlightenment, is that on the far side of adolescence we can become fully autonomous. If, as Kierkegaard assumes, the Other who commands us from on high also loves us with an amazing grace, this is no comfort to that illusion and that fantasy. The point of calling God Father has nothing to do with gender and everything to do with recognizing that love and authority are not mutually exclusive. This is why faith, in Kierkegaard's writings, is inseparable from the possibility of offense.

(5) It will still be the case that moral heteronomy will be material and not just formal; the content of the commandment goes against my self-love precisely in its insistence that I love God and neighbor. This double decentering is what Levinas calls "an inversion of the *conatus* of *esse*" (OB 75). It is not clear whether the trauma involved in this inversion is experienced more deeply in resisting the requirement or in trying to comply with it.

Like Levinas, Kierkegaard finds transcendence in heteronomous, unconditional responsibility. The height that separates us from the God whose command puts in question our identity, our authority, and our essence becomes an utter abyss of absolute difference through sin, our refusal to comply. Before transcendence I am not only commanded but accused and condemned. Because God is love and only then the command to love, God wills reconciliation. Whenever the temptation to offense is overcome and the forgiveness of sins is received in faith, a certain reciprocity is achieved, a mutual love.

But the reciprocity of reconciliation need not frighten Levinas. Although each loves the other, the relation is anything but symmetrical. Nor does the reciprocity render responsibility conditional. I cannot make obedience conditional, as if to say, "I will (try to) love my neighbor if you will love me in return," for God already loves me.

We might put it this way: Silentio frames *Fear and Trembling* with the claim that the faith of Abraham is the task of a lifetime (FT 6–7, 121–23). Now we can see that it is as much the task of a lifetime in the mode of reconciliation as in the mode of obedience, in relation to grace as in relation to law. There it is a matter of obedience to a command that evokes fear and trembling. The command of neighbor love in *Works of Love* is at least as traumatic, not in evoking the same horror but in the fact that I cannot evade its sternness with the assurance that God didn't let Abraham go through with it after all and, in any case, does not require of me what was asked of Abraham. But here Kierkegaard also wants to thematize reconciliation, bridging the abyss opened up by sin. However, the bridge of reconciliation does not diminish the height of authority. The desire for reconciliation does not arise from my *conatus essendi*, free from the possibility of offense. Reconciliation requires (1) that I acknowledge the legitimacy of the divine authority, (2) that I acknowledge my fault in failing to love as I have been commanded, and (3) that I accept forgiveness, leaving me deeply indebted to the one who forgives. Reconciliation is grace, but not cheap grace. That is why Kierkegaard reminds us that it is not so much we who are running around looking for reconciliation. "It is indeed God in heaven who through the apostle says, 'Be reconciled'; it is not human beings who say to God, 'Forgive us'" (WL 336). Similarly, in *Sickness unto Death*, Anti-Climacus notes the possibility of offense at the forgiveness of sin and counters this with the command "Thou shalt believe in the forgiveness of sins" (SUD 115).

Reconciliation also is commanded! If we understand this we will understand how faith is the task of a lifetime in relation to grace as well as to law. We will realize that just as we can never say we have completed the task of loving our neighbor, so we have never completed the task of being reconciled to God. In reconciliation there is reciprocity. And there is rest. "COME HERE TO ME, ALL YOU WHO LABOR AND ARE BURDENED, AND I WILL GIVE YOU REST" (PC 11, 16, 23). But neither the reciprocity nor the rest of reconciliation compromises responsibility. The task of loving my neighbor and the task of being reconciled to God remain uncompleted. Transcendence is not transcended.

# Transcendence, Heteronomy, and the Birth of the Responsible Self

*The shattered cogito: this could be the emblematic title of a tradition, one less continuous perhaps than that of the cogito, but one whose virulence culminates with Nietzsche, making him the privileged adversary of Descartes.*[1]

In his Gifford Lectures, published as *Oneself as Another,* Paul Ricoeur makes it clear that he will not try to put this Humpty Dumpty back together again. He seeks rather to develop a "hermeneutics of the self [that] is placed at an equal distance from the apology of the cogito and from its overthrow . . . at an equal distance from the cogito exalted by Descartes and from the cogito that Nietzsche proclaimed forfeit" (OA 4 and 23). The "arduous detours" of this hermeneutics pass through a series of questions. "Who is speaking of what? Who does what? About whom and about what does one construct a narrative? Who is morally responsible for what? These are but so many different ways in which 'who?' is stated" (OA 19).

It is a similar project that Cal Schrag undertakes in his Ryle Lectures, *The Self after Postmodernity.*[2] He is quite specific about the nature of the cogito that has had such a great fall. It is "a sovereign and monarchical self, at once self-sufficient and self-assured, finding metaphysical comfort in a doctrine of an immutable and indivisible self-identity" (SAP 27). It is "a self-identical monad, mute and self-enclosed, changeless and secured prior to the events of speaking

. . . a fixed, underlying substratum . . . a prelinguistic, zero-point center of consciousness" (SAP 33).

Like Ricoeur and Jean-Luc Nancy,[3] Schrag thinks that "a jettisoning of the self understood in these senses does not entail a jettisoning of every sense of self . . . a new self emerges, like the phoenix arising from its ashes" (SAP 9). And, like Ricoeur and Nancy, he thinks this new, emergent self, at once more plausible philosophically and more familiar experientially, is best understood in terms of Who questions rather than What questions, as if the self were a nature or an essence (SAP 4, 12–13).

Schrag's self is doubly emergent. It emerges theoretically in the aftermath of the critiques that have shattered the cogito. But it emerges experientially as well. The self's identity is not a fact or a given prior to experience but a process worked out in experience (SAP 26, 37). It has a narrative character (SAP 19–28). Its unity is a matter of convergence without coincidence, or, in Ricoeurean language, it is a matter of *ipse* identity rather than *idem* identity (SAP 33–35). In Rylean language, selfhood is a task word rather than an achievement word.[4]

In speaking of the self "after postmodernity," Schrag might seem to suggest that he simply wants to leave postmodernity behind, that he simply identifies it with Nietzsche's replacement of the cogito with the will to power in its amoral diversity. So we are not surprised to find a critique of Lyotard as giving too extreme an account of the dispersal of the self in the plurality of its language games (SAP 28–35) and of Foucault as reducing ethics to aesthetics (SAP 68–71). But Schrag finds Derrida to be in important respects an ally and quotes two passages as illuminating his own project. In one of them Derrida says, "I don't destroy the subject. I situate it. That is to say, I believe that at a certain level both of experience and scientific discourse one cannot get along without the notion of the subject. It is a question of knowing where it comes from and how it functions."[5] It is such a view of the self that Schrag articulates in terms of narrative convergence as a task rather than preestablished coincidence as a guarantee prior to experience.

Derrida affirms the narrative concept of the self as the "common concept" of "autobiographical anamnesis" that "presupposes *identification*. And precisely not identity. No, an identity is never given, received, or attained; only the interminable and indefinitely phantasmatic process of identification endures. Whatever the story of a return to oneself . . . no matter what an odyssey or bildungsroman it might be . . . it is always *imagined* that the one who writes should know how to say *I*." It is just here that he radicalizes the concept of a narrative self. "It is necessary to know already in what language *I* is expressed, and I *am* expressed. Here we are thinking of the *I think*, as well as the grammatical or linguistical *I*, of the *me* or *us* in their identificatory status as it is sculpted by cultural, symbolic, and sociocultural figures . . . the *I* of the kind of anamnesis called autobiographical . . . is produced and uttered in different ways depending on the language in question. It never precedes them; therefore it is not independent of language in general."[6] This is an example of what Derrida means when he says of the subject, "I situate it."

The second citation is from Derrida's answer to Nancy's question "Who comes after the subject?" After affirming the significance of the Who? form of the question, he says, "I would add something that remains required by both the definitions of the classical subject and by these later nonclassical motifs, namely a certain responsibility. The singularity of the 'who' is not the individuality of a thing that would be identical with itself, it is not an atom. It is a singularity that dislocates or divides itself in gathering itself to answer to the other, whose call somehow precedes its own identification with itself."[7]

Here it is not just language in general but the call of the Other that precedes the subject. Schrag notes and welcomes this Levinasian turn in Derrida's thought. It has seemed to many that postmodernism in one or another of its modes has undermined the possibility not only of moral theory in familiar forms but also of the responsible self itself.[8] Among the French poststructuralists, none has sought more assiduously than Derrida to undermine this claim, to show that the shattering of the cogito is not the end of obligation. It is precisely this dimension of Derrida's thought to which Schrag appeals. For all three of the schemes he employs in seeking, with Ricoeur, to locate the self between Descartes and Nietzsche require a responsible self. In his critique of the subordination of ethics to aesthetics he finds in Nietzsche and Foucault, he reaffirms Kierkegaard's three existence spheres: the aesthetic, the ethical, and the religious. Over against Weber and Habermas, who reduce the culture spheres to science, morality, and art, he reaffirms religion as a culture sphere.[9] And in asking who the self is, he replies by exploring the four-dimensional self in discourse, in action, in community, and in transcendence. Each of these grids calls for a self who is responsible in relation to the Other. In fact, each one calls for an account of the relation between the religiously responsible self and the morally responsible self. In Schrag's view, some forms of religion and morality may be so tied to the cogito that they perish with its shattering, but not religion or morality as such.

Derrida's reply to Nancy is even more Levinasian than the reference to "a certain responsibility" reveals. In a long parenthesis immediately preceding it, he speaks of the self's " 'yes, yes' that answers before even being able to formulate a question, that is *responsible without autonomy*."[10] This passage recalls another very Levinasian challenge by Derrida to the autonomous self:

> Language has started without us, in us and before us. This is what theology calls God. . . . Having come from the past, language before language, a past that was never present and yet remains unforgettable—this 'it is necessary' [to speak] thus seems to beckon toward the event of an order or of a promise that does not belong to what one currently calls history. . . . Order or promise, this injunction commits (me), in a rigorously asymmetrical manner, even before I have been able to say *I*, to sign such a *provocation* in order to reappropriate it for myself and restore the symmetry. That is no way

mitigates my responsibility; on the contrary. There would be no responsibility without this *prior coming* (*prévenance*) of the trace, or if autonomy were first or absolute. Autonomy itself would not be possible, nor would respect for the law (sole 'cause' of this respect) in the strictly Kantian meaning of these words.[11]

For Derrida in his Levinasian mode, heteronomy is prior to autonomy and is the condition for the possibility of whatever autonomy is possible for the self I am! And this autonomy consists, not in self-legislation but in agreeing with and thus appropriating a saying prior to my own self-consciousness! Whenever I first say I, it has already been spoken, I have already been laid claim to!

Schrag also challenges the autonomy of the cogito and locates the self as the who of action "*between* autonomy and heteronomy" (SAP 59). But because he assimilates this dyad with that of acting/suffering and active voice/passive voice, he can only deny that his emerging self is "a self caught within the constraints of heteronomy, determined by forces acting upon it" (SAP 59). He denies both autonomy and heteronomy.

Derrida's is the more radical critique of the autonomy of the "modern" self, for in denying autonomy he affirms a certain heteronomy. For him the question of heteronomy is not that of forces before which the self is passive (though he doesn't deny these); it is rather the question of a voice before which the self is responsible. It is moral autonomy, rather than ontological autonomy, that needs to be teleologically suspended, *aufgehoben*, recontextualized, relativized in a prior moral heteronomy. It is significant that Derrida makes this point with reference to "what theology calls God," to language that is prior to the who of discourse, the who of action, and the who of community. With (more than) a little help from Levinas, Derrida brings us to the who of transcendence.

* * *

I want to explore this heteronomy as the transcendence that simultaneously shatters the cogito and creates the responsible self. I believe Schrag needs it to carry out his project and that, while it is not explicit in his discussion of autonomy and heteronomy, it is implicit in the way he draws on both Levinas and Kierkegaard in developing his own argument.[12]

Accordingly, it is to these two thinkers I turn, first of all to a 1970 essay of Levinas's entitled "No Identity," which discusses heteronomous transcendence not only in relation to the responsible self but also in relation to the question of the self-identity. It begins with a quotation from the Babylonian Talmud, "If I do not answer for myself, who will answer for me? But if I answer only for myself, am I still myself?" (NI 141). The first question, in agreement with Ricoeur, Derrida, and Schrag, reminds us that the self must remain on the scene and not simply disappear. The second question reminds us that the self is not "a sovereign and monarchical self, at once self-sufficient and self-assured, finding metaphysical comfort in a doctrine of an immutable and indivisible self-identity."[13] I am essentially relative and am myself only in and through my relation to an Other to whom or for whom I am answerable. But in that answerability I am myself. So we know from the outset that the title, "No Identity," does not signify the simple disappearance of the self. It is not the denial of any identity whatever, but of the monadic, atomic identity that is prior to relation and thus prior to responsibility.

Levinas's point of departure is the "end of humanism" and "death of man" slogans of structuralist human sciences, "the apocalyptic ideas or slogans of intellectual high society" that "impose themselves with the tyranny of the last word, but become available to anyone and cheapened" (NI 141). This charge of dogmatic fadishness doesn't sound especially friendly, but Levinas does not wish to dismiss these ideas. He rather affirms the "methodological" truth of human sciences "distrustful of an ego that hearkens to itself and feels itself but remains defenseless against the illusions of its class or the phantasms of its latent neurosis" (NI 141). We can't escape the insights of Marx and Freud. They lead to what we might call a political rather than a purely epistemic critique of

> the legislative sovereignty of the transcendental consciousness. . . . [D]o not the contradictions that rend the rational world, allegedly issued from transcendental legislation, ruin the identity of the subjective? That an action could be obstructed by the technology destined to render it efficacious and easy . . . that a politics and an administration guided by the humanist ideal maintain the exploitation of man by man and war—these are singular inversions of rational projects, disqualifying human causality, and thus transcendental subjectivity understood as spontaneity and act also. Everything comes to pass as though the ego, the identity par excellence from which every identifiable identity would derive, were wanting with regard to itself, did not succeed in coinciding with itself. (NI 142)

So ringing is Levinas's endorsement of the apocalyptic slogans of structuralism that he favorably quotes Blanchot's anti-humanism: "To speak nobly of the human in man, to conceive the humanity in man, is to quickly come to a discourse that is untenable and undeniably more repugnant than all the nihilist vulgarities" (NI 141–42). At this point Levinas sounds like the assistant professor who has just assumed the self-appointed role as campus terrorist.

Having paid attention to the opening talmudic quotation, we are not surprised by the "Yet" with which Levinas signals that he does not swallow the end of humanism hook, line, and Saussure, or, if you prefer, Levi-Strauss, Lacan, and Foucault. In their structuralist mode, the human sciences are "the preemption of certain significations" (NI 142). Appropriately suspicious, with Marx and Freud, of a putative rationality blind to its own blindnesses, they are blind to their own positivist prejudices in seeking to imitate the objectivism of mathematical physics. Thus they eliminate the subject and inwardness (a very Kierkegaardian term to which Levinas is not at all allergic) altogether. "The inwardness of the self-identical ego is dissolved into the totality which is without recesses or secrets. The whole of the human is outside. That can pass for a very firm formulation of materialism" (NI 142).

With this last remark Levinas calls our attention to the affinities between the philosophical behaviorism and eliminative materialism of Anglo-American philosophy of mind and French-structuralist anti-humanism.[14] Levinas agrees with all these materialisms when they say, "Identity seems to be not strictly inward. *I is an other.*" But he refuses to draw the conclusion they draw, that meaning "would have to be sought in a world that does not bear human traces" (NI 143).

Ceding to its critics the self-sufficient ego always able to return to itself enriched in its *idem* identity by the loot it brings back from its excursions into the world,[15] Levinas nevertheless seeks to retain a certain inwardness, an "impossible inwardness . . . an impossibility we learn of neither from metaphysics nor from the end of metaphysics. There is a divergency between the ego and the self, an impossible recurrence, and impossible identity. No one can remain in himself: the humanity of man, subjectivity, is a responsibility for the others, an extreme vulnerability. The return to the self becomes an interminable detour" (NI 149). In this inwardness we have what Schrag is looking for, a self that has not disappeared before the assaults of Nietzsche and Heidegger, structuralism and poststructuralism, behaviorism and eliminative materialism, but that, on the other hand, is not yet there either. It is emerging, becoming, a process or rather a task not yet completed. It is "an ego ceaselessly missing itself" (NI 149).

How does Levinas argue for this inwardness, this *ipse* identity, this "non-coincidence of the identical" (NI 149)? He does this by denying primacy and ultimacy to questions about free action in the causal sphere, about "making the best of a bad situation" (NI 145). There are three presuppositions to such freedom. First, reference to a bad situation implies that there are forces that oppose me or impose themselves on me. I can affirm myself only by seeking to overcome or at least to manage these. The other two presuppositions concern that by which the will, as practical reason, is guided as it seeks to make the best of a bad situation. One of these is its own interests, its *conatus essendi*, in whose service it seeks to overcome or at least to manage the opposing and imposing forces. The other is that by which the will is guided in seeking its own ends, its representations. The self in question here "delivers itself over to freedom, which is always correlative with an intentionality" (NI 145).[16]

Levinas does not deny this dimension of our lives, nor offer us a new theory of how it works. His description blends together Aristotle's theory of practical reason with Heidegger's analysis of the link between representation and the will to power. Rather, he relativizes free action by recontextualizing it in a horizon whose fundamental fact it is not. That fundamental fact he here calls vulnerability, and it is in terms of this concept that he makes his signature gesture, the teleological suspension of freedom in responsibility.

It is obvious that this vulnerability cannot signify our weakness in the face of causal forces, whether external or internal.[17] For the purpose of this notion is to decenter the stage on which the battles of freedom in that sense are fought. Levinas asks rhetorically, "Does human causality correspond with the meaning of subjectivity . . . does free action answer to subjectivity's vocation?" (NI 145). In a phrase Levinas never tires of using, he calls this vulnerability a passivity "more passive than every passivity" (NI 146). The paradox of this phrase can be eliminated by speaking of a passivity more passive than every causal passivity, for Levinas is explicit that he is not speaking about the causal "openness of every object to all others" (NI 145) as described in Kant's third analogy of experience. This openness "cannot be interpreted as a simple exposedness to being affected by causes. . . . The impotency or humility of [this] 'suffering' is on the hither side of the passivity of undergoing. . . . In vulnerability there lies a *relationship with the other* which causality does not exhaust" (NI 146).

We are fully prepared for Levinas to develop this trans-causal vulnerability in terms of inwardness, especially after he reminds us of the *Aufhebung* of freedom in responsibility by saying that "where the other is from the first under my responsibility, 'something' has overflowed my freely taken decisions, has slipped into me, *unbeknownst to me,* thus alienating my identity" (NI 145).[18]

But we are not at all prepared to hear the openness of vulnerability described as "the denuding of the skin exposed to wounds and outrage . . . the aptitude, which every being in its 'natural pride' would be ashamed to admit, 'to be beaten,' 'to receive blows.' 'He offered his cheek to the smiters and was filled with shame,' says, admirably, a prophetic text" (NI 146).[19] Levinas describes this all too physical vulnerability all too literally as nakedness. In *Totality and Infinity* it was the face of the Other that was naked as its gaze made me a responsible self.[20] Now it is I who am naked in the vulnerability that constitutes my responsibility.

But where is the inwardness in all this? How does getting beaten take us to "the hither side of the passivity of undergoing"? The first clue is in the nature of the relationship to the Other. Because the vulnerable self is "being *for another* . . . [because] the subject is *for the other*," the suffering is "suffering for the suffering of the other" (NI 146–47) rather than simply suffering from the Other. Levinas describes the relation as a certain sensibility, which we could express in the familiar words "I feel your pain." But his very physical descriptions make it clear that it goes beyond "I feel your pain" to "I share your pain," becoming victim myself.

Whether we are speaking of empathy or an even more radical sharing of the Other's suffering, the second and crucial factor is the quasi-voluntary nature of the sensibility, to which I can easily enough become desensitized. Speaking of the prophetic text he has just quoted, Levinas writes, "Without introducing a deliberate searching for suffering or humiliation (turning the other cheek), it suggests, in the *primary suffering*, in *suffering as such*, an unendurable and harsh *consent* that animates the passivity and does so strangely despite itself."

This consent is what takes us to "the hither side of the passivity of undergoing" (NI 146, emphasis added). We must speak its quasi-voluntary nature, because it is prior to the realm of free action and the voluntary in the usual sense. We could also call it quasi-transcendental, transcendental because it is prior to experience and choice and quasi- because it does not originate in the meaning-constituting subject of intentionality but in the pre-experiential answering to a pre-experiential call or accusation.

Levinas proceeds to spell out this "passivity more passive than every passivity" (NI 146) in terms familiar to readers of *Otherwise Than Being*: obsession, substitution, expiation, election, hostage, and persecution. Similarly, he speaks of "being implicated prior to my freedom," of "the accusation prior to any fault," of being "responsible even for their responsibility," of a saying that has "a meaning prior to the truth it discloses," that is, of "the saying that precedes the said," and of "the surplus of meaning over the being that bears it" (NI 147–51).

This is not the place to explore these crucial themes but only to note their intimate connection, in Levinas's mind, with the question of self-identity, on which we must keep focused.[21] The consent that takes us beyond the realm of causal forces is the uncoerced abdication of the "self-enclosed," "self-sufficient," "self-assured," monadic self, secure in its "immutable and indivisible self-identity."[22] Whenever I would say I intend the world, take a position, or decide whether to love or hate my neighbor, I find that my neighbor has already intruded into the inner sanctum of myself and has become a dimension of myself in a way to which I have already consented.[23] The "deportation or drifting of identity" (NI 145), the "strange defeat or defection of identity" (NI 148) of which Levinas speaks, has always already happened. And it is a good thing. For this "difference that opens between the ego and itself, the *non-coincidence* of the identical, is a fundamental *non-indifference* with regard to men" (NI 149, emphasis added).

In other words, having "no identity" in the sense carefully delineated in this essay is a condition for the possibility of being a responsible self. Kant said, "I have therefore found it necessary to deny *knowledge,* in order to make room for *faith.*"[24] As we have seen, Levinas says, "I have found it necessary to deny freedom, in order to make room for responsibility." Now he reformulates that to read, "I have found it necessary to deny identity, in order to make room for responsibility." In the case of freedom, of course, he does not deny it but rather displaces it, making it subsequent and subordinate. In the case of identity, however, he does flatly deny that a certain kind of identity is to be found anywhere than in the fantasies of those who, whether philosophically sophisticated or not, make their own *conatus essendi* primary and essential and the rights and needs of the Other secondary and accidental. So, far from the shattering of the cogito taking us beyond good and evil into cynical nihilism or arrogant aestheticism, it is the repentance that responsibility requires.

At least it can be. If one sets up a simple either/or between the self as an ontologically guaranteed self-identity prior to experience and relation on the one hand and, on the other, "a world that does not bear human traces" (NI 143), the end of humanism and the death of man could signify the demise of responsibility as well. If, however, the self survives the death of its false pretensions, the story could be quite different, and it is clearly such a story Levinas wants to tell.

That is why there is nuance in his denial of identity. The self does not simply disappear into causal nexus like a stone in a pond whose ripples last but a moment. Where Ricoeur speaks of *ipse* identity and Schrag of the emerging narrative self, Levinas speaks of "the uniqueness of the irreplaceable" (NI 150). I am uniquely irreplaceable just by virtue of a responsibility for the Other than I cannot transfer to anyone else. This is my identity. It is mutable, because my responsibilities change, and divisible because I have it by virtue of the vulnerability by which the Other becomes essential to who I am. "If I answer only for myself, am I still myself?" the Talmud asks. No, Levinas replies, but when you answer for another as one who has been elected to be for the Other, you become for the first time yourself.[25]

In this way "a defense of man understood as a defense of the man other than me, presides over what in our day is called the critique of humanism." In spite of structuralist scientism, "man has not ceased to count for man," and this is the meaning of youth, precisely in Paris, 1968. "Able to find responsibilities again under the thick stratum of literature that undo [*sic*] them . . . youth ceased to be the age of transition and passage . . . and is shown to be man's humanity" (NI 151).

This new humanism after the end of humanism could also be called the self after postmodernity. It enables Levinas to give nuance to the theme of alienation he introduced earlier, when he said that in responsibility the Other "has slipped into me . . . thus alienating my identity" (NI 145). But no sooner does he say this than he puts it in question. I am alienated from a certain identity, to be sure. But

> is it then certain that in the deportation or drifting of identity, caught sight of in the inversion of human projects, the subject would not signify with all the dash of its youth? Is it certain that Rimbaud's formula "I is an other" only means alteration, alienation, betrayal of oneself, foreignness with regard to oneself and subjection to this foreigner? Is it certain that already the most humble experience of him who *puts himself in another's place*, that is, accuses himself for another's distress or pain, is not animated with the most eminent meaning of this 'I is an other'? (NI 145).[26]

Three times Levinas asks, Is it certain? Someone should do a study of his rhetorical questions, designed to cut against the grain. Are they not his best arguments? He uses still another one to point in still another way to the possibility of an "eminent," nonalienating meaning to "I is an other." "Or shall the strange defeat or defection of identity confirm the human election—my own, to serve, but that of the other for himself?" (NI 148). Election is a central theme in both Jewish and Christian theology. It means to be chosen of God for salvation and to be a light to the nations. To be sure, for Levinas the concept is intimately intertwined with such severe notions of obligation as hostage, substitution, and expiation, just as for Jewish theology election and the law are inseparable. In this context, where Levinas evokes the Bible, by which "we Westerners are nourished . . . but in a way that owes nothing to the certainty of the *cogito*," he twice makes reference to Psalm 119. The longest chapter in the Bible, it is a hymn of praise for the gift of the law and a plea for help in living up to it. The law is light and wisdom, not oppression and slavery.

Yet we cannot and should not downplay the fact that responsibility comes as heteronomy. Theologically, in the biblical traditions, the law comes from a radically transcendent God, not from the self-legislation of human reason. Philosophically, on the Levinasian analysis, responsibility is born with the incursion of the Other into my very identity as the saying that demands my nonindifference.[27] The command of the Other and the consent I find myself already to have given keep this from being the causal heteronomy of those subjected to forces they cannot control. But the consent is already a reply and not a legislation. It is not constitutive of the meanings that confound it even as it confirms them. The responsible self is not autonomous. The astonishing claim of Levinas is threefold: the responsible self is born from transcendence; transcendence means heteronomy; but heteronomy does not mean alienation. For "no one is enslaved to the Good" (OB 11; cf. 15, 43, 105).

\* \* \*

No one doubts that the God of Kierkegaard's *Fear and Trembling* is a heteronomous transcendence. Is this God also the shattering of the cogito and the birth of the responsible self?

When Schrag first turns to Kierkegaard it is to *Either/Or*, more specifically to Judge William's admonition to the young aesthete to choose himself. This conversion to the ethical sphere from the aesthetic would be an existential paradigm shift of truly revolutionary import. Perhaps it would be, as Judge William clearly thinks, the birth of the responsible self. If so it would not be necessary to proceed to *Fear and Trembling*. We could stay with the highly user-friendly God of whom the Judge speaks so often and so glibly, the God who confirms but never challenges his bourgeois complacency; we would not need to proceed to the "terrifying" and "repelling" God of Abraham, whom one can approach only with a "shudder" and a "*horror religiosus*" (FT 9, 33, 61). But since Schrag evokes *Either/Or* in developing the self in action and not the self in transcendence, and since we expect Kierkegaard, like Levinas, to seek the birth of the responsible self in transcendence, this hope may be premature. Let us see.

The choice Judge William urges on his young friend is not the choice of good over evil in a particular situation, which is secondary, but the choice of good and evil rather than aesthetic categories as those of highest importance for shaping and evaluating his life. It is the decision to enter the ethical sphere, to play a different game with different goals and different rules (E/O II, 166–69).

The Sartrean overtones of the notion of self-choice are undermined when Judge William equates choosing oneself with receiving oneself and with becoming oneself: "when the soul comes to be alone in the whole world, then before one there appears, not an extraordinary human being, but the eternal power itself, then the heavens seem to open and the I chooses itself, or, more correctly, receives itself. . . . He does not become someone other than he was before, but he becomes himself" (E/O II, 177).[28]

This choice is the decision to be a responsible self. After a person "has found himself, has chosen himself absolutely, has repented of himself, he then has himself as his *task* under an eternal *responsibility*. . . . But since he has not created himself but has chosen himself, *duty* is the expression of his absolute dependence and his absolute freedom in their identity with each other (E/O II, 270, emphasis added). Just because Judge William presupposes what Sartre denies, namely, that the self is created by God, self-choice can never signify an absolute autonomy. In choosing myself I accept responsibility to One who has chosen me. There is more than a hint of heteronomy here.

For Levinas, too, self-choice always presupposes the Other's prior presence as one to whom and for whom I am responsible. But in his terms, the self-choice of which Judge William speaks would be an empirical, voluntary ratification of the quasi-transcendental consent that has always already been given. Moreover, the content of this choice as presented by the Judge would be the moral order of a certain society, what Levinas would call a political order of justice trying to take into account the presence of the third. But the birth of the responsible self takes place between two, before the third appears on the scene. So while this choice might signify the responsible self learning to walk, it cannot be the birth of that self.

Nor can Judge William's account of the transition from the aesthetic sphere to the ethical be an adequate account of the birth of the responsible self for Kierkegaard. In the first place, while he talks a lot about God and, in the passage just cited, speaks of being alone before "the eternal power itself," he does not analyze the God-relation nor explore what it might mean to be alone before God, what it might mean for the birth of the responsible self to take place between two, before the third appears on the scene. Second, and as a consequence, the religious is for him no more than a cultural sphere. Judge William is never alone before God but always surrounded by, immersed in, and in a very real sense indistinguishable from respectable, Danish, bourgeois, Lutheran society. Hegel could only be proud of one who embodied his concept of *Sittlichkeit* so well. The institution of marriage that the judge commends so highly to the young aesthete, whom he no doubt suspects of "living in sin," is precisely the social practice that Hegel makes basic to his account *Sittlichkeit* in the *Philosophy of Right*.[29]

But Kierkegaard cannot rest here. As Schrag notes with appreciation, he wants to articulate a transcendence that can critique and relativize all the culture spheres, not only science, ethics, and art, but even religion (SAP 118–25). So we'll have to proceed to *Fear and Trembling* after all. Silentio's Abraham is Kierkegaard's analysis of what it means to be alone before God, and in its teleological suspension "the ethical is reduced to the relative" (FT 70). It is not just a secular humanism, if you like, that is marginalized to make way for the religious. In context it is perfectly clear that the ethical sphere is that of both Hegel and Judge William, which already includes, in both cases, religion as a cultural sphere. Kierkegaard will eventually call it Christendom. We must go beyond such an ethical sphere to find the self in transcendence; and it is only there, for Kierkegaard as for Levinas, that we will find the birth of the responsible self.

Abraham is alone. We see this most dramatically in Problema III, which explores Abraham's silence before Sarah, his wife, Isaac, his son, and Eliezer, his servant.[30] The tragic hero, Agamemnon, or Jephtha, or Brutus, can explain himself when called upon to sacrifice a child. For while he does a terrible and painful thing, it is justified by the universal, not just by the needs of the society of which he is a member but by the ethical standards they share (*Sittlichkeit*). Everyone can be expected to understand that he is doing the right thing. They can weep together. The knight of faith has no such support. He cannot expect even his family to understand and approve. They cannot weep with him but only shrink back in horror.

Largely on the basis of the loneliness of Abraham, Kierkegaard is often presented as having an atomic or monadic theory of the self. Thus, for example, Mark Taylor writes, "While Hegel is the genius whose vision inspires recent forms of socialism, Kierkegaard remains the greatest theoretician of contemporary individualism."[31] Nothing could be further from the truth. Abraham is alone only to secular or pantheistic eyes for which the only actual Other is a human person. But Abraham is alone—before God. *Coram Deo* means that the knight of faith is never alone. In a variety of texts and in his appeal to "that single individual" whom he hopes to find as his reader, Kierkegaard regularly seeks to isolate the individual, to help reflect the individual, not out of every relation, but out of every finite relation, to be freed for the infinite relation, alone, like Abraham, before God.

In spite of their disagreement as to whether the neighbor is the middle term between me and God or God is the middle term between me and my neighbor,[32] there is also a deep agreement here. The self is always already in relation, and a hierarchical, asymmetrical relation at that. Prior to experience, prior to the choice of an aesthetic, ethical, or religious "lifestyle," the (pre)transcendental trauma has already occurred. An Other has already slipped into me, unbeknownst, depriving me of any possibility of a self-enclosed identity. The invasion of my innermost identity by this Other is the birth of the responsible self. Whatever responsibilities I may incur in whatever culture spheres into which I enter are relativized by an absolute duty, prior and higher. That this absolute duty is to God, for Kierkegaard, and not in the first instance to my family or to my society, is the thrust of the three "Problems" that make up the bulk of *Fear and Trembling*.

There is another difference between Levinas and Kierkegaard, but I believe this one to be only apparent. Paradoxical as it may seem, given his sustained critique of ontology, Levinas's account is ontological, at least as we usually use the term; it concerns the very being of the self. To be sure, the traditional ontologies he challenges affirm the identity of the self in some quite strong sense, while he insists, "No identity." But this is not so much to abandon ontology as to give a different account of the being of the self, and, in the process, of being itself. He begins with a "negative ontology," invoking traditional categories such as identity but under a negative sign, and proceeds to new, affirmative, ethical categories, such as vulnerability and so forth.[33] Levinas nicely expresses the primacy of his ethical categories by identifying the self's horizon as "not a world but a kingdom . . . the kingdom of the Good." Accordingly, philosophy is "the wisdom of love" rather than the love of wisdom (OB 52, 162).

Similarly, Kierkegaard's positive account of the self is in ethical terms, for example, the absolute duty to God with which Silentio explicates the teleological suspension of *Sittlichkeit* and Christendom. But the contrast for him is more often a "negative epistemology" than a "negative ontology." He doesn't use the ontological language in which I have just interpreted his account of the incursion of God into the self. He shatters the cogito, not so much in terms of its self-identity as of its performance, by challenging the ultimacy of its knowledge claims. Thus for Silentio the sign of transcendence is "the paradox" and "the absurd."[34] (Similarly, Climacus will go on to challenge the cogito as recollection in *Philosophical Fragments* and as speculation in *Concluding Unscientific Postscript*.)

In a variety of writings, not least in *Fear and Trembling*, Kierkegaard sets faith against reason. But we should not take this to be a Promethean defiance of faith before Reason as some cosmo-ontological first principle. It is precisely to protest against the identification of the cogito with such a principle that he pits faith against reason, which is always human reason in its finitude and fallenness. Thus, Abraham has faith "by virtue of the absurd" which is absurd in the light not of divine reason but of "human calculation." To find oneself alone with God is to lose confidence in the absoluteness of "one's own understanding" along with "everything finite, for which it is the stockbroker" (FT 35–36).[35] Just as the amnion must break if the baby is to be born and the shell must be cracked if the chick is to be born, so the cogito must be shattered at the birth of the responsible self.

That Kierkegaard uses epistemic terms rather than the language of self-identity strikes me as a superficial difference for two reasons. First, a self that loses its (presumed) epistemic and moral autonomy at the same time is a self whose self-enclosed self-identity has been dramatically compromised, even if one does not use such language to express the trauma. Second, Levinas's own critique of "ontology" is largely epistemic. Thus his sustained critique of intentionality, thematization, representation, transcendental apperception, and so forth. There is an essential interchangeability of ontological and epistemological categories. As Catherine Pickstock puts it, "an ontology separated from theology is reducible to an epistemology."[36] Apart from transcendence, being becomes convertible not with intelligibility in itself but with intelligibility *for us*. Being is that which gives itself to be fully comprehended by *human understanding*. Thus, speaking of the simple natures on which the entire edifice of our knowledge is founded, Descartes assures us that they "are known *per se* and are wholly free from falsity. . . . Whence it is evident that we are in error if we judge that any one of these simple natures is not completely known by us. For if our mind attains to the least acquaintance with it . . . this fact alone makes us infer that we know it completely."[37]

Whenever the soul or the cogito or the transcendental ego represents this kind of epistemic hubris it becomes the unbirthing of the responsible self or, perhaps, the birth of the irresponsible self. For the responsible self, as presented by Levinas and Kierkegaard, is triply heteronomous before transcendence. In terms of its being, its knowing, and its doing, it is essentially given over to an Other. It is not the self-identical, self-contained, and self-sufficient self in which "modernity" placed its hopes. Postmodernity is the boy who shouts, "The emperor has no clothes," the investigative journalism that exposes the Wizard of Oz for the sham he is. To rediscover the self "after postmodernity" is to discover a radical, heteronomous responsibility; and this is to resist the cynicism of dis-illusionment.

\* \* \*

Schrag seeks the birth of the responsible self beyond modernity, beyond cynical, nihilistic postmodernity, and, briefly, at the conclusion of his argument, beyond classical theism, claiming that "the classical metaphysics of theism comes up lame in locating the source and dynamics of transcendence" (SAP 138). I believe that Schrag is mistaken on this point and that whatever its weaknesses, one of the greatest strengths of classical theism is its articulation of divine transcendence.

By classical theism I do not mean the attempt of philosophical theology to establish the existence and nature of God by means of pure reason. I rather mean simply belief in a personal Creator and Redeemer who is not only infinite and eternal but, above all, loving. Such a view of God is the widely shared core of Jewish, Christian, and Muslim monotheism. In the Christian context, it is shared not only by those most classical of classical theists, Augustine and Aquinas, but also by two other groups: on the one hand theologians like Luther, Calvin, and Barth, who seek in various ways and degrees to pull Jerusalem away from Athens and the Platonic or Aristotelian frameworks so important to Augustine and Aquinas, and on the other hand lay believers who neither read nor write academic theology.

Classical theism presupposes and presents a triple transcendence. First, there is cosmological transcendence. God is "outside" or "above" or "beyond" the world. This is not to deny that God is intimately present to the world and to every creature in it. It is rather to affirm a crucial existential asymmetry. The world cannot exist without God, but God can exist without the world. This is the meaning of creation. God is not a world-soul that is actual only in union with the world as its body. Nor is God the source from which the world emanates as heat and light from a fire. For while there cannot be the heat and light without the fire, so there cannot be the fire without the heat and light that radiate from it. This asymmetry distinguishes classical theism from every emanationist and pantheistic way of thinking.

Cosmological transcendence is first, not as the axiom of a deductive system but in a Hegelian sense. It is the thinnest, most abstract, least adequate, but nevertheless necessary way of thinking God's transcendence. At first glance it does not appear to be a shattering of the cogito or the birth of the responsible self. In fact, it could all too easily become a theory that, like a trophy bride or other forms of conspicuous consumption, serves as a sign of our superiority, placing us at the center rather than decentering us. "Lord, I thank Thee that I am not a pantheist."

But as classical theism thinks through the meaning of creation more concretely, two further forms of divine transcendence emerge. The first of these is epistemic transcendence, and this comes in two forms. To begin with, the need for special revelation is affirmed. On a spectrum that finds Aquinas at or near one end and Karl Barth at or near the other, classical theists disagree about the nature and extent of the knowledge of God available to us by unaided human reason. But they agree that whatever knowledge, if any, we have in this way, it is not enough. God needs to provide us by grace and beyond our own natural powers, with knowledge that corrects and supplements our "natural" thinking about God. Thus, for example, we have Augustine telling us what he did not find in the books of the Platonists but only in the Bible and complaining about the "presumption" of the Platonists who are content with the results of philosophical speculation.[38] And the Sunday school child, who has never heard of Augustine, knows the same thing:

> Jesus loves me. This I know.
> For the Bible tells me so.

This is indeed a dangerous supplement, for it is the shattering of the cogito. Truth is defined as the *adaequatio res et intellectus*, but classical theism tells us that our best efforts never achieve adequation but rather stand in need both of correction and of supplementation. What clearly and distinctly seems to me to be the case, even with the help of methodological carefulness, is not the measure of being. If I would know how things really are I need to be tutored by the God without whom I could not exist but who can exist without me. Thus the epistemic corollary: I cannot truly know God without God's help; but God's knowledge, which simply is the truth, does not need my assistance.

The second moment of epistemic transcendence intensifies the first. It comes in the affirmation of the incomprehensibility of God. God is "wholly other" not just ontologically as the only uncreated being, but epistemically as well. Even with the help of divine revelation, God remains mysterious and exceeds our conceptual grasp. Thus, for example, Aquinas regularly insists that in that in this life, even with the help of divine revelation, our intellect never sees the divine essence, which "surpasses our intelligence and is unknown to us: wherefore *man reaches the highest point of his knowledge about God when he knows that he knows him not,* inasmuch as he knows that that which is God transcends whatsoever he conceives of him."[39] Our knowledge never achieves adequation. Strictly speaking, it is never true.

Even in a state of rapture or in the life to come, when the blessed apprehend the divine essence, they do not comprehend God. For when "the thing known exceeds its grasp, then the knowing power falls short of comprehension."[40] Only a cogito that no longer sees this humbling as humiliation can be happy in heaven.

This epistemic transcendence casts a different light on two points at which Schrag's critique of classical theism seems to have Aquinas especially in mind. The God of Kierkegaard's religiousness B, he says, "is not a metaphysical entity, as proposed by the proponents of classical theism. One finds no alleged proofs for the existence of a supernatural being in the writings of Kierkegaard . . . because the very project of a metaphysics of theism becomes problematized, deconstructed, if you will, through the dynamics of 'existential faith'" (SAP 135).

Though some of my best friends are Thomists, I am not. In fact, my sympathies lie more with Kierkegaard than with the *doctor angelicus.* However, it seems unnecessary to me to use Kierkegaard to deconstruct Aquinas's "metaphysics of theism" for the sake of divine transcendence. The proofs of God's existence can seem to be a quintessentially onto-theological gesture, the positing of a Highest Being who is not only (1) the key to the meaning of the whole of being but also (2) the means by which the whole of being becomes fully intelligible to human understanding. Epistemic transcendence would be lost.[41] The proofs are clearly one way of making the first gesture. But, then, whoever affirms God as Creator makes this move, whatever the epistemic basis for the affirmation. Aquinas would be making the second, crucial gesture, however, only if it were assumed that God, the key to the meaning of the whole of being, were fully intelligible to us. And that Aquinas repeatedly and emphatically denies. For him it is just the opposite. The affirmation of God as Creator is the acknowledgment that neither God nor the world can be fully intelligible to us.[42] Where God remains mysterious, metaphysics in its onto-theological constitution is already overcome. When Aquinas says that full intelligibility is available to the divine but not to any created intellect, he is paraphrasing Kierkegaard, whose Climacus writes, "Existence itself is a system—for God, but it cannot be a system for any existing spirit" (CUP I, 118).

Schrag also says that Kierkegaardian transcendence "focuses attention away from the categorial constraints of a theo-metaphysics that is destined to construe transcendence as a quasi-scientific cosmological principle" (SAP 134). Once again, this suggests Aquinas, for whom God is surely a cosmological principle. But then God is a cosmological principle for anyone who affirms God as Creator. But it does not follow that God is nothing but a cosmological principle. For classical theism, cosmological transcendence is only the abstract beginning; we have already seen it spill over into epistemic transcendence for both Aquinas and Kierkegaard, and will shortly see ethical transcendence emerge as well.

But before turning to that theme we should look briefly at the "quasi-scientific" character of God as cosmological principle. Aquinas comes to mind again because he treats theology as a "quasi-scientific" discipline. But the 'quasi' is utterly important. For Aquinas *scientia* requires insight into the essence of the entities dealt with by a particular science.[43] In the case of God that is precisely what we do not have. Just as our knowledge of God is by analogy rather than by adequation, so theology has the form of science while lacking the *Wesensschau* that is its essential ingredient. Kierkegaard might well agree, for subjectivity is not the elimination of objectivity but its dangerous supplement. It is only "quasi-scientific." Aquinas's "theo-metaphysics" deconstructs itself precisely to preserve the transcendence of God. In the process, the cogito is dethroned. It is no longer the Czar of cognition, the King of knowledge. As long as transcendence is the issue, I see no need to drive a wedge between Kierkegaard and the likes of Aquinas, nor to turn to Tillich's project of "transcending theism" in search of the "God beyond God" (SAP 136). Along that path it just might be transcendence itself that gets transcended.

A final question. Is the shattering of the cogito represented by classical theism also the birth of the responsible self? This brings us to the question of ethical transcendence, which brings cosmological and epistemic transcendence to their most concrete, or, if you prefer, most existential completion. One could easily show that this is just what happens in Aquinas. But our interest is with Kierkegaard. When his writings are read not only up to *Concluding Unscientific Postscript* but beyond that to include such writings as *Works of Love*, it becomes clear that for him the highest form of transcendence is neither cosmological nor epistemic (though he affirms both), but rather ethical/religious transcendence, or, as we have come to call it, existential transcendence.[44]

## Transcendence, Heteronomy, and the Birth of the Responsible Self

In their own ways Descartes and Kant tried to unite the concept of God as Creator with radical human autonomy at the epistemic and ethical levels. In doing so they opened the door to the thorough-going loss of transcendence in Spinoza and Hegel.[45] Rather than fixing a great gulf between Levinas and Kierkegaard on the one hand and classical theism on the other, I suggest we see the former pair as seeking to restore the sense of transcendence that comes to us from the radical monotheism we sometimes call classical theism. It is the original home of that shattering of the cogito that is the birth of the responsible self.

PART 4. REVERSAL

# The "Logic" of Solidarity

*What human beings strive for in general is cognition of the world; we strive to appropriate it and to conquer it. To this end the reality of the world must be crushed as it were; i.e., it must be made ideal.*[1]

It is because he thinks that Hegel lets the cat out of the bag with words such as these that Levinas's own philosophy is an attempt to accomplish "**the radical reversal, from cognition to solidarity**" (OB 119, emphasis added). The nature of this reversal as spelled out by Levinas and Kierkegaard is the theme of our final two chapters. It presupposes the divine breakthrough into human life discussed in the previous chapters. In spite of the different theologies (chapters 3 and 4) there is the structural convergence expressed in the themes that articulate divine transcendence: the immediacy of revelation as a voice not our own, either individually or collectively (chapters 1 and 2) and the traumatic heteronomy in which the responsible self is born with an essentially intersubjective (non)identity (chapters 5 and 6).

If there is a 'logic' of solidarity, we will have to speak of it in scare quotes because of the sustained assault Levinas (and in due course, Kierkegaard)[2] makes on the dominant understanding of the logos in western philosophy, an understanding he would find nicely expressed in the epigraph from Hegel's Lesser Logic. Since that assault is fundamental to his being unashamed, after Nietzsche and even after Auschwitz, to speak of peace and love and justice,[3] it is appropriate to inquire whether there is another 'logic' that guides the journey he maps out "from cognition to solidarity." What 'argument,' what 'evidence' will emerge from his critique of the logocentrism that has prevailed from Plato to Husserl, and even to Heidegger and Derrida, that might sustain, if not optimism, at least hope for our life together?

Even Heidegger and Derrida? Is not their destruction and deconstruction of the history of ontology the decisive break with the logos of Plato, Descartes, Hegel, and Husserl? Well, no. Each takes up a negative stance toward the tradition, to be sure, but Levinas does not see either as the decisive rupture, the "radical reversal" that is needed. "It is true that philosophy, in its traditional forms of ontotheology and logocentrism—to use Heidegger's and Derrida's terms—has come to an end . . . [but] . . . The speculative practice of philosophy is by no means near its end. Indeed, the whole contemporary discourse of overcoming and deconstructing metaphysics is far more speculative in many respects than is metaphysics itself. Reason is never so versatile as when it puts itself in question" (DEL 33).

How is it, then, that these two remain within the speculative horizon of the discourses they seek to undermine? Following leads in Husserl, Heidegger stands in "opposition to classical intellectualism" and its search for a "reason liberated from temporal contingencies, a soul, co-eternal with the Ideas" (Si 177–79). For him ontology does not occur "in the triumph of human beings over their condition, but in the very tension whereby this condition is assumed. . . . To think is no longer to contemplate, but to commit oneself. It is to be engulfed by that which one thinks, to be involved" (IOF 3–4).[4]

In this way Heidegger runs the risk of "drowning ontology in existence. . . . And yet the philosophy of existence is immediately effaced by ontology . . . [because] this existence is interpreted as comprehension." Being is inseparable from "openness," from "understanding," and from "truth" (Si 122–23). By interpreting being-in-the-world as disclosure (TI 28, 65, 67, 71, 75; TrO 346–47), Heidegger shows that he has revised without really disrupting the western scene "where spirit is taken to be coextensive with knowing" (GP 155; cf. OB 99 and BI 100–101).

Derrida makes essentially the same critique of Heidegger, whose preoccupation with proximity, light, and unveiling he sees as a nostalgic clinging to the metaphysics of presence that renders his analysis of human temporality far tamer than its press releases suggest.[5] Derrida would be a left-Heideggerian, giving the name deconstruction to Heidegger's destruction once it is freed from the romanticism and mysticism that keep appearing as its "on-the-other-hand."

Accordingly, Levinas has a different kind of problem with Derrida, whom he associates with the Kant of the First Critique (WO 3, 5–6) and thereby with the skeptical dimension of reason's self-questioning (DEL 22).[6] "Whereas [Derrida] tends to see the deconstruction of the Western metaphysics of presence as an irredeemable crisis, I see it as a golden opportunity for Western philosophy to open itself to the dimension of otherness and transcendence beyond being" (DEL 28). In other words, Levinas sees Derrida as part of the Heraclitean, skeptical, nominalist traditions whose challenge to the aspirations for pure presence in Plato and his footnotes is not an ethical plea for the widow, the orphan, and the stranger but a purely epistemological squabble about how high on the divided line it is actually possible to climb. Skepticism denies knowledge in order to make room for faith or opinion, which is precisely **not** what Levinas is up to (TI 24; GP 155). In this sense deconstruction is as speculative as the metaphysical tradition it seeks to undermine. "Philosophy is not separable from skepticism, which follows it like a shadow" (OB 168) or like the "legitimate child" (WO 5) it can never disavow.[7] Skepticism is one of the tricks Reason can perform, the versatility by which it puts itself in question.

No doubt Levinas has Derrida especially in mind when he writes, "The privilege of presence is called into question by an entire current of contemporary French philosophy . . . proceeding from a reflection on all the conditionings and all the 'mediations' of supposedly immediate experience" (BM 314). Since the "supposedly immediate experience" under discussion is the various forms of pure presence sought and claimed by the mainstream philosophical tradition as necessary conditions for *episteme, scientia, adequatio rei et intellectus,* clear and distinct ideas, *Wissenschaft, absolutes Wissen,* apodictic certainty, and so forth, insistence on various mediations of the cave, "political, social, epistemological, psychoanalytical, linguistic, poetic" (BM 314), and so forth, is best conceived as a skeptical contribution to the quarrel over the divided line.

Levinas, who knows not only the French philosophies of mediation but also the assaults of Husserl (in spite of himself)[8] and Heidegger on the myth of the given, is the great defender of immediacy. "The immediate is the face to face" (TI 52).[9] But this does not mean that he espouses the "supposedly immediate experience" that the French and Germans (not to mention the Americans) have worked so hard to expose as wishful thinking. The ethical immediacy of the face challenges the contemporary orthodoxy that everything is mediated without reverting to anything like the scene in Plato's *Phaedo* where the naked soul, shorn of all caveish mediations, and the forms, too pure (like Aristotle's God) to need such cleansing, revel in an orgy of immediacy, ready-made for each other and directly present to each other. Over against the immediacies of recurring Platonism and the mediations of recurring skepticism, Levinas posits an immediacy that questions the ultimacy of the debate between them. As we shall see subsequently, his assault on knowledge does not presuppose skepticism; accordingly he does not view Derrida's contribution to that tradition as a stage on the journey from cognition to solidarity.[10]

If the deepest problem with philosophy's beloved logos is neither that it is too abstract and needs a Heideggerian *Lebens* or *Existenzphilosophie* to bring it to concreteness, nor that it is too ambitious and needs a Derridean skepticism to exhibit its finitude and teach it humility, what is its tragic flaw? In a word—power. Knowledge is the will to power of a thoroughly egoistic *conatus essendi*;[11] as such it is the reduction of the other to the same. To paraphrase William James, the object of knowledge is other to the subject of knowledge, but not so very damn other. In knowledge "the object's resistance as an exterior being vanishes" as it becomes "an exteriority surrendering in clarity and without immodesty its whole being to thought" (TI 124). The universal of thought is "the ruse of the hunter who ensnares all that a being contains of strength and irreducibility" (IOF 126). In other words, "the *outside of me* is *for me*" (TrO 345; cf. BTK 60–61; TO 68).

This is what it means to say that the history of philosophy has been the refutation of transcendence.[12] The first principle of knowledge is neither the law of noncontradiction nor the principle of sufficient reason but the Pistol principle: "the world's mine oyster."[13] In this mode philosophy is ideology by its very nature, even before putting itself at the service of some technological or social purpose (GP 172; BI 103; cf. DEL 28; BM 313). Whereas Foucault says that knowledge always functions as social power, Levinas argues that even if the purely epistemological domain is an abstraction from more concrete social scenes, knowledge is already power in its (abstract) purity simply as knowledge.

He expresses this thesis in a variety of ways. Sometimes it is with a recurring list of epithets describing the hegemony of knowledge over its object. Thus, in an early essay, to conceive is to assimilate, to dominate, to hunt, to deny the independence of a being that belongs to me. While murder is the total negation of the Other, knowledge is "a partial negation which is violence" (IOF 126–27). In a later essay, knowledge is the taming or domestication of its object, and the relation is one of mastery, possession, and domination (OB 100–102). These and closely related descriptions such as grasping, conquering, and absorbing proliferate throughout the Levinasian corpus, with the image of possession perhaps being the most frequent.[14]

Especially in *Totality and Infinity*, Levinas develops his assault on knowledge in terms of enjoyment (and its extension in the satisfaction of need through labor and possession into dwelling). He poses the question, "What is the relation between theoretical intentionality of the objectifying act, as Husserl calls it, and enjoyment?" (TI 122). As I see it he gives three answers to this question, only the third of which concerns us here. First, he claims that the object of knowledge is always in the first place the (potential) object of enjoyment rather that some abstraction such as a substance in which qualities or properties inhere. This is his version of Heidegger's argument giving priority to *Zuhandenheit* over *Vorhandenheit*. It is also his critique of Heidegger inasmuch as he argues that the object of use, for example, the hammer, is derivative in relation to the object of enjoyment.

Second, with reference to the subject of knowledge, he argues for the conditioned character of transcendental subjectivity. As someone with needs that call for satisfaction, including, but not limited to, physical needs, the knowing subject is immersed in the world he or she only subsequently constitutes and comprehends.

Finally, with reference to the relation of subject to object, Levinas suggests a powerful analogy between knowing and enjoying or perhaps even an identity in the sense that knowing is one of the human modes of enjoyment. Throughout his development of this theme one is reminded of Hegel's witty argument against the reality of sense-objects with reference to the Eleusinian Mysteries, which involve the eating of bread and the drinking of wine:

> For he who is initiated into these Mysteries not only comes to doubt the being of sensuous things, but to despair of it; in part he brings about the nothingness of such things himself in his dealings with them, and in part he sees them reduce themselves to nothingness. Even the animals are not shut out from this wisdom . . . for they do not just stand idly in front of sensuous things as if these possessed intrinsic being, but, despairing of their reality, and completely assured of their nothingness, they fall to without ceremony and eat them up.[15]

For Levinas as for Hegel eating is a paradigm of the process in which apparent transcendence is revealed to be immanence, in which the other is reduced to the same (TI 128–29). In enjoyment the other is that which the same "lives from" (TI 122). The world is there for me, at my disposal, because it belongs to me. As I feed on it, I satisfy and maintain myself by absorbing it into myself (TI 33, 37; TO 350, 68–69). As examples of the kinds of not-very-other-other I can feed on, Levinas cites "the bread I eat, the land in which I dwell, the landscape I contemplate" (TI 33).

Contemplation as eating? Yes. Levinas says that representation "nourishes itself and lives from the very being it represents to itself" (TI 168). This is true in two senses, corresponding to the second and third answers he gives to the question of the relation of knowledge to enjoyment. One the one hand, intentionality emanates from a body that needs to eat. But, on the other hand, intentionality is itself a kind of alimentation. Echoing Hegel's "in part he sees them reduce themselves to nothingness," Levinas writes,

> In the intelligibility of representation the distinction between me and the object, between interior and exterior, is effaced. . . . Intelligibility and representation are equivalent notions: an exteriority surrendering . . . its whole being to thought. . . . Intelligibility, the very occurrence of representation, is the possibility for the other to be determined by the same without determining the same, without introducing alterity into it. . . . It is the disappearance, within the same, of the I opposed to the non-I. (TI 124)

In short, representation is digestion. We move beyond this world of enjoyment only in the ethical relation in which transcendence is real and not imaginary (TI 172). Short of this we remain in splendid isolation, free from any solidarity that cannot be reduced to voluntary association. "In enjoyment I am absolutely for myself. Egoist without reference to the Other, I am alone without solitude, innocently egoist and alone. Not against the Others . . . —but entirely deaf to the Other . . . without ears, like a hungry stomach" (TI 134; cf. TO 68–69).

But what does this phrase "alone without solitude" mean? It signifies the quasi-or-pseudo-alterity of the object of enjoyment, including the object of knowledge. "Without solitude" signifies that something else is present beside the enjoying/knowing self. "Alone" signifies that this something else is there to be absorbed, digested. "Between the I and *what it lives from* there does not extend the absolute distance that separates the same from the other. . . . The primary agreement, to live, does not alienate the I but maintains it, constitutes its *being at home with itself.* The dwelling, inhabitation, belongs to the essence —to the egoism—of the I . . . the happiness of enjoyment affirms the I at home with itself" (TI 143).

This image of the self at home with itself in the midst of that from which it lives recalls another Hegelian text and introduces a third way in which Levinas expresses his assault on knowledge (along with the possession/domination epithets and the enjoyment motif ). Hegel describes absolute knowledge as the moment in which "self-consciousness has equally superseded this externaliza-tion and objectivity too, and taken it back into itself so that it is in communion with itself in *its* otherness as such."[16] I prefer the older, Baillie translation of "in seinem Anderssein als solchem bei sich" as "at home with itself in its otherness as such."[17] For I am truly at home whenever what is numerically distinct from me is nevertheless mine.

This is not just the message of the Hegelian phenomenology, but of the Husserlian as well. "Phenomenology thus teaches us that consciousness is at once tied to the object of its experience and yet free to detach itself from this object in order to return upon itself, focusing on those *visées* of intentionality in which the object emerges as *meaningful,* as part of our lived experience" (DEL 14).

In this "journey" of *exitus* and *reditus,* "thought thus moves out of itself towards Being, without thereby ceasing to remain in its own proper sphere (*chez elle* [*bei sich*]), always equal to itself. . . . Thought *satisfies* itself in Being" (BI 105). This is why, although we can speak of consciousness "losing itself and finding itself" on the "detour of ideality" in which it grasps its object "across an ideality and on the basis of a said," we must also acknowledge that "this adventure is no adventure. It is never dangerous; it is self-possession, sovereignty, ἀρχή" (OB 99).

This absence of adventure and risk Levinas also expresses as the refusal of the knowing subject to move beyond itself "without return" (TrO 345, 347). This refusal is the essence of the autonomy that defines the western logos. Levinas's "logic" calls for a truly heteronomous experience, which can also be called a work of goodness:

> But then we must not conceive of a work as an apparent agitation of a ground which afterwards remains identical with itself, like an energy which, in all its transformations, remains equal to itself. Nor must we conceive it as a technical operation, which . . . reduces an alien world to a world whose alterity is converted into my idea. . . . *A work conceived radically is a movement of the same unto the other which never returns to the same.* To the myth of Ulysses, returning to Ithaca, we wish to oppose the story of Abraham who leaves his fatherland forever for a yet unknown land, and forbids his servant to even bring back his son to the point of departure. (TrO 348)

Ulysses triumphs over his enemies and returns home as the conquering hero to dwell with his own and to enjoy what is his. Abraham's story lacks both the return to dwelling and enjoyment and the violence that makes it possible. That is why the former is a symbol for the logic Levinas seeks to disrupt, while the latter signifies the heteronomy and transcendence that take us beyond the correlation of being and *intentio,* of essence and *episteme.*

As a reader of the Hebrew Bible, Levinas might well have contrasted Adam to Abraham as well. In the creation story of Genesis 1, Adam is given dominion over all the earth, to enjoy it as food. In the creation story of Genesis 2, the food motif recurs in the form of the Garden of Eden, and Adam is presented as the one who names the living creatures. This linkage between naming and power would not surprise Levinas. One of his earliest assaults on knowledge states the themes he will develop again and again: comprehension as the violence that denies the otherness of the other by bringing it into my power and making it belong to me; and comprehension as the enjoyment that enacts this possession prior to any use that would demonstrate the freedom of ownership. In this context, comprehension is identified with naming. In contrast to the ethical relation to the Other, comprehension "does not invoke a being, but only names it, thus accomplishing a violence" (IOF 9).[18]

If we were to try to symbolize Levinas's critique of naming as violence from a narrative less ancient than the book of Genesis or *The Odyssey,* we might turn to Toni Morrison's *Beloved.* There the slave, Sixo, is accused by his master, schoolteacher, of stealing a shoat. Although the former admits that he killed, cooked, and ate the shoat, he denies that this was stealing. "What is it then?" asks the master in exasperation.

"Improving your property, sir."

"What?"

"Sixo plant rye to give the high piece a better chance. Sixo take and feed the soil, give you more crop. Sixo take and feed Sixo give you more work."

The narrator continues, "Clever, but schoolteacher beat him anyway to show him that definitions belonged to the definers—not the defined."[19]

We might summarize Levinas's indictment this way: knowledge divides the world into subjects who define and objects that get defined, and to be defined is to be another's possession, nourishment for the other to "live from."

\* \* \*

**Objection:** Levinas has let his phenomenological background mislead him. While he speaks in general of knowledge, comprehension, understanding, consciousness, representation, and the correlation of thought and being, he often speaks a more specifically Husserlian language of intentionality, thematization, and the correlation of noema and noesis. But he has allowed his talk about intentionality as thematizing or objectifying act to suggest, illegitimately, that all thematizing is thingifying, in some pejorative sense of the term.

We should remind ourselves of Heidegger's distinction between calculative and meditative thought, or of Buber's distinction between I-It and I-Thou (or I-You) thinking. Thematizing can be unconcealment in the mode of letting be, and we can thematize the other precisely as Other, as a Thou and not an It.

So we should listen to Jim Marsh, when he distinguishes eight different kinds of objectivity, only one of which (not thematization) essentially involves thingifying, domination, manipulation, and so forth. He concludes "that objectification of myself and other persons at times can be legitimate and enlightening." Conceptual thought is not necessarily strategic, instrumental, calculative thinking.[20]

**Response:** Levinas will accept both conclusions, but ask, Where is the objection? Regarding the first, of course, thematizing knowledge can be both legitimate and enlightening. The point has never been to deny a place to intentionality and the life forms built along the "detour of ideality." It has been only to recognize the ineluctable elimination from these spheres of the transcendence without which the ethical and religious life is impossible. To speak of ethics as first philosophy is not to call for the abolition of everything else but only for the teleological suspension of thematizing that takes us beyond intentionality to something more deeply human. There will still be a place for knowledge. But it will be secondary, and the human spirit will no longer be defined in terms of its cognitive achievements. Paradoxically, being, as that which gives itself to representational thought, will not be what is most fundamentally real.

With regard to the second point, the distinction between intentionality in general and its specific form as instrumental reason, Levinas will respond in the words of Kierkegaard's Climacus, "It is just as you say, and the amazing thing is that you think that it is an objection" (PF 52). For it is just by insisting on this distinction that Levinas has made his thesis so counterintuitive to so many of our philosophical habits; and this is exactly what Levinas does when he insists, again and again, that it is knowledge as such, prior to and independent of any ontic use for which it is designed or actually employed, that is violent. That is a central theme of his analysis of knowledge as enjoyment and of his example of contemplating a landscape as a mode of "living from."

This means, of course, that to intend the other as a person rather than as a thing is not to experience "the radical reversal, from cognition to solidarity" but only to make a move appropriate to cognition. Levinas insists that I-It and I-Thou are not two modes of intentionality. Rather, I-It covers the whole domain of intentional objects, and I-Thou "designates what is not intentional but what for Buber is rather the condition of all intentional relations." Thus 'he,' 'she,' and 'they' as well as 'it' "belong to the sphere of the It" (BTK 63). In other words, Buber's critique of Subject-object thinking as I-it thinking is not yet the reversal of the intentional relation toward which Levinas is moving.[21]

**Objection:** But this is totalizing thinking at its worst. A classification that tosses everything into the same bin is not very illuminating. Yet Levinas lumps every kind of cognitive awareness together under the label Representation, or Intentionality, or Thematizing. If such distinguishing marks as possession, enjoyment, and returning (or remaining) home don't distinguish one kind of knowledge from another, what is their purpose?

**Response:** Formally speaking, statements of the form—all Xs are Ys—can be illuminating. This is especially true if no Zs are Ys so that Y-ness signifies a uniform, possibly essential, difference between Xs and Zs.

More specifically, Levinas is making the strong claim that all representation or intentional consciousness has certain characteristics **and** that it is just these characteristics that distinguish the thematizing posture from the ethical relation, thereby undermining solidarity. The distinguishing marks of knowledge as philosophically affirmed (or denied, in the case of skepticism) do not distinguish the noema in which a thing is represented (or present, if you like) as a thing from one in which a person is represented (or present) as a person; but they do distinguish "the detour of ideality" from the directness of the face to face. "In speech we are not only thinking of the interlocutor, but speaking to him" (ET 41).[22] If I exceed the limits of intentionality when I speak to the Other, how much more is this the case when the Other speaks to me or looks at me, two of the most frequent ways in which Levinas characterizes transcendence.

Intentionality totalizes by making everything mine. Levinas's theory (a mode of representation to be sure) is not as such the rupture of this totality. But it points to the ethical relation that interrupts the egoism of knowledge and that precedes the egoism of action and feeling. Over against knowledge, comprehension, disclosure, revealing, recollection, representation, intentionality, thematizing, and so forth, there are proximity, enigma, an-archy, teaching, the ethical relation, the face to face, saying, command, even substitution.

What these latter terms signify is not the abyss of unmeaning upon which our islands of meaning float;[23] nor, as we have already seen, a slide down the divided line to the realm of faith and opinion. In Platonic imagery we are talking about the *epikeina tes ousias*, which Levinas renders as *au-delà de l'essence*; this takes us above the divided line, not beyond intelligibility but to "the first intelligible" (Si 185, 188; cf. TrO 352, "first discourse"). What this means is that notions like meaning, intelligibility, and rationality are not restricted to the meanings given to them by the mainstream of the philosophical tradition.

Meaning does not need to be restricted to the notions of being or essence as presence (GP 154; BI 100; DEL 23). There is a meaning, "different and more ancient" than the one implicated in the identification of thought with knowledge, that deserves to be called "meaning, *par excellence*" (BI 112, 100).[24] The experience in which this meaning arises is one that "approaches the transcendent in a signification which it will not have ascribed to it" (TrO 348). In other words, there is a "signifyingness which is different from the much-discussed 'meaning-endowment,'" the Husserlian *Sinngebung* (OB 100; cf. TI 51; FC 22).

Just as there is another meaning, so there is another intelligibility. "To intelligibility as an impersonal logos is opposed intelligibility as proximity" (OB 167). Levinas defines proximity as "*anarchically* a relation with a singularity without the mediation of any principle, any ideality" (OB 100) and as a relation to the Other that is "not equivalent to a rapport between subject and object" (Si 182).[25] Thus it is clear that the move beyond intentionality is not conceived as a move beyond intelligibility but as access to an "intelligibility before the light, before the present of the initiative with which the signification of logos . . . signifies being" (OB 78). This is the realm of the "first intelligible" mentioned above.

According to another definition, proximity "signifies a *reason* before the thematization of signification by a thinking subject, before the assembling of terms in a present, a pre-original reason that does not proceed from any initiative of the subject, an anarchic reason" (OB 166). It should come as no surprise that there is another reason, "pre-original" and "anarchic," corresponding to the "first intelligible." "We must ask if beyond the intelligibility and rationalism of identity, consciousness, the present, and being—beyond the intelligibility of immanence—the signifyingness, rationality, and rationalism of transcendence are not understood" (OB 154–55). The latter involves a "reasonable significance which Reason does not know!" (BM 320) and moves among reasons "that 'reason' does not know" (GP 172). If the Reason that does not know is spelled with an uppercase R, this points to the near monopoly it has enjoyed throughout the history of western philosophy. If that same 'reason' then appears in quotation marks, this signifies a serious challenge to its hegemony.

On the one hand that challenge is negative vis-à-vis the logos. True ethical responsibility involves "undoing the logos" (OB 102; cf. TI 172). The trauma of transcendence involves "a breakup of the omnipotence of the logos" (GP 173). This "undoing" and "breakup" are the reversal of which Levinas speaks insofar as they lead to responsible solidarity rather than mere skepticism. But it should not surprise us that Levinas should say about the experience of the inviolability of the face, "We have entered the age of logic and reason!" (DF 9). If there is a *ratio* that "reason" does not recognize, there may well be a logic that eludes the "logos."

Before seeing how such a logic might be a logic of solidarity, we must consider what may be the most serious objection of all to the onslaught Levinas unleashes against knowledge.

**Objection:** Like most continental philosophers, Levinas presupposes the Copernican revolution. When knowledge is conceived as constitutive of its objects in the Kantian sense, it is easy to see how their otherness is compromised. When Levinas says that knowledge reduces the other to the same, he is just restating the Kantian admission that when knowledge constitutes its objects it does not know them as they are in themselves (transcendence) but only as they appear to us (immanence).[26]

But Kantian-style antirealism is only the bias of continental philosophy. Both classical Aristotelian-Thomistic realism and the various more recent realisms of analytic philosophy provide no basis for viewing knowledge as possession or domination, and that is just one more sign of their superiority to the transcendental idealisms of Kantian origin whether continental (e.g., Husserl, Heidegger, Gadamer), analytic (e.g., Goodman, Putnam), or the curious blend of the two one finds in Rorty. Properly understood, the mind is a mirror of nature insofar as 'snow is white' is true if and only if snow is white.[27]

**Reply:** Levinas's critique of cognition as understood by main strands of the western tradition is directed as much against the realisms of the tradition as against its idealisms. He often seems to be a Kantian about representational knowledge outside the immediacy of the face to face. For him "every representation is essentially interpretable as a transcendental constitution" (TI 38). The basic meaning of transcendental subjectivity is that "no signification precedes that which I give to myself" (GP 157).

Sometimes this transcendental idealism is expressed in the language of Kant and Fichte. So it is not surprising that Levinas should then repeatedly describe the ethical relation as the breakup of transcendental apperception (OB 141, 148, 151–52, 163–64; GP 159, 165, 171, 173). Again, in speaking of knowledge as a taming or domestication of its other, Levinas contrasts the proximity of the face as being " 'older' than the a priori. . . . For this relationship is not an act . . . not a position in the Fichtean sense. Not everything that is in consciousness would be posited by consciousness" (OB 100–101). Sounding almost like Nietzsche, Levinas takes the "bestowal of sense" in transcendental idealism to have a voluntary character to it. "Intentionality is thus an intention of the soul, a spontaneity, a *willing*, and the sense bestowed itself, in some way, what is *willed*: the way in which beings or their Being manifest themselves to thought in knowledge corresponds to the way in which consciousness 'wills' this manifestation. . . . Cognitive intention is thus a free act" (BI 101). It is this priority of freedom over responsibility that is the reduction of the other to the same.

On other occasions, the a priori is described in Heideggerian terms as "fore-knowledge" or "pro-ject" (BM 316). But most frequently the vocabulary is Husserlian. Although phenomenology set out to challenge "the idealist notion of the subject," because it "rediscovers the universe within the subject which constitutes it, it is still an egology" by Husserl's own admission. Moreover, in this context epistemology becomes first philosophy "not only as a propaedeutic of knowledge but also as a theory of the absolute." The ego is absolute because of its power over the constituted object (BTK 61).[28]

Over against the Husserlian version of transcendental idealism, Levinas interprets the "radical reversal, from cognition" in terms of "an intentionality of a wholly different type" (TI 23). It will involve "meaning prior to my *Sinnge-bung*" (TI 51) and "*signification without a context*" (TI 23).

These themes will be developed more fully in the next chapter, but it should be clear here that Levinas is not a transcendental idealist in either the Kantian, or Fichtean, or Husserlian sense. Transcendence is compromised by the transcendental ego and its horizons. Whatever validity these analyses may have for representational knowledge and the ontology implicit within it, the ethical/religious relation and the responsible self required for authentic solidarity require a foundation, if that is the right word, of an entirely different sort.

It would seem that Levinas's only defense against the realist objection would be to concede and declare himself a realist. But instead he turns to face, as it were, another foe, saying, in effect, "But even on a realist construal of knowing, knowledge is possession, enjoyment, returning home with booty from the battle, the reduction of the other to the same."

Levinas finds it "surprising" that Husserlian phenomenology should take a transcendental turn "after the realist themes the idea of intentionality seemed to approach" (TI 123).[29] But even if this development was in some sense inevitable,[30] Levinas interprets representational intentionality on the realist side of the street as frequently as on the idealist side. Thus he regularly speaks of intentionality or representation in terms of the adequation of thought and being; and when he does so, instead of denying adequation as a good Kantian would, he continues to make all the familiar complaints about knowledge as the abolition of the alterity of the object.[31]

It would be possible to read these passages as referring to Husserlian adequation, the fulfillment of intention in intuition, a notion fully compatible with the transcendental turn in Husserlian phenomenology.[32] But in his adequation texts Levinas regularly invites us to read this notion in terms of the classically realist notion of truth as *adaequatio rei et intellectus*. Italics have been added to the following passages to highlight this invitation. Husserl's surprising transcendentalism affirms

> that the object of consciousness, while distinct from consciousness, is *as it were* a product of consciousness. . . . In clarity an object which is first exterior *is given* [his italics], that is, is delivered over to him who encounters it *as though* it had been entirely determined by him . . . the object's resistance as an exterior being vanishes. This mastery is total and *as though* creative . . . the thinker who submits to what is thought does so "gracefully," *as though* the object, even in the surprises it has in store for cognition, had

been anticipated by the subject. . . . Thus the exteriority of the object represented *appears* to reflection to be a meaning ascribed by the representing subject. (TI 123–25)

Or again, in adequation, being stands "on the brink of illusion . . . *as though* the *given* [his italics] were drawn from oneself, *as though* the meaning it brings were ascribed to it by me. Being bears in itself the possibility of idealism" (TrO 346; cf. TO 68). In this *Philosophie des Als-Ob*, Levinas performs a kind of epoche on the transcendental turn in Husserl, turning back toward the realist moment in phenomenology. This is why, in addition to Husserl and Heidegger, whom Levinas portrays as transcendental idealists, he does not hesitate to include three transcendental realists as targets of his assault on knowledge: Plato, Aristotle, and Hegel. Nor, in doing so, does he impose a Kantian reading on them.

A steady polemic against the Socratic/Platonic doctrine of knowledge as recollection runs throughout *Totality and Infinity* (43, 51, 61, 171, 180, 204), precisely on the grounds that transcendence is reduced to immanence.[33] In recollection, "Reason is alone" (TO 68; cf. 77). A similar "immanence of the real to reason" is found in Aristotle's correlation of knowledge and being, both as ontology and as onto-theology (EF 76–77; cf. TrO 346, EL 20).

Levinas sees Hegel as the culmination of this tradition (EF 78, TrO 347). For Kantian anti-realism in all of its many modes, the Copernican revolution seriously compromises the transcendence of the object of knowledge, for it enters our experience and thought only on our terms in an accord with whatever a priori anticipations we bring to experience. Anti-Kantian realism purports to preserve more transcendence than Kantian anti-realism. It is a double claim. First, the real is and is what it is independently of our knowledge of it.[34] Second, we can have knowledge of the real as it is "in itself." Our knowledge can correspond to it, can perfectly mirror it, can be, to use classical language, *adaequatio intellectus et rei*.

Hegelian idealism is as much a version of this realism as any rationalist or empiricist versions of scientific realism.[35] And it is Hegel who lets the cat out of the bag, who shows how minimal is the transcendence of the realists' object. Thought must be in conformity with being, to be sure, but this conformity is not so much submission as conquest. First, he interprets Kant's transcendental unity of apperception this way: "The Ego is what is originally identical, at one with itself, and utterly at home with itself. If I say 'I,' this is the abstract self-relation, and what is posited in this unity is infected by it, and transformed into it. Thus the Ego is, so to speak, the crucible and the fire through which the indifferent multiplicity is consumed and reduced to unity." Hegel then adds the passage that is the epigraph to this chapter according to which cognition is the appropriation, conquering, and even the crushing of the world.[36]

Thus the fate of the "reality of the world" whose defender the realist purports to be. Whatever independence the realist gives to the object of knowledge with one hand is taken back with the other. In his inaugural address at Heidelberg in 1816, Hegel told his students,

> I hope I may succeed in deserving and winning your trust. At first, however, I can claim nothing from you except that you bring with you above all a trust [Vertrauen] in Science and a trust in yourselves. The courage for truth, faith in [Glaube an] the power [Macht] of the mind [des Geistes] is the first condition of philosophy. Because man [der Mensch] is mind, he must consider himself worthy of the highest and cannot think highly enough of the greatness and power of his mind. With this faith nothing will be so obstinate and hard as not to reveal itself to him. The at first hidden and concealed essence of the universe has no power [Kraft] to withstand the courage for knowledge. It must disclose itself before him, lay its riches and its depths before his eyes, and give them for his enjoyment.[37]

There are thinly disguised sexual overtones in the notion that the object must disclose itself before the eyes of the knower and give itself for his enjoyment. Feminist epistemology might well see Hegel's account as all too masculine. Knowledge is portrayed as if it were the rape of a mortal by a god. For there are theological overtones as well. The theological virtues of trust and faith[38] are directed by the knower toward himself as the bearer of Reason and the producer of Science. The thing in itself, which for Kant is the thing as known by God,[39] is fully exposed to the human subject because in its philosophical mode it has become the divine subject and enjoys divine sovereignty.[40] Of course, the knower, for example, Hegel, did not make the object, for example, the Alps, in the sense in which the God of the Bible is the maker of heaven and earth, including the Alps. But he is, in his philosophical mode as Reason, fully self-aware in the Logic, the Logos that is "God as he is in his eternal essence before the creation of nature and a finite mind"[41] and of which it is said, "All things came into being through him, and without him not one thing came into being" (John 1:3). That is why philosophy can be presented in the Phenomenology as Absolute Knowing, and its bearer in the Encyclopedia as Absolute Spirit. It looks as if anti-Kantian realism is the "crushing" victory of the autonomous subject over the otherness of the object.

Levinas will call this the reduction of the other to the same, label it ontology,[42] and see it as the nerve center not just of Hegel or of modern philosophy but of the mainstream of western philosophy. Hence the passage cited above in which representation is assimilated to enjoyment and the knower, whether understood in realist or transcendental idealist terms, is seen as an egoist, "entirely deaf to the Other, outside of all communication and all refusal to communicate—without ears, like a hungry stomach" (TI 134).

It's alimentary, my dear Watson! The object transcends the subject insofar as it eludes the subject. Mother Hubbard's cupboard may be bare, and Peter Rabbit may elude Farmer McGregor. But had he not, he would have ended up, like his father, in one of Mrs. McGregor's pies. In this case the object's transcendence is transcended as it is consumed, appropriated, conquered, and crushed by the knowing subject, reduced to a means for the subject's enjoyment. Here we have the parable of Descartes's fallible but autonomously absolute subject. Sometimes the object escapes the subject, who fails to achieve truth. But when the object is captured (Hegel will say *begriffen* by the *Begriff*), it is wholly appropriated as the subject's property and assimilated as the subject's sustenance. Moreover, to be so appropriated and assimilated is the raison d'être, the meaning of the being of the object.

Precisely by its purported overcoming of the thing in itself, Absolute idealism is a form of epistemic realism. It is, I believe, with reference to this whole realist tradition, culminating in Hegel, that Levinas describes knowledge, rationality, intelligibility, and manifestation as "being's move" (GP 154). The manifestation of being involves a subjective as well as objective genitive, "as if the very doing of being led to clarity, in the form of intelligibility, and then became an intentional thematization in an experience. . . . Thematic exposition concludes the business of being or truth" (GP 155). Or again, "The . . . disclosure of being to itself would be produced in philosophy. Knowing, the dis-covering, would not be added on to the being of entities, to essence. . . . Philosophy which states essence as an ontology, concludes this essence, this lucidity of lucidity, by this logos. Consciousness fulfills the being of entities" (OB 103). This realist reading of intentionality can be expressed by saying that "being, what is given, what imposes itself . . . the fact that it shows itself, is like an emphasis of its own being. And when I use the expression that it *shows* itself, of course it does so in the being of the subject. . . . So, in this case, being itself is essentially presence" (EL 14–15). It gives itself to comprehension (IOF 3–7); its raison d'être is to be "the alpha and omega of intelligibility" (BI 100).

In the "detour of ideality" that is knowledge, then, "being thus carries on its affair of being." But it does so in a world without surprises (OB 99). This can be expressed by saying that while the subject can be surprised, its identity is not altered, since "alien being is as it were naturalized as soon as it commits itself with knowledge" (TrO 345). Or we can say that in this "extreme accessibility of being" surprise and astonishment disappear "in the truth once it is found" (BI 102). There is discovery and the growth of knowledge. But wherever knowledge is achieved, there being no longer has any secrets; it has given itself completely to the subject that has let it be itself.

It seems that like Husserl, Levinas wants "to affirm both that consciousness bestows sense and that Being commands the modalities of consciousness which reach it, that Being controls what appears as phenomenon. This final phrase receives an idealist interpretation: Being is immanent in thought and thought does not transcend itself in knowledge" (BI 106). But this idealist interpretation is possible only at the point where the realist dream is fulfilled. When being gives itself to thought so completely that there can be talk of adequation between the two, even if this adequation occurs at being's behest, the temptation to talk *as though* thought were the origin of being becomes irresistible. This is why Levinas's assault on knowledge can move back and forth between realist and transcendental idealist modes of discourse so easily. Not only does he see the two theories of knowledge as implying each other; he sees each as implying the same conclusion: "In the final analysis, presence [adequation?] excludes all transcendence" (BI 106). For just this reason, "Reason" undermines solidarity; for instead, of a bond that precedes all my intentional activity and practical action, it allows me to name and define every other, including the neighbor and especially the enemy. This is what Sixo understood. He would have understood the Hegelian epigraph to this chapter according to which knowledge is the crushing of the world and why the realist is not immune to Levinas's critique.

* * *

It is clear now why the journey "from cognition to solidarity" (OB 119) is not a movement from foundation to superstructure but a reversal, a repentant change of direction. So far is knowledge, whether the idealist or the realist version, from being the basis of peace, justice, and love that these latter are only to be found by moving beyond the domain of the former (which is not to move down the ladder to "faith" as mere opinion). It is not by grasping the world but by being grasped from beyond the world that we are delivered from the war of all against all. "In the approach to others *indebtedness* takes the place of the grasp or the comprehension of knowledge" (BI 110). From *Totality and Infinity* through *Otherwise Than Being*, the ground of fraternity, as Levinas often puts it in typical French fashion, is responsibility (TI 214; OB 116). Even when he finds it necessary, in the latter text, to describe responsibility in terms of the extreme passivity of being persecuted or taken hostage, he sees this trauma as the sine qua non of solidarity (OB 102, 117, 159; cf. LP 123). "The putting into question of the I by the other makes me solidary with the other in an incomparable and unique way. . . . Solidarity here is responsibility" (TrO 353).

This means that solidarity is not based upon what we have in common,[43] whether that be some knowable fact about us or some act we undertake together. Thus it is not by belonging to the same genus or having the same causal origin that we are most deeply akin (TI 213–14; BI 110).[44] Nor do we belong together in the first instance by virtue of a social contract rooted in the *conatus essendi* of each. There is a close link in Levinas between the claim that obligation precedes commitment (OB ch. 3–5) and the claim that sociality precedes contract (OB 4–5, 119, 124–25, 159; GP 167).

It follows that in terms of what I can know or need, the Other is a stranger and fraternity exists only "in extreme separation" (EF 84) and "across the abyss that it itself unbridgeable by mere knowledge" (BI 110), even when the Other is, biologically or culturally speaking, kith and kin.

Howard Caygill places great stress on the importance of fraternity in

Levinas's thought, a theme closely related to, if not synonymous with, our theme of solidarity. He writes,

> The dominant liberal tradition of political thought since Kant and Hegel [one would have thought Locke] gives overwhelming primacy to the concept of freedom and then, to a lesser degree . . . of the concept of equality. Yet, as Levinas constantly reminds us, the modern political has been trinitarian since the French Revolution, comprising not only freedom and equality but also fraternity. It is upon the third member of the trinity that Levinas focuses his attention . . . he tries to rethink fraternity on the basis of alterity and thus to derive the concepts of freedom and equality from fraternity rather than leaving it as their supplement.[45]

It is this strange linkage of the Other to the theme of fraternity that motivates the revision in Levinas's answer to the question, What does the face say? In *Totality and Infinity*, the answer is, "you shall not commit murder" (TI 199, 216, 262, 303). Subsequently Levinas finds it necessary to express this categorical obligation in terms that do greater justice to the solidarity implicit in this command. I can avoid murder while remaining indifferent to the Other; but the ethical relation is "the impossibility of indifference—impossible without fail—before the misfortunes and faults of a neighbor" (GP 166). Thus we move to "you shall not usurp my place in the sun" and "you shall not leave me to die alone" (BCI 38).[46] These imperatives are not the first principles of an ethical theory whose task it is to justify them and to derive a moral code from them. They are rather attempts to express in the form of a said meaning that resides first and foremost in saying itself as such.

The first of these formulas is not simply the assertion of natural right in the state of nature, for while it is related to fear it is "fear for the Other" rather than fear of the other (BCI 38; EF 82). That fear asks, "My being-in-the-world, or my 'place in the sun,' my being at home, have these not also been the usurpation of spaces belonging to the other man whom I have already oppressed or starved, or driven out into a third world; are they not acts of repulsing, excluding, exiling, stripping, killing?" (EF 82). This is the fear for the Other that comes to me "from the face of the Other" (BCI 38). In this fear the "impossibility of indifference" just mentioned signals solidarity.[47]

But just as "you shall not commit murder" can mean "leave me alone," so "you shall not usurp my place in the sun" can mean "leave room for me." Neither quite captures the sense in which the call of the Other is a summons that "demands my presence" (BI 109; cf. 112), that "commands me not to leave this mortal to dwell alone" (EL 15). The reference to mortality signifies that it is especially in relation to death, the Other's, not mine,[48] that the bearer of a face must not be left alone. Death may indeed be inexorable, but fear for the other signals "the obligation not to let the other man face death alone" (BCI 38). The Other's death has become "my business," as if my indifference would make me an "accomplice" in it (EF 83). It hardly needs saying that the presence demanded here and the presence demanded by Knowledge (the metaphysics of presence) relate to each other as antipodes.

It may seem as if a solidarity that makes the Other's death "my business" is as strong as one might hope for, or even stronger. But Levinas's account of the bond to which we are bound over in responsibility goes one surprising step farther. On his account I am not merely responsible for the "wretchedness" (TrO 352) or "distress" (MS 97) of the Other, but also "for his responsibility" (II 245). Thus I am responsible "for the pain *and fault* of others" (LP 123, emphasis added; cf. GP 166; OB 112). Usually Levinas disclaims any implication that this responsibility involves guilt or culpability on my part, but he does not hesitate to quote from *The Brothers Karamazov*, if only as hyperbole, "Each of us is guilty before everyone, for everyone and for each one, and I more than others" (GP 168).

All this has ontological implications, which is all right, since Levinas seeks the teleological suspension of ontology, not its abolition. The self is older than the ego (OB 117). This means that "the responsibility for the others, the relation with the non-ego, precedes any relation of the ego with itself" (OB 119; cf. 127). This responsibility is "the *for-the-other*" that comes "before any knowledge I may have of myself, before any reflexive presence of myself to myself, and beyond my perseverance in Being and my repose in myself" (BI 111). It is "as if I were devoted to the other man before being devoted to myself" (EF 83). Neither idealism's *cogito* nor naturalism's *conatus essendi* is the primordial fact about myself.

To put this in terms of my personal identity is to say, "I am 'in myself' through the others. . . . The word *I* means *here I am*, answering for everything and for everyone. Responsibility for the others has not been a return to oneself. . . . I exist through the other and for the other. . . . The psyche can signify this alterity in the same" (OB 112, 114).[49]

This ontology is not first philosophy but is derived from ethics as first philosophy. It starts with the saying and not with the said. For this reason it does not rest on the logic of self identity but expresses the rupture of that logic through the presence of the Other who demands my presence. And yet, even as second philosophy, this ontology has its own logic. Beginning with the Other as the "first intelligible" (Si 185), it seeks to articulate a realm of meaning, intelligibility, and rationality that is the proper ground or foundation of the onto-logic that has so often been taken to be self-evident and self-grounding.[50] We begin to understand this prior logic of solidarity when we see how "you shall not commit murder" entails "you shall not leave me to die alone. Be with me now and in the hour of my death."

History shows, according to Levinas, that communities based on any other foundation, if that is the right word, are violent. Since Levinas means to speak about history and not the state of nature, his reference is not to the primal war of all against all, but to those proud civilizations that seek to base themselves on universal justice. The original face to face is an asymmetrical relation between myself and another. It is when a third party arrives on the scene that it becomes necessary to negotiate the conflicts between the multiplicity of in themselves absolute claims to which this plurality gives rise. Then "the metaphysical relation of the I with the Other moves into the form of the We, aspires to a State, institutions, laws, which are the source of universality. But politics left to itself bears a tyranny within itself . . . how could universal, that is, visible principles be opposed . . . to the face of the other, without recoiling before the cruelty of this impersonal justice" (TI 300).

The primacy Levinas gives to the personal ethical relation over the impersonal principles of a universal, rule-structured justice, deserves careful comparison with Carol Gilligan's attempt to relativize a universalistic ethic of justice to a more concretely personal ethic of care.[51] This is all the more true when Levinas translates "you shall not commit murder" into "be with me now and in the hour of my death."

His view, then, is that we move to solidarity not by rising above the particular interests of clan or contract to the universality of knowledge, even knowledge of justice as construed by traditional ethical theory, but by rising above both the particularity of interests and the universality of knowledge to the particularity of an obligation that requires my presence to the Other. Conscience need not make cowards of us all; it can make us sisters and brothers. But this involves a reversal of the direction in which we were always already heading.

\* \* \*

In its implications for ethics as a branch of philosophy, this reversal is postmodern.[52] How does it stand with Kierkegaard? Vis-à-vis such ideals of modernity as autonomy and objectivity[53] his writings surely represent a call for reversal. "Reason" needs to be (dangerously) supplemented by revelation, objectivity by subjectivity, and self-love by neighbor love. But negatively speaking, much of what he and his pseudonyms present is about the religious subjectivity of hidden inwardness embedded in a sustained critique of certain modes of sociality, referred to variously as the universal (Hegel's *Sittlichkeit*), the present age, the crowd, Christendom, the Established Order, and, as if anticipating Nietzsche, the herd. Positively speaking, much of the Kierkegaardian corpus focuses on the individual, reflected out of these totalities by a voice other than one's own, standing alone—before God—in secret. Is there a logic of solidarity here? A passion for fraternity?

*Works of Love*, as we have seen, represents a decisive break, not with hidden inwardness but with its ultimacy. We are to enter into our closets to pray alone with God, but when we come out, the first one we see is the neighbor whom we are commanded to love, publicly with works of love (WL 51). Thus the first chapter is entitled "Love's Hidden Life and Its Recognizability by Its Fruits." But, like so much of Levinas's writing, this is most easily understood in terms of one-to-one relationships. Neither Levinas nor Kierkegaard moves beyond this to a very full-fledged politics or social theory. But it cannot be denied that there is a greater political élan in Levinas than in Kierkegaard. Charitably, we might say that Kierkegaard did not face the traumas encountered by Levinas as Jew living in the twentieth century. Less charitably, we might say that Kierkegaard shared the social complacency of the Christendom he criticized more than he realized. Whatever the case, Kierkegaard has little to say about solidarity and fraternity on a large scale beyond critique of their counterfeit forms produced by and as the pride of the Present Age.

But there are a few hints that might be developed. The context for developing them is what I call Religiousness C.[54]

In *Philosophical Fragments*, Johannes Climacus contrasts revelation with recollection.[55] In *Concluding Unscientific Postscript* he renders these more concrete. Religiousness A is the Socratic spirituality (not to be simply identified with Platonic speculation) that relies solely on recollection, the assumption that whatever truth we may access is already in us or that it falls within our power to recognize it. Religiousness B relies on revelation for the specifically Christian belief that the eternal has come into time in the God-Man, Jesus Christ. In both *Fragments* and *Postscript*, Christ is the paradox to be acknowledged in faith because this fact is not recognizable by unaided human reason, which is offended by the claim that what is most important to know exceeds its powers. Climacus understands this claim about the Incarnation and the closely related claim about Atonement such that the God in time is not only Teacher but Savior to be essential to Christian faith, and he resists attempts to make Christianity "reasonable" by converting revelation into reason.

Much of the literature on Kierkegaard stops at this point (if it does not, like Levinas, stop already at *Fear and Trembling*). But Kierkegaard wrote a lot more, and it is in this "second authorship" that he moves decisively beyond hidden inwardness and gives us what little social theory he has to offer in a positive way. I call this the movement to Religiousness C as the teleological suspension of Religiousness B. The orthodox Christian doctrines of the Incarnation and Atonement are maintained as articles of faith, but they, or more broadly speaking, doctrinal orthodoxy, are no longer the end of the line. They have their telos beyond themselves. Kierkegaard is interested in "speaking the truth in love" (Eph. 4:15) and in "faith working through love" (Gal. 5:6). The cognitive, whether a matter of faith or reason, is not the highest mode of human existence for Kierkegaard, just as it is not for Levinas. Thus in what I call Religiousness C, Christ continues to be the Paradox to be believed, but also becomes the Paradigm or Pattern or Prototype to be imitated. Only as *imitatio Christi* is the Christian life fulfilled, and this brings it out into the public square; for this is where the life of Christ occurred, except for periodic withdrawals to seclusion for prayer.

A brief look at three passages from Religiousness C. First, an incipient logic of solidarity from one of Kierkegaard's most sustained critiques of "the

Present Age." He writes, "When individuals (each one individually) are essentially and passionately related to an idea and together are essentially related to the same idea, the relation is optimal and normative. Individually the relation separates them (each one has himself for himself), and ideally it unites them" (TA 62). In this text passion is regularly contrasted with reflection, echoing Climacus's contrast between subjectivity and objectivity. The society Kierkegaard envisages does not ultimately rest on knowledge, on having the right political theory, be it liberal or communitarian, radical or reactionary. Its most essential ingredient is personal commitment. Kierkegaard writes, "The spiritual jolting of an individuality is *eo ipso* the indication of decisive religious categories; therefore spirit must not be considered identical with talent and genius, by no means, but identical with resolution in passion" (TA 22). Those who have "commitment issues" will not make good citizens. They will need to be "essentially and passionately related to an idea."

What idea? or better, What kind of idea? One that unites the individuals, to be sure, but only after it has separated them so that "each one has himself for himself." Levinas would speak here of the idea of Infinity and of the nontransferrable, radically individuating responsibility each one has in relation to it. Kierkegaard and his pseudonyms speak of the idea of the Eternal, and often of the more specifically Christian idea of God incarnate. But whether in the more generic or the more specific form, the idea that is needed is one that generates a the nontransferrable, radically individuating responsibility for each one. In *Sickness unto Death* that responsibility is "Thou shalt believe in the forgiveness of sins" (SUD 115), thereby beginning to repair the relation to the power that has established the self. In *Works of Love* is it "You shall love your neighbor as yourself" (WL, First Series). In the first case it involves accepting forgiveness and reconciliation through the death of Christ as Savior; in the second it involves imitating the life of Christ in relation the neighbor.

Here as before the convergence with Levinas is formal and structural. Christ plays no such role in the latter's thought. But whether we are talking about the idea of Infinity à la Levinas, or the idea of Eternity à la Kierkegaard, or the specifically Christian idea of the God in time à la Kierkegaard, the idea is not the content of knowledge so much as the call to infinite, personal, passionate responsibility in response to a claim that defines and identifies us before we can define and identify ourselves.

Such relations and the society built on them are not automatic by any means. Kierkegaard talks about two ways of missing the boat: "if individuals relate to an idea merely *en masse* (consequently without the individual separation of inwardness), we get violence, anarchy, riotousness; but if there is no idea for the individuals *en masse* and no individually separating essential inwardness, either, then we have crudeness" (TA 63). One is reminded here of the remark attributed to Clemenceau that America "is the only nation in history which miraculously has gone directly from barbarism to degeneration without the usual interval of civilization." Kierkegaard's logic of solidarity seeks to be an alternative to both the barbarism that has the wrong kind of idea and the degeneration (he says crudeness, I would say decadence) that is entirely without an idea.

In expounding the text from *Two Ages* it has been necessary to refer to *Works of Love*. But this text has a contribution to make to Kierkegaard's logic of solidarity in its own right. It involves a text we have already considered in a different context.[56] Kierkegaard is discussing the radical equality presupposed in the command to love one's neighbor as oneself, especially since the category of the neighbor includes the enemy (WL 67–68). It *"seems to fit in so little with the relationships of earthly life and with the temporal dissimilarities of the world"* but by virtue of "the perfections of eternity" it is able to be blind to the differences of earthly life. By contrast with the caste system in which outcasts are considered to be "not born," he sees Christianity as "deeply and forever memorably imprinting the kinship of all human beings—because the kinship is secured by each individual's equal kinship with and relationship to God in Christ; because the Christian doctrine addresses itself equally to each individual, teaches him that God has created him and Christ has redeemed him" (WL 69).[57]

For those who relate essentially and passionately to the idea of this kinship (solidarity, fraternity) it has the potential to unite those whom it at the same time separates. Kierkegaard does not develop this potential very far. He is far too comfortable with a blindness to differences of social status that is spiritual and interpersonal without worrying about the suffering caused by various forms of social stratification, the caste systems, if you will, to be found in Christendom. So he makes the indisputable point that Christianity has not eliminated differences and status, but adds that it does not even want to (WL 70–71). But he points to a solidarity whose potential he does not himself develop, one that in principle undermines the logos, the "rationality" of both the hierarchical medieval society that was passing away before his eyes and the (differently) hierarchical liberal modernity that was replacing it.[58]

A third text is quite similar. The first part (No. I) of *Practice in Christianity* is a meditation on Matthew 11:28, "Come Here, All You Who Labor and Are Burdened, and I Will Give You Rest" (PC 5, 11). Anti-Climacus, the pseudonymous author, reflects first on the amazing graciousness of this invitation and then on the opposition it evokes in the form of offense. In a wonderfully dramatic section our author stages a kind of jury trial in which ten representatives of the Established Order discuss whether the Jesus who issues this invitation could be the Christ, the Expected One. Each in his own way votes no. After five "sagacious and sensible" persons give their verdict, the clergyman speaks:

> But the government of the world does not advance tumultuously by leaps, world development is not . . . *revolutionair* but *evolutionair*. Therefore the authentic expected one will look entirely different, will come as the most glorious flowering and the highest unfolding of the established order . . . he

will recognize the established order as the authority, will summon all the clergy to a convention, present to it his achievements, together with his credentials—and then if in balloting he has the majority he will be accepted and hailed as the extraordinary that he is: the expected one. (PC 47)

The biting irony of this text makes it abundantly clear that what Kierkegaard wants us to consider is a dramatic reversal of the status quo. For does not every status quo think like this? But is there a social direction to this reversal, an alternative logic of solidarity? Yes, but once again only in the form of a hint. The clergyman objects to the inviter's "distance from everything that is called the established order . . . his fantastic flight beyond actuality out into association with ignorant commoners[59] . . . his arrogant, revolutionary disdain of all the intelligence and competence of the established order, just to begin all over again from the beginning with the help of—fishermen and tradespeople" (PC 47).

For Religiousness C and its theme of imitating Christ as Pattern, the logic of solidarity will involve an equality in which class privilege, and by extension the hierarchies of race and gender, are neutralized. In this and in related texts Kierkegaard provides us with no developed political theory, much less a political program. Perhaps that is just as well. Both he and Levinas leave it to us to work out the concrete implications (theory) and applications (practice) of the logics of solidarity they present.

# Inverted Intentionality

## Being Addressed

Autonomy is allergic to alterity. If, then, one is to speak of subjectivity and transcendence or, more specifically of intentionality and transcendence, everything depends on how one proceeds. If one begins with a self-sufficient subject, granting autonomy to subjectivity, and then tries to blend alterity into the mix, to use a culinary metaphor, transcendence will be reduced to mere appearance, the *Schein* that is the *Erscheinung* of subjectivity as the true *Wesen*.

This is what happens in Cartesian modernity. The subject is first established as the indubitable center of reference, whose clear and distinct ideas are to be the measure of truth and of being. God, allegedly the highest transcendence, the *tu solus Altissimus* of the Gloria, comes on the scene, to be sure. But too late—only on the onto-theological stage where, as Heidegger puts it in his definition of onto-theology, "the deity can come into philosophy only insofar as philosophy, of its own accord and by its own nature, requires and determines that and how the deity enters into it."[1] The only Oscar for which Descartes's God can be nominated is Best Supporting Actor; for God's role is, ironically, to provide the external guarantee that human thought needs no external guarantees, that Protagoras was right in insisting that "man" is the measure of all things. Of course, Descartes acknowledge the ontic dependence of the subject, who is not *causa sui*, on God, who is. But this affirmation *functions* (1) to keep the censors off his back, and (2) to explain how the subject can be an autonomous absolute even though fallible. Fallibility and method replace sin and salvation. Subjectivity is the independent variable, transcendence the dependent variable, which is to say that transcendence has been absorbed in immanence. Spinoza had good reason to claim that he expressed the Cartesian principle more consistently than Descartes; and Hegel's onto-theological pantheism is as much the fulfillment of Spinoza's project as Spinoza's is the fulfillment of the Cartesian project.[2]

To preserve the authenticity of divine alterity as the highest transcendence, one might insist on starting with God as autonomous and absolute, the independent variable, and blend in human subjectivity as the dependent variable (if I may be pardoned for mixing my culinary and logical metaphors). That is perhaps the appropriate procedure for the theologian within the traditions of the Abrahamic monotheisms,[3] and, in any case, that is how Augustine, Aquinas, Luther, and Calvin proceed as Christian theologians. Thus, for example, in the first paragraph of his *Institutes*, Calvin writes, "In the first place, no one can look upon himself without immediately turning his thoughts to the contemplation of God, in whom he 'lives and moves' [Acts 17:28]."[4] In other words, in a theological context any "Cartesian" attempt to begin with subjectivity immediately collapses in a reference to that which is prior; and Calvin briefly develops this priority of God in both ontological and moral terms as human dependence and depravity. So, in his second paragraph, he presents the proper procedure. "Again, it is certain that man never achieves a clear knowledge of himself unless he has *first* looked upon God's face, and *then* descends from contemplating him to scrutinize himself" (emphasis added).

The phenomenologist may not wish to beg the question at the outset by starting with the subject, thus taking the side of the onto-theologian, or starting with God, thus taking the side of the biblical theologian.[5] Calvin's first suggestion can be helpful here. To begin with the subject is not necessarily to posit the subject as a fixed point of reference. If it turns out to be finite and a fortiori if it turns out to be fallen, it will immediately refer beyond itself, or better, will always already have referred beyond itself. The phenomenologist will be open to the *possibility*[6] that what we try to make first needs to be *aufgehoben* in what is truly First, that it needs to be teleologically suspended in that which is not itself but is its proper home. These references to Hegel and Kierkegaard, respectively, indicate, I should think, that the fates of subjectivity and transcendence are not decided in advance by proceeding in this way; but this will have to be a phenomenology different from those of Husserl and Heidegger, and that is the theme of this chapter.

Kierkegaard's Anti-Climacus gives to the phenomenologist an important enrichment of this strategy. Instead of merely exploring subjectivity in its *possible* relativity to God as Wholly Other, the idea is to explore it in relation to various possible modes of transcendence. Whether, in any given case, autonomy prevails over alterity or vice versa will be the guiding question. The guiding hypothesis might be formulated this way: so much transcendence, so much subjectivity.[7] In other words, the greater the intensity of transcendence, the greater the intensity of subjectivity; or, more specifically, subjectivity is a matter of degree, and it increases with the degree of *self-transcendence* evoked by the *transcendence* to which it is relative. This hypothesis, of course, is not neutral; for it suggests that the self increases as its autonomy decreases and decreases as it becomes more nearly absolute. The hypothesis is a philosophical analog of Jesus' statement "Those who want to save their life will lose it, and those who lose their life for my sake will find it" (Matt. 16:25).[8]

One might even be so bold as to date the birth of postmodernism to Anti-Climacus's definition of sin as despair *before God*. "Sin is: *before God*, or with the conception of God, in despair not to will to be oneself, or in despair to will to be oneself. Thus sin is *intensified* weakness or *intensified* defiance: sin is the *intensification* of despair. The emphasis is on *before God* . . . what lawyers call 'aggravated' despair" (SUD 77). This sounds like the specifically theological stance corresponding to Calvin's second suggestion, and, indeed, it opens the specifically Christian interpretation of despair in *Sickness unto Death* in which Anti-Climacus identifies the self "directly before God" as "the theological self" (SUD 79). But he immediately suggests the more phenomenological strategy of comparing various modes of selfhood in terms of various candidates for being the self's Most Significant Other:

> And what infinite reality [*Realitet*] the self gains by being conscious of existing before God, by becoming a human self whose criterion is God! A cattleman who (if this were possible) is a self directly before his cattle is a very low self, and similarly, a master who is a self directly before his slaves is actually no self—for in both cases a criterion is lacking. The child who previously has had only his parents as a criterion becomes a self as an adult by getting the state as a criterion, but what an infinite accent falls on the self by having God as the criterion! The criterion for the self is always: that directly before which it is a self . . . so everything is qualitatively that by which it is measured, and that which is its qualitative criterion [*Maalestok*] is ethically its goal [*Maal*]; the criterion and goal are what define something. (SUD 79)[9]

We might call this view relational essentialism, according to which *who I am* is a function of my deepest and most defining relation in fact (ontology) and *who I become* is a product of whomever or whatever I choose to be my Most Significant Other (ethics, spirituality).[10] As a heuristic for phenomenological investigation, it opens the door to reflection on various modes of subjectivity in relation to various modes of transcendence.

\* \* \*

Let us begin with a very abstract relation, but one that has tended to dominate modern philosophy, the relation of subject to object. In the previous chapter we have seen that Levinas has a problem both with the realist interpretation of this relation culminating in Hegel and with the transcendental idealist inter- pretation culminating in Husserl (and Heidegger, as he sees it). Since he wishes to overcome the latter's phenomenologies as a phenomenologist, we turn our attention in more detail to his critique of Husserl.[11] The phenomeno- logical slogan "To the things themselves" can sound like an attempt on the part of the anti-Kantian realist to practice Kantian respect for the otherness of the other in the epistemic domain.[12] But to Levinasian ears the correlation (corre- spondence) of intending subject with intended object, of noesis and noema is but another version of the Platonic notion that the truth is within *us* and needs but to be recollected, of the Cartesian notion that *our* clear and distinct ideas are the measure of truth and of being, of the empiricist notion that *our* sense impressions are the measure of truth and being, and of the Hegelian notion of the identity of thought and being within one mode of *our* thought. "To the things themselves" sounds too much like "Tally-ho," the call to hunters and hounds alike to be after the fox (who doubtless has been reading Hegel and has spent the morning chasing Peter Rabbit's cousins). Thus, while the "radical reversal, from cognition to solidarity" (OB 119) means a movement away from both Hegelian realism and Husserlian transcendental idealism,[13] it is against both of these traditions, but especially the latter, that the notion of inverted intentionality comes into play.

A typical mode of intentionality is seeing a physical object. The transcen- dence of this object to subjectivity that intends it is double. In the first place, it gives itself to vision perspectivally in *Abschattungen*. No finite set of these exhausts the infinity of possible profiles or adumbrations that are the being of the object, which always exceeds the phenomena in which it gives itself. Hence what Sartre calls the "transphenomenality of being."[14] In this case, at least, the subject never has the object fully in its grasp. Presence is never complete.

In the second place, just for this reason the object can surprise the subject. Truth is adequation, which means that intuition "fulfills" the intention by confirming what the intention anticipates.[15] But subsequent intuition may falsify the original intention. What I perceive as a building may turn out to be only a facade on a movie set. Intentionality "constitutes" its objects, to be sure, but this plainly does not mean that it creates them either in the sense that the Lord made heaven and earth or in the sense that the artist creates a poem, a painting, or a fictional character. For adequation (truth, knowledge) to occur, the subject must adjust to the object as it gives itself. Here Husserl talks like a common sense realist with an empiricist bent.

For Levinas, it nevertheless means the fatal compromise of the transcen- dence of the object. For the intentional subject turns out to be the independent variable after all. The hounds and the hunters will doubtless have to adjust their course to that taken by the fox, but that does not keep the fox from being the means to the enjoyment of them both. In the hunt, the fox's being is relative, the being of the hounds and hunters absolute. As Levinas reads Husserl,

> The fundamental intuition of Husserlian philosophy consists of attributing absolute existing to concrete conscious life . . . life in the presence of transcendent beings. [N.B.] . . . We shall first describe the absolute character of the existence of consciousness and then show how this existence consists in being intentional. It will then follow that consciousness is the origin of all being and that the latter is determined by the intrinsic meaning of the former. (TIH 25–26)[16]

Consciousness "is an absolute existence. It is relative to nothing, for it is free" (DEH 74). This is because it is "not constituted, but constituting," which corresponds to "man's concern to constitute his own existence freely" (DEH 76, 79).

There is a crucial linkage here among intentionality, constitution, and origin. Thus the vocation of phenomenology lies "in grasping the meaning of objects by putting them back into the *intentions* in which they are *constituted,* and thus grasping them in their *origin* in the mind, in self-evidence" (DEH 71, emphasis added). Fully to understand intentionality as constituting its objects, it is necessary "to show that the *origin of all being,* including that of nature, is determined by the intrinsic meaning of conscious life and not the other way around" (TIH 18, emphasis added). Since, as we have seen, Husserl does not mean the causal origin of the existence of things, we must think in terms of the noncausal origin of their meaning. One way Husserl expresses this, according to Levinas, is that nothing can be "absolutely foreign to the subject" because there is "no imaginable place where conscious life could have or should have been pierced, and in which we would have arrived at a transcendence that could have any other meaning than that of the intentional unity appearing within subjectivity" (DEH 69).[17] Thus it is necessary to transcend not the realism of common sense, but the naiveté with which it "finds itself always before a ready-made object without asking about the meaning of its objectivity" (DEH 72). The meaning of the object's objectivity is that it is essentially and not accidentally there for self-presentation to the subject. As in the hunt the rabbit is for the fox, who in turn is for the hounds and hunters, so the object has its telos outside itself in the subject, and it is precisely by being this Omega to the object that the subject is its Alpha, its origin. Paraphrasing Augustine, the subject says to the object, "You are made for me, and my consciousness is restless until through my intentional acts I have captured and enjoyed you."[18]

Another way to put this is to say that for Husserl the subject's "*access to the object is part of the object's being*" (DEH 95).[19] In other words, "Husserl's step forward beyond Descartes consists in not separating the knowledge of an object—or more generally, the mode of appearing of an object in our life—from its being; it consists of seeing the mode of its being known as the expression and the characteristic of its mode of being" (TIH 32). The object has no meaning but that given to it by the subject, and while empirical subjectivity must adjust to empirical facticity, thus betraying its finitude, this in no way compromises its absoluteness as the object's origin. Levinas writes, "To be sure, the intentionality of consciousness does not designate voluntary intention only. Yet it retains the initiating and incohative pattern of voluntary intention. The given enters into a thought which recognizes in it or invests it with its own project, and thus exercises mastery over it" (OB 101). Only as taken can it be given.

This may seem, as it surely does to Husserl, to be the "triumph of subjectivity."[20] For the temporary (one might say strategic) epistemic subordination of the subject to the facticity of the object is in the service of its ontological supremacy as the origin, the *Sinngeber*, the source without which the object would have no meaning at all. But in terms of our hypothesis, "so much transcendence, so much subjectivity," we are dealing with a very minimal grade of subjectivity. Just as the farmer and the master are hardly selves at all in the presence of their cows and slaves, since the latter provide no qualitative criterion that could be the goal or normative essence of the former, so the subject who intends the object finds that its knowledge, of which it is so proud, to be a special mode of eating and enjoyment, a "rationality" that qualifies its animality only minimally.

Precisely because intentionality is enjoyment the "transcendence" it embodies "does not manage to escape solitude. The light that permits encountering something other than the self, *makes it encountered as if this thing came from the ego.* The light, brightness, is intelligibility itself; making everything come from me, it reduces every experience to an element of reminiscence. Reason is alone" (TO 39, emphasis added). Transcendence is transcended.

For Levinas the intentionality that operates in this subject-object relation permits only the most minimal transcendence, and, in keeping with the formula "So much transcendence, so much subjectivity," only the most minimal selfhood. It's a bit like the farmer who exists only in relation to his cows. There arises a need to turn "beyond intentionality," or, more precisely, beyond *this* intentionality to "an intentionality of a wholly different type" (TI 23).

Perhaps, without leaving the transcendental frame of reference, we should turn from the constituted object to the alter ego, the other constituting subject. Unlike the object that presents itself in *Abschattungen*, the other subject does not give itself to intuition at all. "If it [did], if what belongs to the other's own essence were directly accessible, *it would be merely a moment of my own essence, and ultimately he himself and I myself would be the same. . . . Whatever can become presented, and evidently verified, originally—is something I am; or else it belongs to me as peculiarly my own.*"[21] The mode in which the other subject is "given" to consciousness is not presentation but appresentation, the name Husserl gives to a *"certain mediacy of intentionality."*[22] Perhaps this *awareness of* the other subject is the "intentionality of a wholly different type" in which Levinas hopes to find real transcendence and thereby real subjectivity (TI 23).

Not really. The other subject truly deserves to be called other because the appresentation in which it is "given" to the subject is "a primordially unfulfillable experience."[23] If I am to take seriously the objectivity of the world, I have to take into account the *Sinngebungen* that emanate from a center other than myself. But I can treat those meanings as merely other *Abschattungen*, other perspectives on the object that I must take into account in seeking fulfillment for my own intentions. This is just another dimension of the transphenomenality of being already conceded by Husserl.

Except for the being of the subject itself, it might be replied. But here again transcendence all but evaporates. The other monads are "separate from my monad," to be sure. However, "The only conceivable manner in which others can have for me the sense and status of existent others, thus and so determined, consists in their being constituted *in me* as others. If they get that sense and status from sources that yield a continual confirmation, then they do indeed *exist* . . . but exclusively as having the sense with which they are constituted."[24]

Paraphrasing William James, we can say that like the intentional object, the other subject is other but not so very damn other.[25] This is why Levinas insists, "The Other as Other is *not only* an alter ego. . . . The exteriority of the other is *not simply* due to the space that separates what remains identical through the concept" (TO 48).[26] In critiquing Levinas's critique of Husserl, Derrida refers to this passage and to the one in which Levinas writes that in everyday life, "The other is known through sympathy, as another (my)self, as the alter ego" (TO 47). Then Derrida comments,

> This is exactly what Husserl does not do. He seeks to recognize the other as Other only in its form as ego, in its form of alterity, which cannot be that of things in the world. If the other were not recognized as a transcendental alter *ego*, it would be entirely in the world and not, as ego, the origin of the world. To refuse to see in it an ego in this sense is, within the ethical order, the very gesture of all violence. If the other was not recognized as [transcendental] ego, its entire alterity would collapse. Therefore, it seems that one may not suppose that Husserl makes of the other an other like myself . . . or a *real* modification of *my life*.[27]

But (1) Levinas emphatically affirms the Other as alter ego, so where is the violence of refusing to do so? (2) In doing so Levinas sharply distinguishes the other ego as another origin of the world from objects in the world and thus from being "a *real modification* of *my life*." (3) As another such origin of the world, the alter ego is precisely an other like myself, another instance of the same kind. (4) Levinas does not deny a certain alterity to the Other as alter ego, but denies that the Other is "only" an alter ego because if this were its "entire alterity" that would be very minimal for the two reasons we have seen: the Other's construals can be treated as just so many more *Abschattungen* through which objects are (indirectly) presented to us (as perhaps in a mirror or by inference) and the Other's own existence is "constituted *in me*," albeit in a manner different from the way objects are constituted insofar as appresentation differs from presentation.

* * *

So much transcendence, so much subjectivity. Levinas needs more transcendence than can be found in either the intended object or the alter ego as another intentional center. In company with the latter, the subject is swallowed up in "the collectivity that says 'we,' that, turned toward the intelligible sun, toward the truth, feels the other at its side and not in front of itself" (TO 53)."[28]

Intersubjectivity is the right place to look. But side-by-side co-intentionality is not enough. What is needed is the face-to-face. The side-by-side is not enough because, like the transcendence of the object, the transcendence of the alter ego limns the finitude of the transcendental subject but does not limit its absoluteness. Just as it has to take into account the showings of the object, so it has to take into account the seeings of the alter ego; but precisely in doing this it remains the origin of meaning, truth, and being. As the criteria by which the subject is measured, the object and the alter ego provide a norm, a challenge, a telos for the subject. They must both be taken into account. But all that is required is intellectual virtue. While the tradition interprets intellect in term of rationality, Levinas, deconstructing this self-congratulation with allusions to Hegel and Husserl, interprets it more in terms of clever animality, in terms of capturing, assimilating, enjoying. In any case, moral virtue is nowhere to be found. So far forth we have a philosophy of freedom but not of responsibility. The subject is merely a hungry stomach without ears. So little transcendence, so little subjectivity.

That the side-by-side might be *aufgehoben* in the face-to-face, that epistemic freedom might be teleologically suspended in ethical responsibility, that truth might "presuppose" justice (TI 90), is already hinted at when Levinas insists that intersubjectivity is "not only" and "not simply" a matter of the alter ego. We need to see (1) how to get from the side-by-side to the face-to-face, from the alter ego to the widow, the orphan, and the stranger, and (2) what kind of transcendence we encounter as we do. We do not get from here to there by abandoning phenomenology. We must look for a transcendence that "is reflected *within* the totality and history, *within* experience," but in "an intentionality of a wholly different type" from Husserl's (TI 23).[29]

The difference is threefold. First, we are dealing here with "a notion of meaning prior to my *Sinngebung* and thus independent of my initiative and my power" (TI 51). This "prior" means that by the time my transcendental ego arrives on the scene it is always already too late to be the origin of meaning and thus of truth and being. My intentional acts and their constitutive force are always posterior and never prior; they occur in a world in which meaning has always already been established by another. I am neither the Alpha, the origin of this "object," nor its Omega, its telos, its raison d'être. I am no longer master in the realm where my intentionality involves "reducing the represented to its meaning, the existent to the noema, the most astonishing possibility of reducing to a noema the very being of the existent" (TI 127).

Second, meaning arises as a *"signification without a context"* (TI 23). Husserl's method consists "in discovering the unsuspected *horizons* within which the real is situated . . . beginning with the body (innocently), beginning with culture (perhaps less innocently). To hold out one's hands, to turn one's head, to speak a language, to be the 'sedimentation' of a history—all of this *transcendentally* conditions contemplation and the contemplated" (Si 178; cf. TI 28). These horizons are the concreteness of the transcendental ego. They belong essentially to the cognition that must be transcended for the sake of transcendence. Of course, this does not mean that either the sign (the face of the other as a trace of transcendence) or its meaning occurs nowhere or that I am nowhere when it shows up *"within* [my] experience." What it means is that my horizons of expectation are not are not the condition of the possibility of this experience, that the pre-understandings that I bring with me to the encounter do not limit or dictate the meaning that emerges.[30]

Third, this double negation, namely that here is a meaning that is a function *neither* of my intentional acts *nor* of their horizons, can be put positively. The other that I encounter in the face-to-face *"expresses itself"* and it does so καθ αὐτό (TI 51).[31] Here, Levinas claims, and only here the Husserlian slogan "zu den Sachen selbst" is fulfilled, since in ordinary intentionality my own transcendental *selbst* always plays a decisive, mediating, yea, originating role. Here, Levinas claims, and only here does phenomenology conform to Heidegger's translation of Husserl's slogan—"to let that which shows itself be seen from itself in the very way in which it shows itself from itself [*sich von ihm selbst her zeigt*]."[32]

Each of these themes deserves fuller attention, but together and even in this sketchy form, they can provide an answer to our first question, How do we get from the side-by-side to the face-to-face?—*unless* we understand them in terms of the alter ego. To avoid this possibility we must turn to our second question: What kind of transcendence do we encounter in the face-to-face? It will have to be an alter ego that is "not only" and "not simply" an alter ego but also one whose presence will effect the qualitative leap[33] from the epistemological to the ethical. The face will have to be that which "calls [beings] forth to their full responsibility" so that they are "called upon to answer at their trial" (TI 23). Its infinity "puts the spontaneous freedom within us into question. It commands and judges it and brings it to its truth" (TI 51).[34] Ethics will have to be first philosophy.[35]

If we ask how this leap, this μετάβασις εἰς ἄλλο γένος[36] from the indicative to the imperative, is possible, the answer is simple. "The face speaks" (TI 66). In the passages where we have found the key elements of "intentionality of a wholly different type," Levinas calls explicit attention to his use of the language of calling, questioning, and commanding by attributing the "non-allergic relation, an ethical relation" to "conversation" and to "this aptitude for speech" (TI 51 and 23). One can say that his philosophy of transcendence is a philosophy of language.

But not just any old philosophy of language, and surely not one that revolves around the assertion of empirical facts. Here again we must distinguish the face from the alter ego. The latter, with the help of a very empirical brain, lips, tongue, larynx, and lungs, speaks to me. This is how I become aware of the other's different interpretations, which I must take into account in the service of objectivity. "No, if you look from over here you'll see it's a facade for a movie set and not a real house." Moreover, the alter ego and my transcendental ego, empirically embedded to be sure, converse to negotiate our practical comportment as members of society.

It is at this point that Husserl appears to make a move from the side-by-side to the face-to-face. In his account of social acts and I-Thou relations, he speaks of turning to the other subject. "Ich wende mich an ihn." I do so with the intent to communicate to the other, and precisely with the theoretical practical purposes just mentioned: " 'das ist so und so,' 'das sollst du tun.' "[37]

But while these uses of language hint at the "inversion [of] *objectifying cognition*" that is, the "call from the Other" (TI 67), they do not embody it. The other turns to me and speaks in a similar fashion. We can thus speak of inverse intentionality in that meanings originate elsewhere and in language are directed toward me, but not in such a way that I cannot assimilate them and *become* the constituting origin of both the meanings and their source. This kind of language game may give rise theoretically to science and practically to various kinds of social contract liberalism, but not to the absolute responsibility for the other that arises when it is the face that speaks. The reason lies in the reciprocal, symmetrical nature of this language game. "Wir beide, ich und du, 'sehen uns in die Augen,' er versteht mich, gewahrt mich, I gewahre ihn, gleichzeitig." Husserl continually reminds us that this "*Wechselbeziehung*" is "*füreinander*," "*wechselseitig*," "*vice versa*," and "*zweiseitig*."[38]

By contrast, it is precisely because of the absolute asymmetry of the face-to-face that Levinas has in mind that he calls the face the Infinite and its voice Revelation (TI 62, 66–67, and 73);[39] and this is why he will eventually stress the priority of the saying over the said (OB I, 1 and II, 3–4). What is crucial is not what is said but the mere fact that I am addressed and that this address, whatever its content, has the form of an absolute, unconditioned, categorical imperative.

Nor can I assimilate it so as to *become* its origin. That is what Kant is up to in affirming the autonomy of pure practical reason and what Heidegger is up to when he writes, "*In conscience Dasein calls itself.*"[40] But autonomy is allergic to alterity and is the attempt to absorb it so as to neutralize its bite. This defanging, however, turns out to be the defacing of the other. Abstractly put, it is the reducing of the other to the same; concretely it is the birth of violence from the humanism that dehumanizes. Ethical transcendence is encountered in an inverse intentionality in which asymmetry resists all attempts at assimilation and absorption.[41] Vision is *aufgehoben* in the voice, and the violence of the hungry stomach is teleologically suspended in the vulnerability of the ear to a claim it can never makes its own.

The presence of the face that speaks is, of course, no guarantee that I will welcome it, accepting the responsibility under which it places me. I may be too much in the thrall of the desire[42] to be the center that owns itself, a desire that philosophers praise as autonomy and theologians condemn as the pride that is the original sin. The attempt to reduce the Other to an alter ego may be a symptom of a deeper desire to silence the voice from whom intentionality's arrows are shot toward me rather than emanating from me. Perhaps that is why, when we ask what the voice says, Levinas, who is not eager to answer that question in any detail, answers simply, "You shall not commit murder" (TI 171, 199, 216, 262, and 303). For every act of objectification that silences this voice, including those that "honor" it by treating it as merely a fellow researcher or negotiating partner, is the attempt to kill, not necessarily the biological life, but the moral and spiritual life of the Other.[43]

\* \* \*

Murder or welcome. The alternative sounds a bit like that posed by Kierkegaard and his pseudonyms between offense and faith.[44] In fact, there is more than just a bit of similarity between the two cases. For in the Kierkegaardian corpus offense and faith are alternative responses to the voice of transcendence, in this case the voice of the God whom one does not see face-to-face. Consider three such cases. First, there is Abraham. The story of the (almost) sacrifice of Isaac, to which *Fear and Trembling* is devoted, arises out of a divine command that could never have arisen from the autonomy of pure practical reason.[45] "Take your son, your only son Isaac, whom you love, and go to the land of Moriah, and offer him there as a burnt offering on one of the mountains that I shall show you" (Gen. 22:2). Abraham's faith consists in accepting the absolute and asymmetrical authority of this voice. Autonomy is allergic to alterity; here faith is a "non-allergic" relation to the Wholly Other.[46]

In order to see how deeply Levinasian this is, we need not overlook the deep differences. In *Fear and Trembling* revelation is the voice of the God of Abraham, a divine infinity that is not known only in the face of the human other. God is clearly an independent origin of responsibility and is not restricted to speaking through the human face of my neighbor.[47] Perhaps it is just for this reason that divine speech consists of two distinct types of speech act: promise and command.[48] So we are reminded that in Abraham's case, the command was preceded by promise. "By faith Abraham emigrated from the land of his fathers and became an alien in the *promised land.* . . . By faith he was an alien in the *promised land.* . . . By faith Abraham received the *promise* that in his seed all the generations of the earth would be blessed" (FT 17, emphasis added).[49] Ironically, it was this latter promise that raised the trauma of the command to sacrifice Isaac to the nth degree.

A second divine command is central to *Works of Love.* Kierkegaard's God does not appear only in and as the neighbor, but does command, "You shall love your neighbor as yourself" (Lev. 19:18).[50] Here faith is to show itself in works of love, and to emphasize the heteronomous origin of this command, which explicitly gives rise to the possibilities of offense or the obedience of faith, Kierkegaard contrasts commanded love with two forms of celebrated love: erotic love and friendship. These latter arise naturally out of human understanding and thus generate no offense. In the case of the beloved or the friend the hard part is finding the right and willing person(s). The welcoming is easy. By contrast, the claim of the neighbor is traumatic and threatening, and it is the task of a lifetime to learn to welcome the widow, the orphan, and the stranger (who may turn out to be my enemy).[51] The voice that calls me to erotic love and friendship is an immanent voice; the voice that commands me to love my neighbor is a traumatically transcendent voice.[52] In the language of phenomenology, it expresses an inverse intentionality, a reversal of the cognitive relation as understood by major strands of the western tradition.

In a Lutheran context, the primary purpose of the Law is to reveal to us our sinfulness and turn us to repentance and faith in the Gospel. So it is appropriate that Kierkegaard should write about the command to love our neighbors as we love ourselves before he has Anti-Climacus write about a third command, one that grows directly out of the Gospel itself. "Thou shalt believe in the forgiveness of sins" (SUD 115). The possibilities of offense rather than faith are signs of the transcendence of the voice that speaks here, and they are many. I can be offended that I, a decent, respected, law-abiding citizen should be called a sinner. I can be offended that I cannot make amends for whatever faults I may have, in other words, atone for my own sins so as to avoid becoming dependent on another for forgiveness and reconciliation. I can, in a moment of despairing pride, be offended at the idea that anyone who has done what I have done could ever be forgiven.[53]

Perhaps Anti-Climacus has been meditating on the fact that the Gospel begins, both on the lips of John the Baptist and on the lips of Jesus, with the words "Repent, for the kingdom of heaven has come near" (Matt. 3:2, 4:17), or, as Mark summarizes the early preaching of Jesus, "repent, and believe in the good news" (1:15). The Gospel is good news indeed. That is the very meaning of the word. But to hear and receive it as good news, one must first work through the bad news and the possibility of offense found in that single, dreadful word, Repent! I must overcome the voice within me that says, without too much concern for consistency, "I don't need to repent and receive forgiveness as a gift. I'm a good person. Besides, I can compensate for my own 'mistakes.' In any case, what's the point? I don't deserve to be forgiven, and no one has the right to forgive me anyway."

As the overcoming of the temptation to offense, faith is not a second class form of knowing, down toward the bottom of Plato's divided line. It is the willingness to be vulnerable to a voice not my own, to trust in its promises rather than my own agenda and agency, and to accept the responsibility placed upon me by its commands and offer of forgiveness. Overcoming my allergy to alterity, I become open to Overwhelming Otherness.

We have been exploring the transcendence of the voice that calls me to a unique, inescapable, non-negotiable responsibility, of an inverse intentionality in which, by being addressed by a voice not my own, (a) my transcendental ego is asymmetrically relativized or teleologically suspended in a command whose origin I can never be, and (b) my horizons are *aufgehoben* in a point of view that I do not and cannot occupy. In keeping with our slogan, "So much transcendence, so much subjectivity," we need to ask what kind of subjectivity corresponds to such transcendence. From what we have already seen, we can say two important things about it. First, it is a heteronomous subjectivity, or, to put it another way, it is a decentered subjectivity. It is a subjectivity quite compatible with postmodernism's "death of man," "death of the subject," "end of humanism" motifs; for these slogans are directed at the various forms of the autonomous subject that is allergic to alterity and insists on transcending every transcendence so as to be at once the center and the origin.

Second, it is a responsible self. Both Levinas's critique of the tradition as it culminates in Husserl and Kierkegaard's critique of the tradition as it culminates in Hegel seek (a) to displace knowing from its place as the highest human task, giving that place of privilege to an ethico-religious task, and (b) to resist the reduction of the ethical/religious to *Sittlichkeit*, the laws and customs of my people.[54] The tribunal before which the subject is subpoenaed is not a critique of reason in which our knowledge claims are tested to discover just how far we can comprehend or digest the world in the alimentary canal of our empirical and a priori concepts.[55] It is rather the tribunal in which subjects are "called upon to answer at their trial" in such a way that they are called forth "to their full responsibility" (TI 23) before their neighbor and in that way before God, as Levinas will have it, or before God and consequently before their neighbor, as Kierkegaard will have it.

It is fairly clear how the voice that calls us to responsibility as Levinas and Kierkegaard understand it represents a higher level of transcendence than that of the object of knowledge or the alter ego as partner in knowledge. And it is fairly clear how the subject of knowledge differs from the subject of responsibility. The contrasts between autonomy and heteronomy, centered and decentered, are fresh in our minds. But what warrants the claim that there is "more" or "deeper" or "more authentic" subjectivity in the latter case than in the former? In short, what justification is there for our hypothesis, So much transcendence, so much subjectivity?

One answer to this question would follow the strategy of Johannes Climacus when he claims that the System has no ethics (CUP I, 119, 121). The argument that can be reconstructed from the whole of *Concluding Unscientific Postscript* can be summarized as follows:

> If you start with the knowing subject unencumbered by ethico-religious responsibility, there is no way to bring the latter in later except by arbitrary fiat, and the temptation to do this will be dramatically reduced by the fact that the starting point places the discussion in a hermeneutical circle in which it is already presupposed that in our deepest essence we are knowers. The criterion of the subject is Truth and not Goodness, freedom and not responsibility, objectivity and not subjectivity. In short, while epistemology is not a sin, the epistemological fetishism of modern philosophy, all appearances to the contrary not withstanding, puts us not on the royal road to science but on the fast track to nihilism, a road paved with good intentions about intentional analysis.

Such an argument would be very Levinasian. Our two thinkers have been developing it throughout these pages and have, at the very least, pointed to the hermeneutical circle within which the hypothesis—so much transcendence, so much subjectivity—will have the ring of truth about it. Within that circle we find both Levinas and Kierkegaard, united in spite of deep differences, in the conviction that it's not what you know, it's who you love that makes you truly human.[56]

# NOTES

Introduction

1. *Modern Theology* 8, no. 3 (July 1992), pp. 241–61.

2. Quoted in *Being and Nothingness*, trans. Hazel Barnes (New York: Philosophical Library, 1956), p. 406.

3. (Boston: Little, Brown, and Company, 1929). Subsequent references are to this work. The next five paragraphs are taken from "Levinas, Kierkegaard, and the Theological Task."

4. Abraham as presented in *Fear and Trembling* will appear repeatedly in the chapters below. For Levinas, see the contrast between Ulysses and Abraham in chapter 7.

1. Revelation as Immediacy

1. On the two modes of metaphysics as onto-theology that have these two foundations, see Jean-Luc Marion, "Descartes and Onto-theology," in *Post-Secular Philosophy: Between Philosophy and Theology*, ed. Phillip Blond (New York: Routledge, 1998).

2. Louis Menand, "The Real John Dewey," *The New York Review of Books*, 39, no. 12 (June 25, 1992), p. 52. It is, of course, Richard Rorty who has most explicitly developed the link between American pragmatism and French postmodernism. See especially *Consequences of Pragmatism* (Minneapolis: University of Minnesota Press, 1982).

3. Richard Rorty, *Philosophy and the Mirror of Nature* (Princeton, N.J.: Princeton University Press, 1979), p. 315. Alvin Plantinga identifies such privileged representations as those that are self-evident, incorrigible, or evident to the senses. See his "Reason and Belief in God," in *Faith and Rationality: Reason and Belief in God* (Notre Dame, Ind.: University of Notre Dame Press, 1983), p. 59. This view should not be confused with "weak" foundationalism, which does not require such apodicticity for foundational beliefs.

4. The holisms of thinkers like Wittgenstein, Quine, Sellars, Brandom, and Kuhn are pluralistic, resisting the Hegelian claim of *the* whole and thus any claim to Absolute Knowledge.

5. Jean-François Lyotard and Jean-Loup Thébaud, *Just Gaming*, trans. Wlad Godzich (Minneapolis: University of Minnesota Press, 1985), pp. 44–45; cf. pp. 17, 64. The absence of absolute criteria, of any common measure between various language games, or of any unifying metanarrative is the theme of Lyotard's *The Postmodern Condition*, trans. Geoff Bennington and Brian Massumi (Minneapolis: Minnesota University Press, 1986) and *The Differend*, trans. Georges Van Den Abbeele (Minneapolis: Minnesota University Press, 1988).

6. See Plantinga's volume cited in note 3 above.

7. *The Portable Nietzsche*, trans. Walter Kaufmann (New York: Viking, 1954), p. 198 ("Upon the Blessed Isles"). Heidegger is another source of postmodern atheism. His view that whatever one's "ontic" commitments may be, one adopts an atheistic perspective, outside of religious faith, the moment one begins to philosophize. This is a curious remnant in his thought of an Enlightenment rationalism whose chief opponent he purports to be. For his sharp separation of philosophy from theology see especially the lecture "Phenomenology and Theology," in *The Piety of Thinking*, trans. James G. Hart and John C. Maraldo (Bloomington: Indiana University Press, 1976). Cf. *History of the Concept of Time: Prolegomena*, trans. Theodore Kisiel (Bloomington: Indiana University Press, 1985), pp. 79–80, and *The Metaphysical Foundations of Logic*, trans. Michael Heim (Bloomington: Indiana University Press, 1984), p. 140.

8. Kierkegaard, CUP I, 118. That the thing in itself is quite simply the thing for God is quite clear in the Kantian text. See my "In Defense of the Thing in Itself," *Kant-Studien* 59, no. 1 (1968), pp. 118–41.

9. For Hart see *The Trespass of the Sign* (New York: Fordham University Press, 2000). For Marion see *God without Being*, trans. Thomas A. Carlson (Chicago: University of Chicago Press, 1991).

10. See, for example, *Dialogue and Deconstruction: The Gadamer-Derrida Encounter*, ed. Diane P. Michelfelder and Richard E. Palmer (Albany: SUNY Press, 1989), and Jürgen Habermas, *The Philosophical Discourse of Modernity*, trans. Frederick Lawrence (Cambridge, Mass.: MIT Press, 1987).

11. See note 3 above.

12. Foucault's *Madness and Civilization* was also published, in French, in 1961.

13. It needs to be emphasized that what I've been calling French negativism shares this positive appraisal of critique in relation to the possibility of ethics. The common goal of these writers is not to eliminate the moral life by establishing a world of arbitrary choice, but so see how justice may be possible in a world whose Enlightenment project has failed. Just because their answers differ significantly from those offered by the American debate between liberalism and communitarianism (and the German counterparts stemming from Habermas and Gadamer), they need to be included in the North American debate. For Derrida, see Drucilla Cornell, *The Philosophy of the Limit* (New York: Routledge, 1992); for Foucault, against the background of Nietzsche and Heidegger, see Charles Scott, *The Question of Ethics* (Bloomington: Indiana University Press, 1990); and for Lyotard, see *Just Gaming*.

14. *Just Gaming*, p. 46.

15. This attempt to resist colonization of the subject-subject relation by the imperialism of the subject-object relation links Levinas with a tradition that stretches from Sartre, Marcel, and Buber back through Kierkegaard and Pascal to Augustine. The heart of Levinas's critique of Husserl and Heidegger is that they never really make this move. Here we encounter the notion of inverted intentionality that will be developed in chapter 8.

16. For a dramatic reversal from force to face, see the discussion of *All Quiet on the Western Front* in the Introduction.

17. A trip through the Art Institute of Chicago, focusing on the portraits, provides an excellent commentary on Levinas. Or a study of Van Gogh's portraits in Roland Dorn et al., *Van Gogh Face to Face: The Portraits* (New York: Thames & Hudson, 2000).

18. The debate between Apel and Habermas on the possibility of a *Letztbegründ-*

*ung* for ethics is interesting on this point. Apel's hard line can be viewed as a kind of claim for immediacy, while Habermas's unwillingness to go along, in spite of the strongest constitutional inclination to do so, is an indication of the strength of the philosophical case for the ineluctability of mediation. See *The Communicative Ethics Controversy*, ed. Seyla Benhabib and Fred Dallmayr (Cambridge, Mass.: MIT Press, 1990), pp. 9–10, 338–39. Cf. Georgia Warnke, "Rawls, Habermas, and Real Talk: A Reply to Walzer," *Philosophical Forum*, 21, nos. 1–2 (fall-winter, 1989–90), pp. 197–203. But Apel's claim is theoretical, whereas Levinas's is experiential.

19. See *Phaedo* 100b and *Metaphysics* 1017a and 1022a for the metaphysical meaning. The two senses are combined in Spinoza's definition of substance as "id, quod in se est, et per se concipitur" (*Ethics* I, Def. 3). Here as throughout the Latin tradition *per se* renders καθ αὐτό.

20. Except in the biographical sense. The movement out of the cave and into the sunlight in *Republic*, Book VII, and the ascent up the "heavenly ladder" in *Symposium* 211b are necessary to get to where the true objects of knowledge can be seen. But once there, we throw away the ladder and see them directly. We "contemplate things by themselves with the soul by itself" (*Phaedo* 66e).

21. Edmund Husserl, *Ideas Pertaining to a Pure Phenomenology and to a Phenomenological Philosophy: First Book*, trans. F. Kersten (The Hague: Martinus Nijhoff, 1983), p. 44.

22. *Ideas*, p. 92. Husserl continues, "The spatial physical thing which we see is, with all its transcendence, still something perceived, given 'in person.' . . . It is not the case that, in its stead, a picture or a sign is given. A picture-consciousness or a sign consciousness must not be substituted for perception." Cf. *Cartesian Meditations*, trans. Dorion Cairns (The Hague: Martinus Nijhoff, 1973), p. 57, where Husserl describes evidence as "the *self-appearance*, the *self-exhibiting*, the *self-giving* of an affair . . . or other objectivity, in the final mode: 'itself there,' 'immediately intuited,' 'given originaliter.'"

23. Cf. TI 74, where καθ αὐτό is defined as "signifying before we have projected light upon it." A useful guide in reading Levinas is to track the many different ways in which he says that what we encounter in the ethical relation to the Other is something prior to what the tradition has taken as basic.

24. In context, the first of these passages refers to Heidegger, the second to Husserl. But both apply equally to each. Cf. TI 49, "To think the infinite, the transcendent, the Stranger, is hence not to think an object. . . . The distance of transcendence is not equivalent to that which separates the mental act from its object in all our representations, since the distance at which the object stands does not exclude, and in reality implies, the *possession* of the object. . . . The 'intentionality' of transcendence is unique in its kind; *the difference between objectivity and transcendence will serve as a general guideline for all the analyses of this work.*" Here again we encounter the notion of an inverted intentionality. See note 15 above.

25. The priority of the individual to the community in the last formula is not the temporary priority of the Hobbesian war of all against all, the Lockean natural market, or the Hegelian struggle between master and slave but the permanent priority that places every constituted social order in question. In all these formulas we hear a powerful affinity with Kierkegaard's critique of Hegelian mediation.

26. See *Being and Time*, trans. John Macquarrie and Edward Robinson (New York: Harper and Row, 1962), p. 105 in the context of ¶¶16–17. Here Heidegger denies that disclosure involves the mediation of inference, but this is only to make the world

safe for the mediations of interpretation. Thus disclosure is central to his accounts of Understanding and Interpretation, ¶¶31–32, 63, 68, of Truth, ¶44, and Conscience and Resoluteness, ¶¶54, 60, as thoroughly contextualized affairs. Levinas's early critique of Heidegger is found in IOF.

27. A reminder. We cannot hold Kierkegaard responsible for the views of his pseudonyms any more than we can hold a novelist responsible for the views of his characters. But we can hold him responsible for presenting those views to us. So I shall designate as Kierkegaard's those ideas he presents for our consideration, whether pseudonymously or in his own name.

28. To speak of a personal God is to speak of a God who performs speech acts. That the biblical God is such a God and that the most typical divine speech acts are not assertions but promises and commands is powerfully argued by Nicholas Wolterstorff in *Divine Discourse: Philosophical Reflections on the Claim That God Speaks* (New York: Cambridge University Press, 1995).

29. I have argued that for Hegel transcendental subjectivity resides in historically concrete linguistic/cultural communities. We, in any given case, are the transcendental ego. See *History and Truth in Hegel's Phenomenology*, 3rd ed. (Bloomington: Indiana University Press, 1998), pp. 65, 79–84, 111–15, 122–26, and 137.

30. Silentio reminds us of the Socratic idea of "the superiority of the heaven-sent madness over man-made sanity" (*Phaedrus* 244d).

31. Here the knight of faith believes, by virtue of the absurd, that he will get Isaac back *in this life* because with God all things are possible.

32. Here the knight of faith accepts the paradox that killing Isaac will be a sacrifice rather than murder.

33. On second immediacy, see SLW 399, CUP I, 347n., and JP II, 1123 and pp. 594–95. On the relation to Hegel's notion of immediacy, see my "Kierkegaard and the Role of Reflection in Second Immediacy," in *Immediacy and Reflection in Kierkegaard's Thought*, ed. P. Cruysberghs et al. (Leuven: Leuven University Press, 2003), pp. 159–79. This volume also contains essays on second immediacy by Heiko Schulz, Arne Grøn, and M. Jamie Ferreira.

34. On the social institution and administration of both theoretical and practical norms, see Robert B. Brandom, *Tales of the Mighty Dead: Historical Essays in the Metaphysics of Intentionality* (Cambridge, Mass.: Harvard University Press, 2002), pp. 212–16 and 220–21.

35. On the importance of the hypothetical character of the thought experiment, see my "Johannes and Johannes: Kierkegaard and Difference," in *International Kierkegaard Commentary: Philosophical Fragments and Johannes Climacus*, ed. Robert L. Perkins (Macon, Ga.: Mercer University Press, 1994), pp. 13–32.

## 2. REVELATION AS ENIGMA AND PARADOX

1. *To the Other: An Introduction to the Philosophy of Emmanuel Levinas* (West Lafayette, Ind.: Purdue University Press, 1993). PII appears in this volume, but I cite it from CPP.

2. By Robert Bernasconi, in personal correspondence.

3. See the notion of inverse intentionality as developed in chapter 8.

4. The notion of faith, in its opposition to human reason, as a kind of (divine) madness is especially important in *Fear and Trembling, Philosophical Fragments*, and

*Concluding Unscientific Postscript.* On the New Testament roots of Kierkegaard's interest in the Socratic notion of divine madness, see my *Kierkegaard's Critique of Reason
and Society* (University Park: Pennsylvania State University Press, 1991), pp. 87–88.

5. See the discussion of this Kierkegaardian text in chapter 1, and, for this particular strategy, see note 35.

6. Here I stick with the 1962 translation of Swenson and Hong. In the 1985
translation the Hongs have replaced Reason with understanding, weakening the rhetorical force of the passage considerably. Accordingly, I have altered the translation to
restore Reason.

7. See *Confessions*, VII, 20 in relation to VII, 9.

8. But already in "Philosophy and the Idea of Infinity" we read, "The epiphany of
a face is wholly language" (PII 55), and *Totality and Infinity* gives a thoroughly semantic analysis of the alterity expressed in the human face that commands us from on high.
"The face speaks" (TI 66).

9. As we can learn from either Climacus's thought experiment or from Kant,
simply to raise the question of right (*quid juris*) is to engage in critique. See *Critique of
Pure Reason*, A84 = B116.

10. Levinas is more careful than some in referring to the philosophical tradition he
seeks to undermine. We are not dealing here with western philosophy as a seamless
totality but with its "dominant tradition," with characteristics it has "most often" ex-
hibited. See PII 57 and 48.

11. To put it this way is to suggest that there is an ethical as well as an epistemological dimension to critique. Thus Silentio regularly insists that faith is a matter of humility and courage (FT 33–34, 48–50, 73). Derrida would agree, claiming that even before
ethics is the theme of reflection, deconstruction is already the work of justice. See
"Force of Law: The 'Mystical Foundation of Authority,'" in *Deconstruction and the
Possibility of Justice*, ed. Drucilla Cornell, Michel Rosenfeld, and David Gray Carlson
(New York: Routledge, 1992).

12. Here Levinas speaks of the atheism of philosophy in terms of immanence and
totality, blind or deaf to enigma and transcendence. Cf. PE 49. At PE 53 he specifically
addresses the atheism of Heidegger. The atheism Levinas here seeks to escape is different from the atheism affirmed in TI 57–58 and 77 as a "break with participation" that
immersion in the totality that is overcome in the emergence of the interiority of the self
as I.

13. This distinction between desire and need, fundamental to the argument of
*Totality and Infinity*, is introduced in PII 54–57.

14. The Kierkegaardian overtones of these references to contradiction, paradox,
and scandal (offense) are clear. But when Levinas speaks of the "scandalous absence" of
God there is an unmistakable reference to the Holocaust. See the dedication of *Otherwise Than Being*, "To the memory of those who were closest among the six million
assassinated by the National Socialists, and of the millions on millions of all confessions
and all nations, victims of the same hatred of the other man, the same anti-semitism"
(OB 5). In the light of Auschwitz, he holds that all theodicy is probably "indecent"
(NTR 187). Cf. "Loving the Torah More Than God" in DF.

15. Lessing's claim that "that contingent historical truths can never become a
demonstration of eternal truths of reason" (CUP I, 93) is the crucial stimulus for both
*Philosophical Fragments* and *Concluding Unscientific Postscript*. In other words, Johannes Climacus represents Kierkegaard's attempt to come to grips with the Socratic

assumption as reformulated by Lessing. Lessing's famous essay "On the Proof of the Spirit and of Power" is found in Chadwick, *Lessing's Theological Writings*, ed. Henry Chadwick (Stanford, Calif.: Stanford University Press, 1957).

16. Cf. Levinas's formulation cited above from PII 54, where he also says, "Infinity does not enter into the *idea* of infinity, is not grasped; this idea is not a concept. The infinite is the radically, absolutely, other."

17. Cf. PE 63, "If the other is presented to the same, the copresence of the other and the same in a phenomenon forthwith constitutes an order." The immediacy of revelation discussed in chapter 1 is its refusal to be "assimilated" or "compromised" by the "already familiar order."

18. To describe significations as "triumphant" is to call attention to their historical contingency. It is also to point to the triumph of structure over event, for they represent the *said* that has broken free from the *saying* that gave them birth. It is at PE 65 where the distinction between saying and said, so central to *Otherwise Than Being*, first appears in this essay. Levinas identifies the said, this order of temporarily fixed meaning, as the "context" of signification. In *Totality and Infinity* Levinas presents ethics as presupposing a semantics of *"signification without context"* (TI 23). This is what he means when he says that the Other signifies καθ αὐτό. See the discussion in chapter 1.

19. This would be to give an interesting twist to the Hegelian thesis that a proper skepticism is the necessary preparation for a proper metaphysics. See ¶¶79–82 of *The Encyclopedia Logic* and "Relationship of Skepticism to Philosophy," in *Between Kant and Hegel*, trans. George di Giovanni and H. S. Harris (Albany: State University of New York Press, 1985).

20. This puts him in conversation with Derrida, who repudiates the traditional sign as metaphysical in the pejorative sense. See *Positions*, trans. Alan Bass (Chicago: University of Chicago Press, 1981), especially the interview with Kristeva; "Force and Signification" and "Structure, Sign, and Play," in *Writing and Difference*, trans. Alan Bass (Chicago: University of Chicago Press, 1978); "The Pit and the Pyramid" and "Différance" in *Margins of Philosophy*, trans. Alan Bass (Chicago: University of Chicago Press, 1982); part I of *Of Grammatology*, trans. Gayatri Chakravorty Spivak (Baltimore: Johns Hopkins University Press, 1976); and, perhaps before all else, *Speech and Phenomena*, trans. David B. Allison (Evanston, Ill.: Northwestern University Press, 1973). Derrida's argument that signs are radically ambiguous because the context of their employment can never be either closed or (a fortiori) fully thematized is weaker than Levinas's claim that both God and neighbor disturb the complicity of sign and signified that constitutes every human order or context.

21. Probably the most Kierkegaardian feature of *Totality and Infinity* is the sustained polemic against knowledge as recollection. See, for example, TI 43, 51, 61, 171, 180, 204 and the discussion of this theme in chapter 1. Levinas discusses the trace at length in "The Trace of the Other," in *Deconstruction in Context*, ed. Mark C. Taylor (Chicago: University of Chicago Press, 1986), pp. 345–59.

22. John D. Caputo skillfully develops this same theme from *Repetition* in the Kierkegaard chapter of *Radical Hermeneutics: Repetition, Deconstruction, and the Hermeneutic Project* (Bloomington: Indiana University Press, 1987). In the *Fragments* Climacus simply associates this idea with Socrates, but in the *Postscript* he follows Kierkegaard's own *The Concept of Irony* in distinguishing Socrates from Plato and attributing this speculative idea to the latter.

23. In Levinas's linguistic formulation this view ignores the difference between the

saying and the said, reducing event to essence, and reduces language to a doubling up of phenomena "so that men could point them out to one another." In fact, however, "significations said offer a hold to the *saying* which 'disturbs' them. . . . All speaking is an enigma" (PE 69–70; cf. 65).

24. It is just this feature of the enigmatic that leads Levinas to speak of inwardness and to say that "subjectivity is enigma's partner, partner of the transcendence that disturbs being" (PE 70; cf. 72). It is just this essential link to subjectivity, "whereas the disclosure of Being occurs open to universality" (PE 70), that removes the enigma from ordinary communication. Readers of Kierkegaard need not be reminded of the chiasmic relation of inwardness and indirect communication.

25. It is these four whose common ground Allan Megill seeks to articulate in *Prophets of Extremity: Nietzsche, Heidegger, Foucault, Derrida* (Berkeley: University of California Press, 1985).

26. The importance given to Abraham in *Fear and Trembling* and to Job in *Repetition* is an indication of the degree to which the Kierkegaardian project presents Christianity as a Jewish sect rather than a footnote to Plato.

27. For an interpretation of Kierkegaard along these lines, see Ronald L. Hall, *Word and Spirit: A Kierkegaardian Critique of the Modern Age* (Bloomington: Indiana University Press, 1993).

28. Is this the meaning of loving the Torah more than God? See DF 142–45. In II 247, Levinas suggests that this is a Jewish-Christian issue. That seems to me a mistake.

29. For further discussion, see chapter 3.

30. Like Levinas, Kierkegaard will focus on the difference between the second and third person pronouns, leaving to others the question of the masculine form of the latter.

31. See the Appendix to chapter III of PF; SUD 83, 87, 113–31; and PC 23–26, 36–40, and 69–144. That we should expect a gap between any society's norms (*Sittlichkeit*) and the will of God is the point of the teleological suspension of the ethical in *Fear and Trembling*.

32. Here it is possible to use 'metaphysical' both in the Levinasian sense where it contrasts with 'ontological' and in the more usual sense in which the two terms are virtually synonyms.

## 3. TELEOLOGICAL SUSPENSIONS

1. Jacques Derrida, "Force of Law: The 'Mystical Foundation of Authority,'" in *Deconstruction and the Possibility of Justice*, ed. Drucilla Cornell, Michel Rosenfeld, and David Gray Carlson (New York: Routledge, 1992), p. 28.

2. Cf. the discussion of "French negativism" in chapter 1.

3. Derrida is an important exception with his notion of "religion without religion." For a helpful guide, see John D. Caputo, *The Prayers and Tears of Jacques Derrida: Religion without Religion* (Bloomington: Indiana University Press, 1997).

4. "Violence and Metaphysics," in *Writing and Difference*, trans. Alan Bass (Chicago: University of Chicago Press, 1978), p. 82.

5. Jewish, Christian, and secular readers. See the concluding paragraphs of chapter 2.

6. Cf. John Burnaby, who writes, "It is impossible, if we believe in a God who really exists, not to believe in 'another' world; for that other world is posited with belief

in God. If God exists, He constitutes another world." *Amor Dei: A Study of the Religion of St. Augustine* (London: Hodder & Stoughton, 1938), p. 10.

7. For a fuller account of this structure, see my essay "Kierkegaard's Teleological Suspension of Religiousness B," in *Foundations of Kierkegaard's Vision of Community*, ed. George B. Connell and C. Stephen Evans (Atlantic Highlands, N.J.: Humanities Press, 1992), pp. 111–14.

8. See the account of inverted intentionality in chapter 8.

9. I first suggested this in "Levinas, Kierkegaard, and the Theological Task," *Modern Theology* 8, no. 3 (July 1992), pp. 241–61.

10. In this passage and a related one at DEL 31, Levinas argues that it is precisely this Other between myself and God that keeps God from ever being simply present.

11. We must not let this phenomenological language obscure the anti-phenomenological insistence that to be revealed is to express oneself in seeing and speaking rather than in being seen. For God to be revealed is not for God to be seen. "God thus reveals himself as a trace, not as an ontological presence" (DEL 31).

12. *The Future of an Illusion*, ch. VII.

13. "Violence and Metaphysics," pp. 97, 83, 92. I have argued that Kierkegaard also opens the way for a non-Marxist practice of ideology critique. See *Kierkegaard's Critique of Reason and Society* (University Park: Pennsylvania State University Press, 1991), especially chs. 5 and 7.

14. For a brief account of this kind of religion as *mimesis*, see my *God, Guilt, and Death: An Existential Phenomenology of Religion* (Bloomington: Indiana University Press, 1984), ch. 10. For a helpful analysis of Levinas's polemic against "participation," see John Caruana, "Levinas's Critique of the Sacred," *International Philosophical Quarterly* 42, no. 4 (Dec. 2002), pp. 519–34.

15. "Violence and Metaphysics," p. 87.

16. For this reading of *Fear and Trembling*, see my essay "Abraham and Hegel" in *Kierkegaard's Critique of Reason and Society*,

17. See the discussion of immediacy in chapter 1.

18. His overt target is Hegel, and he does not speak of Christendom. My suggestion, however, is that the "attack upon Christendom" is already under way and that the critique begun in *Either/Or* continues in *Fear and Trembling*. Kierkegaard finds Danish Christendom to be all too Hegelian in taking social norms to be ultimate.

19. Levinas thinks that Abraham is a murderer (though he didn't actually go through with it). Silentio will reply that to say so is to beg the question. For if God commanded Abraham to offer Isaac as a sacrifice it would be just that, sacrifice and not murder. Levinas's critique of *Fear and Trembling* is best found in PN 65–79. What is unfortunate is that he appears to be entirely unaware of *Works of Love* and takes *Fear and Trembling* to be Kierkegaard's definitive word on the relation of religion and ethics. See my "The Many Faces of Levinas as a Reader of Kierkegaard," forthcoming in J. Aaron Simmons and David Wood, *A Conversation between Neighbors: Emmanuel Levinas and Søren Kierkegaard in Dialogue* (Bloomington: Indiana University Press).

20. See my analysis of "third commandment idolatry" in *Suspicion and Faith: The Religious Uses of Modern Atheism* (New York: Fordham University Press, 1998), pp. 205–9.

21. See "Prolegomena to Any Future Philosophy of Religion That Will Be Able to Come Forth as Prophecy," in *Kierkegaard's Critique of Reason and Society*, pp. 1–18.

22. See the quotation of 1 John 4:20–21 above.

23. The "conversation" between Levinas and Kierkegaard is skewed by the fact that Levinas seems not only not to have read this work but also to be entirely unaware of its existence.

24. Obviously Levinas does not appeal to redemption through Christ, but his philosophy, like Kierkegaard's, is one of egalitarian solidarity. See chapter 7.

25. Thus the title of Jamie Ferreira's wonderful book *Love's Grateful Striving: A Commentary on Kierkegaard's Works of Love* (New York: Oxford University Press, 2001).

## 4. Commanded Love and Divine Transcendence

1. The French originals were published in 1975 and 1974, respectively, but "God and Philosophy" was given as a lecture at Catholic, Jewish, and Protestant institutions during 1973–74. As noted earlier, I am treating the Levinasian corpus as essentially simultaneous. For a superb treatment of developmental differences, see Meredith Gunning, *About Face: Development in Emmanuel Levinas's Treatment of Subjectivity*, Ph.D. dissertation, Fordham University, 2006.

2. But see my argument in chapter 3 that Levinas's God is not fully the God of the Bible, even if with Kierkegaard and Heidegger, his "theology" is indeed a critique of much traditional philosophical theology. The critique is made possible by retaining certain formal features of the biblical God.

3. Martin Heidegger, *Identity and Difference*, trans. Joan Stambaugh (New York: Harper & Row, 1969), p. 56.

4. *Identity and Difference*, p. 72.

5. In *The Essence of Reasons*, trans. Terrence Malick (Evanston, Ill.: Northwestern University Press, 1969), Heidegger reduces these two issues to one. Transcendence is simply Dasein's move beyond beings to Being. For Heidegger transcendence is something Dasein does; for Levinas it signifies an "exposure," a "disturbance," and a "passivity" (GP 156, 160–63).

6. For arguments that Aquinas, who is evoked here, is not an onto-theologian after all, see Jean-Luc Marion, "Thomas Aquinas and Onto-theo-logy," in *Mystics: Presence and Aporia*, ed. Michael Kessler and Christian Sheppard (Chicago: University of Chicago Press, 1963), pp. 38–74, and my essay "Aquinas and Onto-theology," *American Catholic Philosophical Quarterly*, 20, no. 2 (2006), pp. 173–91.

7. At GP 162 Levinas describes this coinciding in the language of adequation, derived from both medieval realism and Husserlian phenomenology. John Llewelyn writes that for Levinas "atheism is defined as the restriction of thinking to intentional representation where the thinking and what is represented may in principle be mutually adequate." *Emmanuel Levinas: The Genealogy of Ethics* (New York: Routledge, 1995), p. 160.

8. Cf. the critique of transcendental subjectivity in chapter 1.

9. In *Concluding Unscientific Postscript*, Kierkegaard's Climacus insists that all claims to the identity of thought and being are premature for those who exist in time and that the system betrays its absurdity by pretending to see everything *sub specie aeterni.*

10. And, if antecedent to being, also prior to the transcendental subjectivity to which being shows itself. Levinas's language here evokes Heidegger's talk in *Being and Time* about knowing as a founded mode of being-in-the-world (¶13) and about assertion as a derivative mode of interpretation (¶33). But Levinas is headed in a different

direction and will seek to decenter the present in terms of an ur-past rather than an ultra-future.

11. What Levinas's argument suppresses is the fact that, for example, Aquinas's rational theology, Rudolf Otto's appeal to religious experience, and Karl Barth's theology of revelation all insist that in God's self-showing God remains hidden. All three deny the adequacy of our knowledge of God, in the philosophical sense of the term, though not, of course, its adequacy for religious purposes.

12. I retain Heidegger's term, onto-theology, because it seems to me that only the less interesting part of his critique revolves around the ontological difference; the heart of the matter is a critique of calculative-representational thinking under the rule of the principle of sufficient reason, or so I argue in the title essay of *Overcoming Onto-theology: Toward a Postmodern Christian Faith* (New York: Fordham University Press, 2001). And on this point, Heidegger's project of overcoming metaphysics and Levinas's project of overcoming ontology are deeply akin in their rejection of the primacy of theoretical intentionality.

13. In his critique of Levinas's critique of thematization, Theo de Boer seems to accept at face value the assimilation of Pascal to Plato. See "Theology and the Philosophy of Religion According to Levinas," in *Ethics as First Philosophy*, ed. Adriaan T. Peperzak (New York: Routledge, 1995); see especially p. 168 in relation to p. 162. It should be noted that Levinas does not completely distance himself from Pascal. Although he doesn't mention the heart, he describes his own move beyond ontology as a move "among reasons that 'reason' does not know, and which have not begun in philosophy" (GP 172).

14. See *Pseudo-Dionysius: The Complete Works*, trans. Colm Luibheid (New York: Paulist Press, 1987), pp. 49–50, 53, 63, 135, 138, and 263.

15. There is no explicit reference to Dionysius or negative theology here. But the implication is quite direct in light of Dionysius's description of what lies beyond being as "the truly mysterious darkness of unknowing." *The Complete Works*, p. 137.

16. This is why, although he distances himself from Heidegger, Pascal, and Dionysius, Levinas associates himself with Kant, whom he sees as freeing ethics from ontology. See OB 129.

17. Martin Heidegger, "Language," in *Poetry, Language, Thought*, trans. Albert Hofstadter (New York: Harper & Row, 1971), p. 207. Cf. "The Nature of Language, in *On the Way to Language*, trans. Peter Herz and Joan Stambaugh (New York: Harper & Row, 1971), p. 108. Robert Bernasconi discusses this theme in *The Question of Language in Heidegger's History of Being* (Atlantic Highlands, N.J.: Humanities Press, 1985). When Heidegger says "die Sprache spricht," there is an obvious, if surprising, affinity with structuralism, and Levinas is saying No to both.

18. "The Way to Language," in *On the Way to Language*, p. 123.

19. On the doubling of thought and being, see PE 69–70. On the notion of testimony, see TD.

20. For Levinas's distinction between the sacred and the holy, see "Desacralization and Disenchantment," in NTR. On proximity, see LP.

21. Cf. "The Good assigns the subject . . . to approach the other, the neighbor. This is an assignation to a non-erotic proximity, to a desire of the non-desirable, to a desire of the stranger in the neighbor. It is outside of concupiscence" (OB 122–23).

22. *Phenomenology of Spirit*, trans. A. V. Miller (Oxford: Clarendon Press, 1977),

p. 32. This is, incidentally, as realistic a formula as one could want. Hegel describes scientific surrender as "absorbed in its object" and "immersed in the material."

23. *What Is Metaphysics?* in *Existentialism from Dostoevsky to Sartre*, ed. Walter Kaufmann (rev. ed.; New York: New American Library, 1975), p. 243.

24. *Discourse on Thinking*, trans. John M. Anderson and E. Hans Freund (New York: Harper & Row, 1966), pp. 54–61.

25. See note 16 above.

26. See Jean-Luc Marion,"Descartes and Onto-theology," in *Post-Secular Philosophy: Between Philosophy and Theology*, ed. Phillip Blond (New York: Routledge, 1998), pp. 67–106.

27. The quoted phrase is both the title of an important 1984 essay in which Levinas summarizes much of his thinking and the title of a book of essays on the importance of Levinas for philosophy, literature, and religion. See note 13 above.

28. Bach cantata BWV 140.

29. Quotations from Augustine will be by book and chapter numbers from *The Confessions of St. Augustine*, trans. Rex Warner (New York: New American Library, 1963).

30. The biblical quotation is from Ephesians 5:14. Some scholars think this is an early Christian hymn based on Isaiah 60:1, "Arise, shine; for your light has come, and the glory of the Lord has risen upon you."

31. Heidegger accordingly sharply distinguishes Augustinian from Cartesian self-certainty: "Self certainty and the self-possession in the sense of Augustine are entirely different from the Cartesian evidence of the 'cogito.'" *The Phenomenology of Religious Life*, trans. Matthias Fritsch and Jennifer Anna Gosetti-Ferencei (Bloomington: Indiana University Press, 2004), p. 226.

32. Cf. Romans 13:8–10, Galatians 5:14, and James 2:8.

33. In the two texts from Romans, Kierkegaard thematizes the paragraph just prior to the one that triggered Augustine's conversion.

34. Levinas's analysis of enjoyment is pertinent here. See TI 122–51; OB 61–74.

35. WL 19, 58, 60, 68–74, 81. On the theme of equality in Kierkegaard's writings, see Gene Outka, "Equality and the Fate of Theism in Modern Culture," *Journal of Religion* 67, no. 3 (July 1987), pp. 275–88; "Equality and Individuality: Thoughts on Two Themes in Kierkegaard," *Journal of Religious Ethics* 10, no. 2 (fall 1982), pp. 171–203; and M. Jamie Ferreira, "Equality, Impartiality, and Moral Blindness in Kierkegaard's *Works of Love*," *Journal of Religious Ethics* 25 (1977), pp. 65–85. My own discussion of this theme in *Postscript* is found in *Becoming a Self: A Reading of Kierkegaard's Concluding Unscientific Postscript* (West Lafayette, Ind.: Purdue University Press, 1966).

36. Kierkegaard also suggests a philosophy of language in which constative, assertive, indicative speech acts lose their privilege before the divine command. "The divine authority of the Gospel does not speak to one person about another . . . no, when the Gospel speaks, it speaks to the single individual. It does not speak *about* us human beings, you and me, but speaks *to* us human beings" (WL 14).

37. This chapter was first presented as a lecture in 1967. The notions of substitution and hostage are already found in Talmudic studies from 1964 and 1966. See NTR 49, 85, 87.

38. See the discussion of these formulas in chapter 1.

39. For an attempt to take rights theory beyond this limitation, see Henry Shue, *Basic Rights: Subsistence, Affluence, and U.S. Foreign Policy* (Princeton, N.J.: Princeton University Press, 1980).

40. There is a double hiddenness. My God relation is not a public event. It takes place behind closed doors even if I am among others in a house of worship. And God remains hidden from any brazen and presumptuous inquisitiveness that would seek to see God (WL 9–10). Most emphatically, the priority of the God relation is not the return of the primacy of theory, knowledge, and the I think.

41. John Llewelyn gives just such a reading of Levinas in *Emmanuel Levinas: The Genealogy of Ethics*, ch. 12.

42. On the *there is (il y a)*, compare EE 57–85, TI 190–91, DF 292, and OB 162–65.

43. In *Transcendence and Self-Transcendence* (Bloomington: Indiana University Press, 2004), I have argued that this epistemological transcendence is the presupposition for ethical transcendence, in which the former is teleologically suspended.

44. This is the final sentence of Spinoza's *Ethics*. The original version of this chapter was supported by a grant from the Pew Evangelical Scholars Program, which I am pleased to acknowledge with gratitude.

## 5. The Trauma of Transcendence as Heteronomous Intersubjectivity

1. For example, David Burrell, C.S.C., writes, "So the quintessential theological task becomes one of formulating [the] 'distinction' [between God and the world] so as to assure the required transcendence, while allowing us to have some notion of what it is we are referring to in addressing 'the Holy One,' 'our Father,' or 'Allah Akbar.'" *Knowing the Unknowable God: Ibn-Sina, Maimonides, Aquinas* (Notre Dame, Ind.: University of Notre Dame Press, 1986), p. 2.

2. Peter Berger, *The Sacred Canopy* (Garden City, N.J.: Doubleday, 1967), p. 46.

3. This chapter was originally presented to a Castelli Colloquium in Rome on the subject "Intersubjectivity and Philosophical Theology."

4. *Ethics*, I, 18.

5. That Hegel is as much a pantheist as Spinoza I argue in "Hegel," in *The Blackwell Companion to Modern Theology*, ed. Gareth Jones (Oxford: Blackwell, 2004), pp. 293–310.

6. *Hegel's Science of Logic*, trans. A. V. Miller (New York: Humanities Press, 1969), p. 50. Cf. p. 74, where Hegel identifies the categories that make up the Idea as progressively richer definitions of the absolute, and ¶85 of the "Lesser (Encyclopedia) Logic," where the logical determinations are said to be *"metaphysical definitions of God."*

7. *Philosophy of Right*, ¶1 and Remark.

8. In "The Necessity of Contingency," in *Art and Logic in Hegel's Philosophy*, ed. Warren E. Steinkraus and Kenneth L. Schmitz (Atlantic Highlands, N.J.: Humanities Press, 1980), John Burbidge shows that contingency does not disappear altogether from the Hegelian scheme although the self-actualization of the Idea is itself necessary. On the existential asymmetry of God and the world, see John Burnaby, "If 'God' *means* the world-ground, then God without a world is not God. Now this is precisely what Augustine and Thomas find incompatible with the very idea of creation." *Amor Dei: A Study of the Religion of St. Augustine* (London: Hodder & Stoughton, 1938), p. 41.

9. *Summa Theologiae*, I, Q. 46.

10. *Hegel's Phenomenology of Spirit*, trans. A. V. Miller (Oxford: Clarendon Press, 1977), p. 110. Translation altered.

11. *Philosophy of Right*, ¶158.

12. *Philosophy of Right*, ¶163.

13. *Philosophy of Right*, ¶¶146–47.

14. For a detailed account of the isomorphism of family and state, see my *Hegel, Freedom, and Modernity* (Albany: SUNY Press, 1992), ch. 3.

15. *Phenomenology*, pp. 110–11. Bold type added.

16. *Phenomenology*, pp. 408–409. Bold type added.

17. See note 10 above.

18. Martin Buber, *I and Thou*, trans. Walter Kaufmann (New York: Charles Scribner's Sons, 1970), p. 75, and *Between Man and Man*, trans. Ronald Gregor Smith (New York: Macmillan, 1965), p. 34.

19. *Between Man and Man*, pp. 5–6.

20. Quotations from Augustine will be by book and chapter numbers from *The Confessions of St. Augustine*, trans. Rex Warner (New York: New American Library, 1963).

21. See TH and TI, 34–35, where desire for the wholly other is directed toward "the Most-High."

22. "L'absolument Autre, c'est Autrui" and "*L'Autre en tant qu'autre est Autrui.*"

23. Especially in chapters 4 and 5. Also in GP.

24. See the analysis in chapter 1.

25. Cf. IOF 9–10 for the trans-horizonal, immediate givenness of the Other as face. Already in Husserl Levinas finds the teaching that what we take to be direct intuition is "revealed to be implanted in horizons unsuspected by this thought" (TI 28). And in RR 121 he speaks hermeneutically of the self finding itself "placed within horizons that it somehow had not willed, but with which it cannot dispense." But the immediacy of the face bursts the bounds of our horizons. See the description of the way the Other is first given within the horizons of our cultural context, but as the epiphany of transcendence breaks through the conditions of phenomenality (TrO 351).

26. Rudolf Bernet, "The Traumatized Subject," *Research in Phenomenology* 30 (2000), pp. 160–79.

27. See TI 51–52, 65–67, 74, 77. This theme is also developed in FC and ET.

28. On the theme of teaching in Levinas, see Norman Wirzba's fine essays "From maieutics to metanoia: Levinas' Understanding of the Philosophical Task," *Man and World* (now *Continental Philosophy Review*) 28 (1995), pp. 129–44, and "Teaching as Propaedeutic to Religion: The Contributions of Levinas and Kierkegaard," *International Journal for Philosophy of Religion* 39 (April 1996), pp. 77–94.

29. In *After Writing: On the Liturgical Consummation of Philosophy* (Oxford: Blackwell, 1998), p. 62, Catherine Pickstock writes, "an ontology separated from theology is reducible to an epistemology." For Levinas, the formula might be "ontology, the identity of thought and being that lacks transcendence, is reducible to epistemology," that is, to realism, idealism, phenomenology, and hermeneutics.

30. Cf. Jacques Derrida, who writes "not that I love nonknowledge for itself, on the contrary, I am even ready to think like certain Muslims that 'the ink of the learned is more sacred than the blood of the martyrs,' but sacred, precisely, through something other than knowledge." See *Circumfession*, in *Jacques Derrida*, trans. Geoffrey Ben-

nington (Chicago: University of Chicago Press, 1993), pp. 141–42. See also Derrida's *Adieu: To Emmanuel Levinas*, trans. Pascale-Anne Brault and Michael Naas (Stanford, Calif.: Stanford University Press, 1999), pp. 17–29.

31. On this questioning, see Sylviane Agacinski, "Another Experience of the Question, or Experiencing the Question Other-wise," and Jean-Luc Marion, "L'Interloqué," both in *Who Comes after the Subject*, ed. Eduardo Cadava, Peter Connor, and Jean-Luc Nancy (New York: Routledge, 1991).

32. The three modes of divine transcendence that appear in this chapter, cosmological, epistemic, and practical (ethical/religious) provide the frame for my argument in *Transcendence and Self-Transcendence* (Bloomington: Indiana University Press, 2004). The final two chapters are devoted to Levinas and Kierkegaard.

33. Reference to gestation alerts us to the repeated use of maternity as a symbol of every self's responsibility for the Other. See OB 67–68, 71, 75, 78–79, 104–105, 108, 115. This theme deserves more attention than it gets in feminist discussions of Levinas.

34. For a fuller discussion of this theme, see chapter 6.

35. Augustine writes that "if I do not remain in Him, I shall not be able to remain in myself." *Confessions*, VII, 11.

36. Jacques Derrida, "Violence and Metaphysics," in *Writing and Difference*, trans. Alan Bass (Chicago: University of Chicago Press, 1978), p. 82.

37. Derrida says that language always precedes the 'I'. But this seems to be a weaker point, the priority of the 'already said,' rather than the priority of the Other as saying. This ethical relation he develops in other ways. See *Monolingualism of the Other; or, The Prosthesis of Origin*, trans. Patrick Mensah (Stanford, Calif.: Stanford University Press, 1998), pp. 28–29.

38. Perhaps it would be more accurate to speak of what would be my essence if I were not essentially related to the Other. This way of putting it supports the claim that Levinas doesn't simply overcome ontology but offers an alternative ontology, just as he offers an alternative rationality.

39. See the discussion in chapters 3 and 4.

40. For an argument to this effect, see Jean-Luc Marion, "Thomas Aquinas and Onto-theo-logy," *Mystics: Presence and Aporia*, ed. Michael Kessler and Christian Sheppard (Chicago: University of Chicago Press, 1963), pp. 38–74.

41. See the discussion in chapter 1.

42. Here we encounter Augustine's *facere veritatem*, to which Derrida returns so frequently in *Circumfession*. Typical of the questions Kierkegaard has in mind are the question of the lawyer who asked, "And who is my neighbor?" (Luke 10:29) and of Pilate who asked, "What is truth?" (John 18:38).

43. For Anti-Climacus on offense, see SUD 71, 83–87, 129–31.

44. This account occurs in part I, before the concept of sin has been decisively introduced. Its inclusion can only intensify the offense that must be overcome by faith. At FT 73, Silentio does speak of humble courage, but only to insist that the lack of faith's courage stems from pride. But he doesn't spell out that pride in terms of being humiliated at being helped.

45. Kierkegaard interprets the contrast between the flesh and the spirit in these terms. "No, just because Christianity is truly spirit, it understands by the sensuous some thing quite different from what is simply called the sensuous nature, and it has been no more scandalized by a drive human beings have indeed not given to themselves than it has wanted to forbid people to eat and drink. By the sensuous, the flesh, Christianity

understands selfishness. A conflict between spirit and flesh is inconceivable unless there is a rebellious spirit on the side of the flesh . . . Therefore, self-love is sensuousness" (WL 52–53). The ethic of neighbor love is no more ascetic in essence than it is masochistic.

46. See the discussion of enabling love in chapter 4.

47. For Kierkegaard as for Levinas, and against Heidegger, it is my responsibility that individuates more fundamentally than my death.

## 6. TRANSCENDENCE, HETERONOMY, AND THE BIRTH

### OF THE RESPONSIBLE SELF

1. Paul Ricoeur, *Oneself as Another*, trans. Kathleen Blamey (Chicago: University of Chicago Press, 1992), p. 11. Henceforth OA.

2. Calvin O. Schrag, *The Self after Postmodernity* (New Haven, Conn.: Yale University Press, 1997). Henceforth SAP.

3. See *Who Comes after the Subject?* ed. Eduardo Cadava, Peter Connor, and Jean-Luc Nancy (New York: Routledge, 1991), Introduction.

4. See *The Concept of Mind* (New York: Barnes and Noble, 1949). In her interpretation of the *Phaedrus*, Catherine Pickstock finds "a suggestion that a person's identity is defined and performed . . . by a kind of journeying, an 'identity' which is always *in medias res*." She calls this a "doxological identity" because of Socrates' insistence on praising the god and, ultimately, the Good and the Beautiful. "I" am not just *unterwegs* but turned outside of myself to that which is greater than myself and which calls me to its infinity rather than serving my finite projects. *After Writing* (Oxford: Blackwell, 1998), p. 45. This "doxological dispossession" (pp. 170, 177, 194, 250) is a premodern version of the "self after postmodernity."

5. Quoted in note 3, page 14, from *The Languages of Criticism and the Sciences of Man: The Structuralist Controversy*, ed. Richard Macksey and Eugenio Donato (Baltimore: Johns Hopkins University Press, 1970), p. 271.

6. *Monolingualism of the Other or The Prosthesis of Origin*, trans. Patrick Mensah (Stanford, Calif.: Stanford University Press, 1998), pp. 28–29. The question Who speaks? becomes the sharper question Who speaks in what language? This would be the one-sided triumph of plurality over unity of which Schrag accuses Lyotard only if language games had the kind of monadic self-enclosure that Derrida regularly sees as the denial of difference. John Milbank makes a similar point when he writes, "Objects and subjects are [for postmodernity], as they are narrated in a story. Outside a plot, which has its own unique, unfounded reasons, one cannot conceive how objects and subjects would be, nor even that they would be at all." "Postmodern Critical Augustinianism: A Short *Summa* in Forty-two Responses to Unasked Questions," in *The Postmodern God*, ed. Graham Ward (Oxford: Blackwell, 1997), p. 265. Such narratives include not only the stories of individuals but the meganarratives, the larger, communal stories that constitute the languages in which the individual stories are told.

7. Quoted on SAP 14 from *Who Comes after the Subject?*, p. 100.

8. In *Against Ethics* (Bloomington: Indiana University Press, 1993) and in *Saints and Postmodernism* (Chicago: University of Chicago Press, 1990), John D. Caputo and Edith Wyschogrod, respectively, draw a sharp distinction between these two questions. Even more strongly than Kant, they argue that the moral life does not depend on moral theory.

9. On this point see Schrag's splendid essay "The Kierkegaard-Effect in the Shaping of the Contours of Modernity," in *Kierkegaard in Post/Modernity*, ed. Martin Matuštík and Merold Westphal (Bloomington: Indiana University Press, 1995).

10. *Who Comes*, p. 100, emphasis added.

11. Jacques Derrida, "How to Avoid Speaking: Denials," in *Derrida and Negative Theology*, ed. Harold Coward and Toby Foshay (Albany: SUNY Press, 1992), p. 99.

12. Levinas closely links heteronomy and transcendence when he suggests they are what is lost when Buber presents the I-Thou relation with too much focus on reciprocity, "as a harmonious co-presence, and an eye to eye," which Levinas takes to be different from the face-to-face. See GCM 150.

13. Nor is it "a self-identical monad, mute and self-enclosed, changeless and secured prior to the events of speaking." These are Schrag's definitions of the presumptuous modern cogito, quoted above from SAP 27 and 33.

14. Levinas also associates Heidegger with these philosophies insofar as human beings are but mouthpieces of being (NI 143–44). "But for Heidegger the subject has nothing inward to express" (NI 144, n. 4).

15. Levinas does not distinguish *idem* identity from *ipse* identity. Thus he describes the transcendental I beyond which the Other takes us as "the identity of an *I* that from the start, without objectifying reflection, is a *self*, the identity of an *ipseity*" (OS 1).

16. Cf. IOF 7–10, where Levinas seeks to break from the knowledge is power tradition. Levinas's sustained critique of intentionality is found in DEH and BI. See the analysis of inverted intentionality in chapter 8.

17. With reference to the id, Freud cites Georg Groddeck's claim that "we are 'lived' by unknown and uncontrollable forces." *The Ego and the Id*, ch. 2.

18. Cf. OB 150. Catherine Pickstock, in arguing against Derrida's interpretation of the *Phaedrus*, presents Socratic eros as the priority of the Good and the Beautiful over the soul. Because of this transcendence, the philosophical gaze is reverent rather than violent and "The erotic gaze is therefore neither totalizing nor rationalizing. . . . The erotic gaze institutes an ontologically constitutive loss of self. " See *After Writing*, pp. 32–33.

19. The biblical text is Lamentations 3:30. Cf. Isaiah 50:6, which Handel set to music in *Messiah*. "I gave my back to those who struck me, and my cheeks to those who pulled out the beard; I did not hide my face from insult and spitting."

20. I understand this nakedness both literally, signifying the poverty of the widow, orphan, and stranger who above all are the Other, and symbolically, signifying that the Other comes shorn of anything that would make her attractive or useful to me. No beauty. No bribes.

21. See OB 13–15, for example, for the close link between the concept of substitution and that of the self's identity.

22. These phrases, cited at the beginning of this essay, were used by Schrag to describe the cogito whose shattering he applauds.

23. In OB Levinas speaks of "the other in the same" (25); of vulnerability and exposure as "one-penetrated-by-the-other" (49); of the passivity of proximity as "having-the-other-in-one's-skin" (115).

24. *Critique of Pure Reason*, B xxx.

25. In OB, because "I exist through the other and for the other" (114), "I am 'in myself' through the others" (112). Cf. Augustine, *Confessions*, VII, 11, "if I do not remain in Him, I shall not be able to remain in myself."

26. It is because George Steiner sees only the first meaning to Rimbaud's *Je est un autre* that he sees postmodernism only as a danger to be overcome. See *Real Presences* (Chicago: University of Chicago Press, 1989), pp. 94–110. Levinas repeatedly insists that the intrusion of the Other into the self is not inherently an alienation. See OB 105, 112, 118.

27. Responsibility as non-indifference Levinas also calls Agape or love without concupiscence. See EN 103, 113, 131, 149, 169, 186, 194, 216, 227, and 228.

28. See Edward F. Mooney, "Kierkegaard on Self-Choice and Self-Reception: Judge William's Admonition," in *International Kierkegaard Commentary: Either/Or, Part II*, ed. Robert L. Perkins (Macon, Ga.: Mercer University Press, 1995).

29. I have spelled this out in detail in "Hegel's Radical Idealism: Family and State as Ethical Communities," in *Hegel, Freedom, and Modernity* (Albany: SUNY Press, 1992).

30. But Abraham's silence has been anticipated all along. See FT 21, 60, 67, 71, 76, 79–80. Actually neither Sarah nor Eliezer is mentioned in the Genesis 22 story, but it is clear that Isaac does not know what his father is up to.

31. Mark C. Taylor, *Journey's to Selfhood: Hegel & Kierkegaard* (Berkeley: University of California Press, 1980), p. 10.

32. See chapters 3 and 4.

33. The inescapability of ontological language is a central thesis of Derrida in "Violence and Metaphysics," *Writing and Difference*, trans. Alan Bass (Chicago: University of Chicago Press, 1978). That Levinas does not so much simply abandon ontology as offer an alternative ontology is argued by Adriaan Peperzak in *Beyond: The Philosophy of Emmanuel Levinas* (Evanston, Ill.: Northwestern University Press, 1997). Like Derrida, Levinas recognizes the affinity of his thought for negative theology, though he denies their identity. See OB 44, 147, and especially 150–51.

34. For the first of these, see FT 33, 48–53, 55–56, 62–66, 85, and 88. For the second see FT 34–37, 40, 46–51, 56, 59.

35. I have discussed this theme in relation to Johannes Climacus in *Becoming a Self: A Reading of Kierkegaard's Concluding Unscientific Postscript* (West Lafayette, Ind.: Purdue University Press, 1996), pp. 123–26 and 180–84.

36. *After Writing*, p. 62. By contrast, the self engaged with transcendence, in her case, Socrates, has an " 'identity' which is always *in medias res.* . . . The person who gives praise [to the Good] is not estranged, yet neither can he lay claim to a fixed or completed identity " (45).

37. From Rule XII in *Rules for the Direction of the Mind*. Pickstock cites part of this passage in her analysis of the collapse of ontology into epistemology. See *After Writing*, p. 64.

38. See *Confessions*, VII, 20.

39. *De Potentia Dei*, 7.5.14. For a helpful summary of this theme, see John F. Wippel, "Quidditative Knowledge of God," in *Metaphysical Themes in Thomas Aquinas* (Washington, D.C.: Catholic University of America Press, 1984).

40. *De Veritate*, 8.2. Cf. *Summa Theologiae*, 1.12.1.3 and 1.12.7.

41. I have argued that the intelligibility thesis, which involves the elimination of mystery, is an essential part of Heidegger's critique of onto-theology. I do not commit onto-theology merely by affirming a Highest Being who is the key to the meaning of the whole of being. See the title essay of my *Overcoming Onto-theology* (New York: Fordham University Press, 2001) and "Aquinas and Onto-theology," *American Catholic Philosophical Quarterly* 80, no. 2 (2006), pp. 173–91.

42. That Aquinas's doctrine of creation implies that we cannot fully understand even created beings is argued skillfully by Joseph Pieper in *The Silence of St. Thomas*, trans. John Murray, S.J., and Daniel O'Connor (Chicago: Henry Regnery, 1965), second essay.

43. For a lucid and succinct account of Aquinas's concept of science, see Scott MacDonald, "Theory of Knowledge," in *The Cambridge Companion to Aquinas*, ed. Norman Kretzmann and Eleonore Stump (New York: Cambridge University Press, 1993).

44. On the divine command character of this existential transcendence, see C. Stephen Evans, *Kierkegaard's Ethic of Love: Divine Commands and Moral Obligations* (New York: Oxford University Press, 2004). For the threefold analysis of divine transcendence as cosmological, epistemic, and ethical/religious, see my *Transcendence and Self-Transcendence* (Bloomington: Indiana University Press, 2004). For a detailed commentary on *Works of Love*, see M. Jamie Ferreira, *Love's Grateful Striving* (New York: Oxford University Press, 2001).

45. See chapters 2 and 3 of *Transcendence and Self-Transcendence*.

## 7. The "Logic" of Solidarity

1. Hegel, *The Encyclopedia Logic*, trans. T. F. Geraets et al. (Indianapolis: Hackett, 1991), ¶42, Addition 2.

2. See my essay "Kierkegaard and the Logic of Insanity," in *Kierkegaard's Critique of Reason and Society* (Macon, Ga.: Mercer University Press, 1987), pp. 85–103.

3. There are two kinds of people who can speak this way today: those who ignore Nietzsche and Auschwitz and those, like Levinas, who do not.

4. Heidegger thus agrees with Buber and Marcel "in questioning the spiritual primacy of intellectual objectivism, which asserts itself in science, taken as a model of all intelligibility." But he does not move from a philosophy of existence to a philosophy of coexistence for which what is ultimate is "not truth, but *sociality*, which is not reducible to knowledge and truth" (BM 307).

5. Jacques Derrida, "The Ends of Man," in *Margins of Philosophy*, trans. Alan Bass (Chicago: University of Chicago Press, 1982), pp. 123–34. Cf. "Violence and Metaphysics," in *Writing and Difference*, trans. Alan Bass (Chicago: University of Chicago Press, 1978), pp. 87–92.

6. Kantian interpretations of Derrida are found in Rodolphe Gasché, *The Tain of the Mirror: Derrida and the Philosophy of Reflection* (Cambridge, Mass.: Harvard University Press, 1986), and Irene Harvey, *Derrida and the Economy of Différance* (Bloomington: Indiana University Press, 1986). Both focus on the earlier Derrida, for whom Levinas's account is more fitting than for the later Derrida, who, in part at least under the impact of Levinas, gives greater ethical significance to the other of thought.

7. The important discussion "Skepticism and Reason" at the end of OB should not be taken to suggest that Levinas locates his own project in the skeptical tradition, though he sees a curious parallel. When he says that "the history of Western philosophy has not been the refutation of skepticism as much as the refutation of transcendence" (OB 169) he not only distinguishes himself from the skeptics but suggests that they and their Platonic opponents share an allergy to alterity. Robert Bernasconi sees this clearly when he notes that Levinas "is not himself adopting a skeptical position" and adds that "the evaluation of skepticism is not Levinas's primary concern." Except for that which

can appear only as a trace, he leaves the debate over the divided line to others. "Skepticism in the Face of Philosophy," in *Re-Reading Levinas*, ed. Robert Bernasconi and Simon Critchley (Bloomington: Indiana University Press, 1991), pp. 150 and 152. See note 10 on p. 160 for the fate of the "legitimate child" metaphor in OB.

8. See Ludwig Landgrebe, "Husserl's Departure from Cartesianism," in *The Phenomenology of Edmund Husserl: Six Essays*, ed. Donn Welton (Ithaca, N.Y.: Cornell University Press, 1981).

9. Of course, Levinas does not deny that the human face appears to us contextualized by a wide variety of horizons. He only insists that in the nakedness that gives it is true ethical significance it signifies above and beyond these, freeing itself from the forms imposed upon it by them. See TrO 351–53 and the discussion above in chapter 1.

10. This critique does not take into account what has come to be called Derrida's "Levinasian turn."

11. See Si 189; BI 100, 112; BCI 35, 38; OB 117–18, 125, 127; DEL 24; EL 17.

12. See note 6 above.

13. Shakespeare, *The Merry Wives of Windsor*, II, ii.

14. See, for example, EL 16; TI 46, 49, 75–76; EF 76–77; BTK 68; TO 51; BI 102.

15. Hegel, *Phenomenology of Spirit*, trans. A. V. Miller (Oxford: Clarendon Press, 1977), p. 65. Cf. the epigraph at the opening of this chapter.

16. *Phenomenology of Spirit*, p. 479.

17. Hegel, *The Phenomenology of Mind*, trans. J. B. Baillie, 2nd ed. (London: George Allen Unwin, 1949), p. 790. The German text is found in *Phänomenologie des Geistes*, ed. Johannes Hoffmeister (Hamburg: Felix Meiner, 1952), p. 549. Levinas is surely to be counted among those for whom Hegel's *als solchem* expresses a pious but unfulfilled intention to preserve genuine alterity.

18. Levinas also writes that "in representation the same defines the other without being determined by the other" (TI 125).

19. Toni Morrison, *Beloved* (New York: Penguin, 1987), p. 190. In section 2 of the First Essay of *On the Genealogy of Morals*, Nietzsche writes, "The lordly right of giving names extends so far that one should allow oneself to conceive the origin of language itself as an expression of power on the part of the rulers; they say 'this *is* this and this,' they seal every thing and event with a sound, and, as it were, take possession of it" (Kaufmann translation).

20. James L. Marsh, *Post-Cartesian Meditations* (New York: Fordham University Press, 1988), ch. 3. The quotation is from p. 86. Marsh is not talking specifically about Levinas.

21. See chapter 8.

22. Cf. BTK 64, 68 and Maurice Blanchot, "Our Clandestine Companion" in FFL 45, 55, 97. Derrida summarizes Levinas this way: "I could not possibly speak of the Other, make of the Other a theme, pronounce the Other as object, in the accusative. I can only, I *must* only speak to the other; that is, I must call him in the vocative, which is not a category, a *case* of speech, but, rather the bursting forth, the very raising up of speech." "Violence and Metaphysics," p. 103. Cf. pp. 95, 123.

23. In contrast to the later, "Levinasian" Derrida, the Derrida of *Writing and Difference* comes across as deeply sympathetic to Bataille's Nietzschean dyad of meaning and unmeaning. See "From Restricted to General Economy: A Hegelianism without Reserve" in *Writing and Difference* and my discussion in "Laughing at Hegel," in *Overcoming Onto-theology* (New York: Fordham University Press, 2001), pp. 197–218.

24. The reference to a more ancient meaning of meaning points to the dual origin of philosophy in Greek and biblical experience. See DEL 19, 21. The "tradition at least as ancient" as mainstream Platonism is, of course, Plato's own notion of "the good above Being" (PII 53). But Derrida speaks of Levinas's summons "to depart from the Greek site . . . toward a prophetic speech"; the "more ancient volcano" he portrays as underlying the effusions of the Greek logos is plainly Sinai. "Violence and Metaphysics," p. 82.

25. Cf. LP. The reference to an-archy points to the link, explicit in the passage cited, between proximity and the trace. On this latter topic, see TrO and MS. Also see Robert Bernasconi's discussion in "The Trace of Levinas in Derrida," in *Derrida and Différance*, ed. David Wood and Robert Bernasconi (Evanston, Ill.: Northwestern University Press, 1988) and "One-Way Traffic: The Ontology of Decolonization and Its Ethics," in *Ontology and Alterity in Merleau-Ponty*, ed. Galen A. Johnson and Michael B. Smith (Evanston, Ill.: Northwestern University Press, 1990).

26. This implies that only on the "foundation" of the "radical reversal" here at issue is a robust realism possible. Traditional realisms compromise their object as much as Kantian idealism, as argued below.

27. The period at the end of this sentence needs to be read aloud. For the realist the relevant truth condition is that snow is white period, not relative to this or that conceptual scheme.

28. Cf. "The Phenomenological Theory of Being: The Absolute Existence of Consciousness," chapter 2 of Levinas, *The Theory of Intuition in Husserl's Phenomenology*, trans. André Orianne (Evanston, Ill.: Northwestern University Press, 1973).

29. "The attitude of the *Logische Untersuchungen* is a realist one." *The Theory of Intuition*, p. 54.

30. See *The Theory of Intuition*, p. 91.

31. See TI 27, 123–25; BI 103–7; TrO 346; BM 313.

32. It is worth noting, however, that this notion is most fully developed in the *Logische Untersuchungen*, especially Investigation VI, which Levinas reads in realist terms. See note 29 above.

33. On this theme, see Norman Wirzba, "From maieutics to metanoia: Levinas' Understanding of the Philosophical Task," *Man and World* 28 (1995), pp. 129–44, and chapter 1.

34. N.B. Kant holds to this view as well. That is what the thing in itself is all about. So defining realism simply in terms of the ontic independence of the real isn't very helpful. Even so radical an anti-realist as Richard Rorty has his version of this claim. "We need to make a distinction between the claim that the world is out there and the claim that truth is out there. To say that the world is out there, that it is not our creation, is to say, with common sense, that most things in space and time are the effects of causes which do not include human mental states. To say that truth is not out there is simply to say that where there are no sentences there is no truth, that sentences are elements of human languages, and that human languages are human creations. . . . The world is out there, but descriptions of the world are not." Thus, while world cannot "propose a language for us to speak," once we are inside a language game, it can "cause us to hold beliefs" and, for that matter, to abandon them. See *Contingency, Irony, and Solidarity* (New York: Cambridge University Press, 1989), pp. 4–6.

35. For an interpretation of Hegel's idealism as realism, see Kenneth Westphal, *Hegel's Epistemological Realism* (Dordrecht: Kluwer, 1989). In the light of this passage it is not surprising that Heidegger's turn to "*letting be*" does not impress Levinas (IOF 6).

36. Hegel immediately proceeds to deny a Kantian, "subjective" interpretation of this crushing. See *The Encyclopedia Logic*, trans. R. F. Geraets et al. (Indianapolis: Hackett, 1991), §42, *Zusatz* 1.

37. *Sämtliche Werke: Jubiläumsausgabe in zwanzig Bänden*, ed. H. Glockner (Stuttgart: Frommann-Holzboog, 1927–30), vol. XVII, pp. 21–22. Hegel repeats this almost verbatim in his Berlin inaugural address of 1818, but asks that his students bring with them "trust in Science, faith in Reason, trust and faith in yourselves." In a Lutheran context, these uses of 'trust' and 'faith' are anything but innocent. See vol. VIII, p. 36.

38. Luther refuses to reduce faith to its cognitive component and makes trust as crucial an ingredient as belief or assent.

39. For the textual argument, see my "In Defense of the Thing in Itself," *Kant-Studien*, 59, no. 1 (1968), pp. 118–41.

40. This is how both Hegel and Husserl overcome the thing in itself.

41. *The Science of Logic*, trans. A. V. Miller (New York: Humanities Press, 1969), p. 50. Cf. pp. 63 and 74, *The Encyclopedia Logic*, §85.

42. Following Heidegger, Levinas sees phenomenology as "the science of the 'meaning' of being" distinct from "the knowledge of the properties of being" (TIH xxxii). Cf. p. 131, where Levinas writes that "the study of the objectivity of objects is reduced to the clarification of the very existence of being. . . . Our problem [as phenomenologists] is the very meaning of being in each of the special cases in question." There is also an Hegelian point to Levinas's use of 'ontology' for what others might call epistemology. The study of thought *is* the study of being.

43. This may explain why Levinas speaks of solidarity, fraternity, and sociality, but shies away from the language of community. See EF 84.

44. It may seem strange, then, for Levinas to say that fraternity involves "the commonness of a father. . . . Monotheism signifies this human kinship" (TI 214)—but only if we forget that he has just said, "Paternity is not a causality," and that he regularly rejects theologies of God as first cause in favor of theologies of God as the deepest source of the obligation that shines through the face of the Other.

45. *Levinas and the Political* (New York: Routledge, 2002), pp. 3–4.

46. See the discussion of these themes in chapter 1.

47. At this point the critique of Heidegger for lacking an ethics takes the form of observing that *Dasein* never worries whether its *Da* is occupying someone else's place (EL 19; EF 82, 85). See next note.

48. Here the critique of Heidegger is that the *Jemeinigkeit* of *Being and Time* gives us a *Dasein* concerned only for its own death (DEL 26; BCI 39; BI 110–12). See previous note.

49. On the "here I am," *me voici*, see GP 168, 170; BCI 38; EL 16. On the relational character of the self's identity, see chapter 6.

50. Thus "conscience" turns out to be "the condition of consciousness *tout court* and of disclosure" (IOF 128; cf. TrO 352). The ethical relation stands in a similar founding relation to knowledge (BM 316), to intentionality (BTK 63), and to thematizing (OB 120).

51. See Carol Gilligan, *In a Different Voice* (Cambridge, Mass.: Harvard University Press, 1982); see also Nell Noddings, *Caring: A Feminine Approach to Ethics and Moral Education* (Berkeley: University of California Press, 1984). This affinity with Gilligan has an obvious bearing on the ongoing discussion of Levinas and the feminine.

52. Levinas is the paradigm of a "heteronomic" but not a "heteromorphic" postmodernism. For this helpful distinction, see John D. Caputo, *Against Ethics* (Bloomington: Indiana University Press, 1993), ch. 3.

53. In *Postscript* Climacus affirms objectivity for the "what" of knowledge, though he insists that truth of this sort is always approximation at best and never adequation. But he also insists that the "what" be teleologically suspended in a "how" where subjectivity prevails, not epistemic subjectivism but ethical/religious decision and commitment.

54. See "Kierkegaard's Teleological Suspension of Religiousness B," in *Foundations of Kierkegaard's Vision of Community*, ed. George B. Connell and C. Stephen Evans (Atlantic Highlands, N.J.: Humanities Press, 1992), pp. 110–29, and "Kierkegaard's Religiousness C: A Defense," *International Philosophical Quarterly* 44, no. 4 (Dec. 2004), pp. 535–48.

55. See chapter 1.

56. See chapter 3.

57. It is clear that creation is not merely a causal concept for Kierkegaard but needs to be understood in terms of grace, as a gift.

58. For this social context, see Bruce H. Kirmmse, *Kierkegaard in Golden Age Denmark* (Bloomington: Indiana University Press, 1990), especially part 1.

59. If "ignorant commoners" are "beyond actuality," one might as well be honest and call them "not born."

## 8. Inverted Intentionality

1. Martin Heidegger, *Identity and Difference*, trans. Joan Stambaugh (New York: Harper & Row, 1969), p. 56. Cf. Jean-Luc Marion, "Descartes and Onto-theology," in *Post-Secular Philosophy: Between Philosophy and Theology*, ed. Phillip Blond (New York: Routledge, 1998), pp. 67–106.

2. Just as for Descartes the human subject is the measure of being and truth, but only in the mode of clear and distinct ideas, and for Spinoza only in the mode of the "third kind" of knowledge, so for Hegel the human subject is autonomous and absolute only in the mode of the philosopher, who operates at the level of *Vernunft* and its *Begriffe* and not at the level of *Verstand* and its *Vorstellungen*. On the relation of the onto-theological pantheisms of Spinoza and Hegel to each other and to the very different traditions of Augustine and Aquinas, and Kierkegaard as well, see my *Transcendence and Self-Transcendence* (Bloomington: Indiana University Press, 2004).

3. Even apart from, but not in conflict with, claims to divine revelation, the acknowledgment of theology's embeddedness in tradition is an abandonment of claims to autonomy. No matter how one parses 'Scripture and tradition,' it is a double abdication from autonomy.

4. John Calvin, *Institutes of the Christian Religion*, trans. Lewis Ford Battles (Philadelphia: Westminster Press, 1960), vol. I, p. 35.

5. Given the hermeneutical circle in which I work, I have given Christian examples. But 'biblical' can be taken here in its generic reference to the Book and thus, in the context of the Abrahamic monotheisms, to the Jewish Bible, the Christian Bible, or the Koran.

6. Jean-Luc Marion affirms that the difference between phenomenology and theology is that what the latter affirms as actual the former describes as possible. See

"Metaphysics and Phenomenology: A Summary for Theologians," in *The Postmodern God: A Theological Reader,* ed. Graham Ward (Oxford: Blackwell, 1997), pp. 280 and 293; "In the Name: How to Avoid Speaking of 'Negative Theology,'" in *God, the Gift, and Postmodernism,* ed. John D. Caputo and Michael J. Scanlon (Bloomington: Indiana University Press, 1999), pp. 39 and 63; and *Being Given: Toward a Phenomenology of Givenness,* trans. Jeffrey L. Kosky (Stanford, Calif.: Stanford University Press, 2002), pp. 234–36 and 242.

7. With apologies to Marion's different, if not unrelated, formula: "so much reduction, so much givenness." See *Reduction and Givenness: Investigations of Husserl, Heidegger, and Phenomenology,* trans. Thomas Carlson (Evanston, Ill.: Northwestern University Press, 1998), p. 203.

8. The words "for my sake" are important. This loss of life is not the despair of weakness, that lacks the courage to be, nor the despair of defiance, that lacks the humility to be; it is rather the faith of self-transcendence that reaches out beyond itself to that which is greater than itself. "He must increase, but I must decrease," says John the Baptist (John 3:30), to which Jesus replies, as it were, "In that very decrease is your authentic increase. This is how to become a self."

9. Hegel treats *Mass* (measure) and *Massstab* (standard, criterion) in his Logic of Being under Quantity. It signifies far too external a relation to be anything's essence and goal.

10. This view is to be sharply distinguished from the "biological" essentialism that stretches from Aristotle to Hegel, according to which a being's essence is a kind of metaphysical DNA that unfolds from within. (Perhaps Nietzsche's will to power should be included here as well.) Hegel's holism represents a relational ontology, but I think it can be shown (though not here) that the structures of Aristotelian biologism tend to neutralize this. Such an argument would appeal to the ultimacy of self-conscious self-relation in his philosophy of spirit. It would appeal in part to the argument by Jürgen Habermas that monological reason prevails over dialogical reason and in part to the argument of Adriaan Peperzak that the unfolding of theoretical and practical reason rather than the quest for recognition is fundamental to the mature philosophy of objective spirit. See Jürgen Habermas, *The Philosophical Discourse of Modernity,* trans. Frederick Lawrence (Cambridge, Mass.: MIT Press, 1987), and Adriaan Peperzak, *Modern Freedom: Hegel's Legal, Moral, and Political Philosophy* (Dordrecht: Kluwer, 2001). The emphasis on choice reminds us of Kierkegaard's existence spheres or stages on life's way.

11. Levinas describes Husserlian phenomenology as "the conclusion to which one of the characteristic traditions of philosophy leads" (BI 100–101).

12. Heidegger reads it this way when he tells us that phenomenology means "to let that which shows itself be seen from itself in the very way in which it shows itself from itself." *Being and Time,* trans. J. Macquarrie and E. Robinson (New York: Harper & Row, 1962), p. 58. At the outset of his discussion of phenomenology, Heidegger explicitly cites the slogan "To the things themselves!" See p. 50.

13. See the argument to this effect in the previous chapter.

14. *Being and Nothingness,* trans. Hazel Barnes (New York: Philosophical Library, 1956), pp. xlvi–l.

15. See especially Husserl, *Logical Investigations,* trans. J. N. Findlay (New York: Humanities Press, 1970), Investigation VI, First Section.

16. Cf. p. 28, "This absoluteness does not concern only the truths pertaining to

consciousness and their certainty but also the very existence of consciousness itself. To posit as absolute the existence of consciousness means more than the fact that it is absurd to doubt it."

17. Levinas himself puts the second passage cited in quotation marks, as if quoting Husserl, but gives no reference.

18. What Heidegger says of the sciences, Levinas finds to be true of phenomenology in its quest to be rigorous science, namely, that its objectivity represents "a certain limited submission to what-is, so that this may reveal itself. This submissive attitude taken up by scientific theory becomes the basis of a possibility: the possibility of science acquiring a leadership of its own." "What Is Metaphysics," in *Existentialism from Dostoevsky to Sartre*, ed. Walter Kaufmann (New York: New American Library, 1975), p. 243.

19. Cf. p. 97, *"the essence of beings is in the truth or the revelation of their essence."* Emphasis Levinas's in both cases.

20. It is with good reason that Quentin Lauer's *Phenomenology: Its Genesis and Prospect* (New York: Harper & Row, 1965) was originally published as *The Triumph of Subjectivity* (New York: Fordham University Press, 1958).

21. Husserl, *Cartesian Meditations*, trans. Dorian Cairns (The Hague: Martinus Nijhoff, 1973), 109, 114. Emphasis added to show that Levinas's reading is on target.

22. *Cartesian Meditations*, p. 109.

23. *Cartesian Meditations*, pp. 114–15.

24. *Cartesian Meditations*, p. 128. Not even God is exempt. "The monad invites God himself to be constituted as meaning for a thought responsible to itself" (TIH 83).

25. James is reported to have said that for his colleague Josiah Royce, "the world is real but not so very damn real."

26. Emphasis added. N.B. Levinas does not deny that the Other is an alter ego, but only that it is "not only" and "not simply" such.

27. Violence and Metaphysics," in *Writing and Difference*, trans. Alan Bass (Chicago: University of Chicago Press, 1979), p. 125.

28. Levinas treats Heidegger's *Miteinandersein* as but a variation on this theme.

29. Cf. TI 29, where he writes that "not every transcendent intention has the noesis-noema structure." It turns out that we must move beyond Heidegger as well. See IOF.

30. Both in *Reduction and Givenness* and in *Being Given: Toward a Phenomenology of Givenness*, trans. Jeffrey L. Kosky (Stanford, Calif.: Stanford University Press, 2002), Jean-Luc Marion seeks to establish a phenomenology more radical than Husserl's precisely by refusing to let the transcendental ego and its horizons be the conditions of the possibility of experience, or, to speak phenomenologically, of givenness. Like Levinas (see especially IOF), Marion sees the phenomenological Heidegger in *Being and Time* as reformulating but not abandoning these arbitrary, a priori restrictions.

31. Cf. TI. 65, 67, 74–77, 181, 262 and the discussion in chapter 1 here. This Greek phrase is translated in Latin as *per se*, literally, through itself.

32. *Being and Time*, p. 58.

33. The Kierkegaardian language here is deliberate.

34. These themes are often repeated, but I have here cited them from the very pages, cited above, in which the threefold distinctiveness of "intentionality of a wholly different type" is set forth.

35. In addition to EF, see TI, Section IC, entitled "Truth and Justice."

36. In Aristotelian logic one gets a fallacy of four terms if one jumps from one genus to another midargument. Lessing describes the leap between metaphysical faith and historical knowledge in these terms. See "On the Proof of the Spirit and of Power," in *Lessing's Theological Writings*, trans. H. Chadwick (Stanford, Calif.: Stanford University Press, 1957), p. 54. Kierkegaard's Johannes Climacus is preoccupied with these themes both in *Philosophical Fragments* and in *Concluding Unscientific Postscript*.

37. *Husserliana*, vol. 14, *Zur Phänomenologie der Intersubjectivität. Zweiter Teil: 1921–1928*, ed. Iso Kern (The Hague: Martinus Nijhoff, 1973), pp. 166–67; vol. 15, *Zur Phänomenologie der Intersubjectivität. Dritter Teil: 1929–1935*, ed. Iso Kern (The Hague: Martinus Nijhoff, 1973), p. 474; and vol. 4, *Ideen zu einer reinen Phänomeno-logishen Philosophie*, II, *Phänomenologishen Untersuchungen zur Konstitution*, ed. M. Biemel (The Hague: Martinus Nijhoff, 1952), p. 194. Husserl here develops a theory of communicative action not unlike that of Jürgen Habermas, with special focus on what the latter calls "constative" and "regulative" speech acts. See Habermas, *The Theory of Communicative Action*, trans. Thomas McCarthy (Boston: Beacon Press, 1981), vol. I, pp. 328 and 445 (figures 16 and 17, respectively, along with the textual analysis). Thus Husserl speaks of "der aktuelle Konnex der Mitteilungsgemeinschaft" and of "die Grundform der kommunikativen Einigung." Vol. 15, p. 475.

38. *Husserliana*, vol. 14, p. 167; vol. 4, p. 194; and vol. 15, pp. 471–73.

39. See the discussion of revelation in chapters 1 and 2.

40. *Being and Time*, p. 320.

41. When speaking of obsession as persecution, Levinas says that this "inversion of consciousness . . . cannot be defined in terms of intentionality." We need not assume that he has changed his mind. For he continues, "where undergoing is always also an assuming, that is, an experience always anticipated and consented to" (OB 101). Inverted intentionality is not *that* kind of intentionality. In other words, the inversion of consciousness of which he speaks cannot be defined in terms of the objectifying, constituting intentionality that presents objects and appresents the alter ego. It is rather "an intentionality of a wholly different type."

42. 'Desire' is here used in its ordinary sense, which Levinas calls need or concupiscence.

43. A profound phenomenology of this rejection is found in Sartre's discussion of "Concrete Relations with Others" against the background of "The Look" in *Being and Nothingness*.

44. By Kierkegaard himself especially in *Works of Love*; by Johannes Climacus in *Philosophical Fragments*; and by Anti-Climacus in *Sickness unto Death* and in *Practice in Christianity*. In relation to the latter, see my "Kenosis and Offense: A Kierkegaardian Look at Divine Transcendence," in *International Kierkegaard Commentary: Practice in Christianity*, ed. Robert L. Perkins (Macon, Ga.: Mercer University Press, 2004), pp. 19–46.

45. There are cultures in which child sacrifice is practiced as a socially sanctioned rite. Silentio makes it abundantly clear that in his version of the story Abraham does not belong to such a society.

46. N.B. Here the otherness of the Wholly Other is not ontological but ethical; it is not an essence that exceeds my powers of comprehension but a command that contravenes my natural desire while compelling nevertheless. Following Spinoza, Levinas calls this desire *conatus essendi* in *Otherwise Than Being*, and following Nietzsche, Heidegger calls it the will to power that wills itself. See "The Word of Nietzsche: 'God Is

Dead,'" in *The Question Concerning Technology*, trans. William Lovitt (New York: Harper & Row, 1977), especially pp. 74–85.

47. Derrida's reflections on *Fear and Trembling* are closer to Levinas than to Kierkegaard. Since the face reveals genuine transcendence, "every other is wholly other" (*tout autre est tout autre*). Thus "this extraordinary story" exhibits "the very structure of what occurs every day" in my encounters with the singular, human other who cannot be subsumed without remainder under any general or universal rule. 'God' is the name for this structure. See *The Gift of Death*, trans. David Wills (Chicago: University of Chicago Press, 1995), pp. 66–68, 77–78.

48. This suggestion emerges with great force in Nicholas Wolterstorff's aptly titled book *Divine Discourse: Philosophical Reflections on the Claim That God Speaks* (New York: Cambridge University Press, 1995). In Lutheran terms that Kierkegaard would have appreciated, command and promise correspond to Law and Gospel. Levinas seems to be allergic to any form of gospel.

49. The two references to the promised land presuppose the earlier command/promise, "Go from your country and your kindred and your father's house to the land that I will show you" (Gen. 12:1). The pseudonymous author, Silentio, emphasizes the heteronomy of faith, which he describes as "unreasonable," at least by the standards of "worldly understanding," which Abraham had to leave behind.

50. This command is taken up in Jesus' summary of the law. See Matthew 22:34–40, Mark 12:28–31, and Luke 10:25–28.

51. Kierkegaard explicitly includes the enemy in the concept of the neighbor, echoing Jesus in the Sermon on the Mount, Matthew 5:43–48. See WL 67–68.

52. On the theme of trauma in Levinas, see Rudolf Bernet, "The Traumatized Subject," *Research in Phenomenology* 30 (2000), pp. 160–79 and chapter 5 here.

53. Anti-Climacus presents the command to believe in the forgiveness of sins in a section entitled "The Sin of Despairing of the Forgiveness of Sins (Offense)" (SUD 113).

54. This Hegelian notion is very close to what Levinas calls "politics" and "history," contrasting both with morality. See TI 21–22. For both Levinas and Kierkegaard inverse intentionality signifies the reversal from autonomous freedom to heteronomous responsibility. As we saw in chapter 7, Levinas also speaks of a reversal "from cognition to solidarity." Most sympathetic readers wish that both thinkers, but especially Kierkegaard, had given greater thought to the link between responsibility and solidarity, had given us more of a positive politics to go with their critique of violent and complacent politics.

55. Kant calls the critique of pure reason "a tribunal which will assure to reason its lawful claims, and dismiss all groundless pretensions." *Critique of Pure Reason*, A xi. The pre-and-post-Kantian epistemologies of modernity are similar tribunals, though often with different verdicts.

56. In his earlier writings Levinas avoids the language of love in favor of the language of justice. But later, especially in *Entre Nous*, he affirms love in the sense of agape, which he designates as "love without concupiscence" as the proper welcome of the other. For his early suspicion of love talk, see "The I and the Totality," ironically included in *Entre Nous*.

# INDEX

# Index

realism, 6, 80, 125, 130, 141, 165n29, 172nn26,34; anti-Kantian, 127–28, 141; anti-realism, 125, 172n34; epistemic, 129; medieval, 161n7; scientific, 127

reason, 4, 14, 22, 29–30, 32, 62, 85, 107–108, 116, 124, 127–28, 130, 143, 147, 175n10, 178n55; for Aristotle, 99; and autonomy, 148; and faith, 106; for Gadamer, 24; for Hegel, 24, 173n37; and intentionality, 122; and knowledge, 48, 150; and philosophy, 72; and revelation, 134; for Socrates, 30

reciprocity, 90–91, 93

recollection, 4, 25, 86, 127; and immanence, 86; and knowledge, 30, 32, 34, 61, 85; and revelation, 21, 25, 27, 29, 85, 89, 134; and transcendence, 39

reconciliation, 92–93

religion, 37, 53, 54; as cultural sphere, 96, 104; and ethics, 38, 47, 50–51, 53, 160n19; as social phenomenon, 75. *See also* Christianity; Judaism; theology

Remarque, Erich Maria, 3; *All Quiet on the Western Front*, 3

reminiscence, 28–29, 143

repentance, 79, 86, 101, 149

representation, 18, 51, 60, 81, 99, 119, 123; and enjoyment, 128; and intellect, 61; and responsibility, 87; and will to power, 99

responsibility, 15, 64, 81, 83–84, 87, 92–93, 96, 102, 132, 135, 148, 150, 167n47, 169n27; birth of responsible self, 104–108, 110–11, 115, 150; and fraternity, 130; and freedom, 99, 101, 145, 151, 178n54; and heteronomy, 103; and repentance, 101; and solidarity, 178n54

revelation, 1, 4, 21, 22, 24–26, 35, 41, 54, 62, 87, 89, 109, 115, 147–48, 158n17, 162n11; and authority, 26; and reason, 29, 134; and recollection, 21, 25, 27, 85, 134; and teaching, 83; and transcendence, 21

Ricoeur, Paul, 12, 79, 94–97, 102; *Oneself as Another*, 94

Rimbaud, Arthur, 102, 169n26

romanticism, 116

Rorty, Richard, 79, 125, 153n2, 172n34

Royce, Josiah, 176n25

Ryle, Gilbert, 95

salvation, 41, 53, 103, 139

Sarah (Bible), 105, 169n30

Sartre, Jean-Paul, 3, 72, 79, 82, 104, 141, 154n15; *Being and Nothingness*, 177n43

Saussure, Ferdinand de, 98

Schrag, Cal, 94, 96, 97, 99, 102, 107, 109, 167n6; *The Self after Postmodernity*, 94

science, 96, 98, 128, 151, 173n37

Scriptures. *See* Bible, Christian

secularism, 33

self-consciousness, 77

selfhood, 82, 88, 140, 143. *See also* self-identity

self-identity, 5, 19, 38, 75, 83, 87–88, 92, 94–95, 97–98, 101, 102, 106–107, 132, 168n15

self-knowledge, 32

Sellars, Wilfrid, 153n4

signification, 17, 32–34, 39, 49–50, 124–26, 146, 158nn18,20

sin, 25, 40, 41, 67, 79, 92, 93, 139, 140, 148, 149, 166n44

skepticism, 117, 124, 170n7

Socrates, 19, 24, 26, 29, 32, 34–35, 85–87, 134, 157n15, 158n22, 167n4, 168n18, 169n36. *See also* maieutics; reason, for Socrates; teaching

solidarity, 6, 115, 124–25, 130–31, 133–37, 141, 161n24, 173n43

speech, 63; divine, 148; rational, 30. *See also* command, divine; language

Spinoza, Baruch, 47, 50, 76, 111, 139, 174n2, 177n46

Steiner, George, 169n26

Stoicism, 72

structuralism, 17, 20, 49, 98–99. *See also* poststructuralism

subjectivity, 37, 56–87, 110, 135, 150–51, 174n53; subject and object, 141, 167n6; transcendental, 60, 98, 118, 125, 138–45, 151, 159n24, 161n10. *See also* intersubjectivity

suspension, teleological: of autonomy, 97, 99; of ego, 150; of epistemic freedom, 145; of ethical, 22, 23, 53, 55, 105; of knowledge, 85; of ontology, 132; of the religious, 51, 52–53; of transcendence, 84; of thematizing, 122; of violence, 148

Talmud, 38, 49, 62, 97–98, 102

Taylor, Mark, 105

teaching, 19, 24–26, 35, 80, 81, 85, 123; and revelation, 83. *See also* maieutics; Socrates

**MEROLD WESTPHAL** is Distinguished Professor of Philosophy at Fordham University. His most recent book is *Transcendence and Self-Transcendence* (Indiana University Press, 2004).

Lightning Source UK Ltd.
Milton Keynes UK
UKHW021815240322
400569UK00009B/346

9 780253 219664